TABLE OF CONTENTS

France

THE
COUNTRY

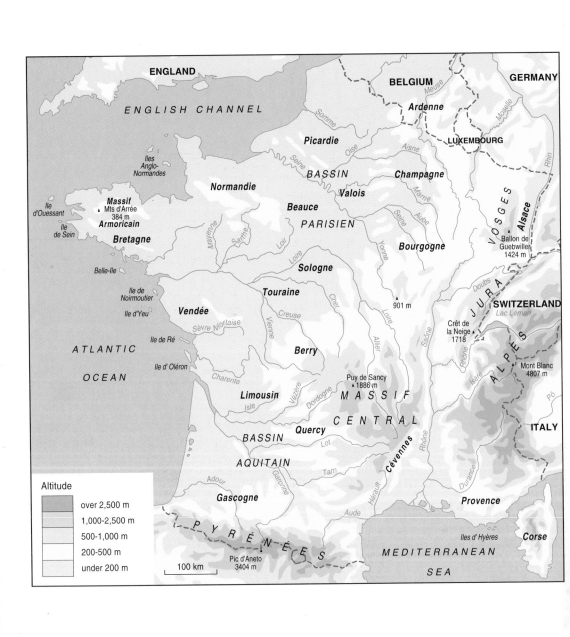

ENGLAND

BELGIUM

GERMANY

ENGLISH CHANNEL

Meuse

Ardenne

Picardie

Oise

LUXEMBOURG

Somme

Aisne

Moselle

Iles Anglo-Normandes

Normandie

BASSIN

Champagne

Rhin

Seine

Valois

Marne

VOSGES

Île d'Ouessant

Massif
▲ Mts d'Arrée
384 m
Armoricain

Beauce

PARISIEN

Seine

Aube

Alsace

Ballon de
Guebwiller
1424 m

Île de Sein

Bretagne

Mayenne

Sarthe

Loir

Yonne

Bourgogne

Belle-Île

Loire

Sologne

Doubs

JURA

Île de
Noirmoutier

Touraine

Cher

Loire

Saône

901 m

SWITZERLAND
Lac Léman

Île d'Yeu

Vendée

Creuse

Vienne

Crêt de
la Neige ▲
1718

ALPES

ATLANTIC

Île de Ré

Sèvre Niortaise

Berry

Allier

Mont Blanc
4807 m

Île d'Oléron

OCEAN

Charente

Vézère

Puy de Sancy
▲ 1886 m

Rhône

Isère

Limousin

Isle

Dordogne

MASSIF

ITALY

Quercy

Lot

CENTRAL

Rhône

Pô

BASSIN

AQUITAIN

Tarn

Cévennes

Adour

Garonne

Hérault

Durance

Gascogne

Aude

Provence

Iles d'Hyères

Corse

Altitude

	over 2,500 m
	1,000-2,500 m
	500-1,000 m
	200-500 m
	under 200 m

PYRÉNÉES

100 km

MEDITERRANEAN

Pic d'Aneto
3404 m

SEA

Geography

France has a surface area of 550,000 km², which makes it the largest country in Western Europe – bigger than Spain, Germany and Sweden. It lies on the western edge of the continent of Europe and shares borders with six neighbouring countries: Belgium and Luxembourg to the north; Germany and Switzerland to the east; Italy to the south-east; and Spain to the south-west. This geographical position gives France two salient advantages. On the one hand, partly due to its excellent communications network, it is a sort of crossroads at the heart of the European Union, linked to the east with the vast industrial and urban area stretching from the mouth of the Rhine to the plains of the Po River; to the north-west, it is within easy reach of the industrial centres of the United Kingdom and to the south it forms an integral part of the Mediterranean arc running from Catalonia to central Italy. The French coastline provides access by sea to Northern Europe, America and Africa via the North Sea, the Atlantic Ocean and the Mediterranean, which are amongst the world's busiest waters. Mainland France is compact and forms a hexagon of which no side is longer than

The Canal de Bourgogne
at La Bussière-sur-Ouche
(Côte-d'Or)

A great diversity of landscapes

The cliffs of Étretat
(Seine-Maritime)

Cirque de Salazie
in the overseas
department of Réunion

The confluence
of the Vienne and Loire
rivers at Candes-
Saint-Martin
(Indre-et-Loire)

1,000 km. Within these boundaries, France has exceptionally varied scenery; this, together with its rich cultural heritage, helps make it popular with tourists.

A very varied topography

West of a diagonal line from Bayonne to Sedan, France is relatively low-lying, with altitudes mostly below 200 metres. The plains and plateaux of the Paris basin and the Aquitaine basin cover most of this area. Although there are no high mountains, the landscapes are strikingly varied, partly because they have been formed in quite different ways. Some coastal plains, such as those in Flanders, emerged from the sea as tides and rivers left deposits. The low plains of Beauce, Brie and Picardy were created by sedimentation: they were formed by limestone and clay being deposited on the sea-bed during the Mesozoic Era and Tertiary Period. There are also lush alluvial plains like those of the Seine and Loire rivers. The land rises around the rim of the Paris basin. To the north lie the Ardennes, an ancient Hercynian massif worn down by a long period of erosion; to the north-east is the Lorraine versant of the Vosges; to the south, the Massif Central; and to the west the Massif Armoricain. The pattern is repeated around the Aquitaine basin, which is bordered by the Massif Central to the east and the Pyrenees to the south.

Farmland
in the Lauragais (Aude)

The relief of the south-eastern half of the country is more undulating. There are medium-altitude mountains ranging from 500 to 1,700 metres, of which some are ancient Hercynian massifs. This is the case of the Vosges and the Massif Central, which were thrown outwards at the time of uplifting of the Alpine ranges. They have rounded peaks and steep-sided valleys which make access extremely difficult. The Massif Central also contains many extinct volcanoes, such as the Cantal and the Puy de Dôme. Other ancient massifs which are less extensive, such as the Maures and the Estérel with their ravines carved out by Mediterranean downpours, have more impressive scenery, even though their peaks reach no higher than 900 metres. The Jura is also medium-altitude, but it is a comparatively recent massif which was formed in the Tertiary Period. It is made up of folds of sedimentary rock containing large amounts of limestone and is more dramatic, with alternating mountains and valleys and some breathtakingly high peaks. Many of the rock-folds are crossed by narrow transverse valleys called cluses, which make communications easier than is usual in mountain areas. This medium-altitude mountain scenery is also found in the northern and southern Pre-Alps, where the mountains often reach heights of over 2,000 metres. More violent folding and greater erosion have resulted in steep slopes which in places make the mountains look higher.

France's high mountains are found especially in the central Alps and Pyrenees. Both ranges began to form over 50 million years ago, in the Tertiary Period, in the zone where the crustal plates supporting

Europe and Africa collided. The tops of these mountain ranges, which extend beyond France's borders, reach high altitudes – Mont Blanc, in the Alps, rises to 4,807 metres and Vignemale, in the French Pyrenees, to 3,298 metres (though Aneto, in the Spanish Pyrenees, is higher at 3,404 metres). The scenery is majestic, largely as a result of glacial erosion – craggy summits, jagged rows of peaks and deep U-shaped valleys. In the south-eastern part of the country, all these mountains, be they ancient or more recent, leave little room for plains. Such plains as there are follow the coastlines as, for example, in the Languedoc and eastern Corsica, or stretch between mountains, as in the Saône and Rhône valleys.

The Pyrenees viewed from the outskirts of Aurignac (Haute-Garonne)

France is drained by four major rivers, which provide focal points for industrial and urban development. The Loire (1,012 km long) and the Garonne (575 km) flow somewhat unevenly and are therefore unsuitable for modern river transport, but their estuaries shelter thriving ports like Nantes-Saint-Nazaire and Bordeaux. The other rivers, which flow more evenly and have been provided with the requisite structures on and around them, are important waterways. These are the Seine (776 km), which has made Rouen and Le Havre the major ports serving Paris and the surrounding area, and the Rhône (522 km in France) which is well maintained between Lyon and the sea. In addition, the Rhine, which forms the border between France and Germany for a distance of 190 km, is one of the most important navigable waterways in the world.

The same degree of diversity is found along France's coasts (5,500 km long) which have extremely varied scenery. Along the Channel, in the regions of Artois, Picardy and Upper Normandy, the coastline is made up of steep, often vertical cliffs. These are cut into by estuaries such as those of the Somme and the Seine and are being eroded by the force of the sea. Rocky coasts, which fringe the ancient massifs and the younger mountains, have a more complex history. The sea has sculpted them into bays and promontories, sometimes bordered by islets, as in Brittany, Provence and western Corsica. This has produced a jagged coastline which has provided harbours for ports but requires consummate navigation skills. Sandy beaches are found along the edges of plains and plateaux in Flanders, Les Landes, the Languedoc and eastern Corsica. Although popular with tourists, these make it difficult to build harbours. Lastly, marshy coastlines such as the Camargue and Poitevin areas, which were historically unsuitable for human habitation, can now be visited by tourists and are often part of nature reserves.

Temperate Climate

France is located between latitudes 41° and 52° North, on the western edge of the Eurasian continent, and so lies within the northern temperate zone. It is generally subjected to west winds bringing in air from the sea which result in a mild coastal and inland climate. But in winter, continental anticyclones sometimes cause cold winds like the bise (a keen, dry north or north-east wind) to sweep through France. All in all, a combination of maritime influences, latitude and altitude produce a varied climate.

In the west, the climate is predominantly oceanic, with a high level of rainfall brought in by Atlantic depressions, often in the form of light showers, and spread evenly over the year. This climate typically results in mild winters, particularly in the south, and cool summers. The weather is often changeable, with cloudy skies, rain and sunny spells following in swift succession.

The Brittany coast : Cap de la Chèvre (Finistère)

As we move inland, the climate deteriorates. In Alsace and Lorraine, the climate takes on continental characteristics, with hot, stormy summers, colder winters and less plentiful rainfall. In the south-west, the oceanic climate produces hotter summers and more autumn sunshine.

The Mediterranean climate prevails in the south-east and Corsica, giving clear skies, hot dry summers and mild winters. This area often receives more than 2,500 hours of sunshine per year. Rainfall comes mainly in spring and autumn, often in the form of heavy showers which accelerate the process of erosion and sometimes cause terrible flooding. There are strong winds such as the mistral, which sweeps down the Rhône valley, or the tramontana which blows over the Languedoc. Frosts and snow are unusual on the coastal plains but the climate soon becomes colder in the mountains of the hinterland. The Mediterranean climate is suitable for fragile crops such as grapevines and other fruit, and perhaps most favourable of all for summer tourism, especially as the sea can be as warm as 23° or 25°C in summer off the Mediterranean coasts.

Lastly, higher areas have a mountain climate, with cooler temperatures and more plentiful rainfall. In high mountain areas, the number of days when temperatures are below freezing may be over 150 per year and the mantle of snow may last for up to six months. Because the climate varies with altitude, there are different bands of vegetation. Broad-leaved trees gradually give way to conifers, which in turn are replaced by low-growing alpine plants above 2,000 m. But there are considerable differences between the slopes, according to which way they face. *Adrets* (south-facing slopes) are most suitable for building villages and growing crops, whilst *ubacs* (north-facing slopes) often remain wooded.

Natural Resources

Forests

Its relief, geology and climate mean that France has a high farming potential. Most regions have plenty of good farmland, whose varieties include the limon soil of the Paris basin, the brown earth of the Atlantic forests and the red earth of the Mediterranean regions. With 16 million hectares of forests – 29% of its territory – France has the highest proportion of forested land in the European Union. The area covered by woods and forests has almost doubled in the last century, and has continued to increase since the end of the Second World War, owing to reforestation projects and the drift away from farming. In regions with an oceanic climate, forests are mainly broad-leaved – oak-trees preferring sunny areas and beeches thriving in cooler, damper parts. In Mediterranean regions, the need to adapt to dry summers means that evergreens tend to dominate. Of the broad-leaved trees, the holm oak thrives on chalky soil and the cork oak on siliceous soil. The most prevalent conifers are the maritime pine, Aleppo pine and Corsican pine. In mountain forests, broad-leaved trees grow in the valleys and on the lower slopes. Higher up, they give way to conifers, which are more resistant to the cold winter temperatures. These conifers are mainly spruce and fir trees in areas with high precipitation such as the Vosges, the Jura and the northern Alps. But in dry areas like the southern Alps, larches, which lose their needle-like leaves in winter, make up most of the forest cover.

Despite their large surface area, French forests yield only 33 million m³ of wood per year. Production does not meet demand and the balance of trade for lumber and byproducts shows an annual deficit of over 16 billion francs (2.6 billion

Beech forest in the Vosges

dollars). This shortfall can partly be explained by the extremely fragmented nature of forest ownership. The State and local authorities have control over only 4 million hectares, most of which are in the Paris basin, the Loire Valley and north-eastern France. These forests are administered by the National Forestry Office and are admirably managed. But the situation is very different for the remaining 11 million hectares, which belong to 3.7 million private owners, two thirds of whom own less than a hectare. These small properties often produce little timber.

Fishing

Its annual catch of approximately 850,000 tonnes makes France the fourth biggest fishing nation in the European Union, behind Denmark, Spain and the United Kingdom. Most fishermen use traditional methods, working from small boats near the coast, particularly in Brittany and the Mediterranean. The last few years have seen a resurgence of this type of fishing, which serves the fresh fish market. Industrial fishing, which uses high-tonnage ships with sophisticated equipment for locating fish and preserving them once caught, is a centre of economic activity in large specialised ports like Boulogne, Lorient and Concarneau. These ships generally spend one or two weeks at sea, but may make trips of several months when fishing off the coast of Africa or tropical America.

For the last two decades, the French fishing industry has been in serious difficulty. Catches are falling and there is a deeper and deeper trade deficit (it now exceeds 11 billion francs [1.8 billion dollars] a year). The number of fishermen (there are 16,500 today) has halved since 1970 and the number of boats has likewise fallen (to 6,500 today). The problems come from depletion of fish stocks, pollution of some coastal waters and increasing competition from both industrial and third-world countries. In addition, the setting-up of the 200-mile exclusive economic zone has deprived French boats of the right to fish in some traditional fishing grounds, thus forcing them to move out into the cold waters of the Arctic Ocean and the North Atlantic, and the tropical waters of the Atlantic.

Binic harbour
(Côtes-d'Armor)

In 1983 the adoption of a European fisheries policy led to the introduction of several measures to prevent over-fishing in EC waters, regulate the market for fish, finance the restructuring of the fishing fleet and conclude agreements with countries outside the EC. The French government adopted some financial measures to alleviate the social consequences of the slump in Breton fishing ports in 1993 and

1994. Fish-farming, however, is enjoying a remarkable development. Oysters are chiefly produced on the coast of Charentes, Brittany
and Normandy and in the Arcachon basin. Mussels come from the bay
of l'Aiguillon, the Brest bay area and the bay of Mont Saint-Michel. Producers have been exploring new possibilities in the last two decades,
with salmon- and sea-trout-farms in Brittany and bass in the Etang de
Thau salt-lagoon on the Languedoc coast.

Energy and mineral resources

Although France's subsoil is rich in building materials
(gravel, sand and limestone for cement factories) and raw materials
such as kaolin, talc, sulphur, salt and potash, it has few mineral and
energy resources. Coal production is steadily declining (in 1997 the figure was only 8 million tonnes) and all the mines are set to close by
2005. Hydrocarbon resources are even more limited (2.1 million tonnes
a year of oil, and 2.9 billion m^3 of natural gas) and satisfy less than 5% of
French energy needs. France is better supplied with uranium, of which
almost 1,000 tonnes are produced annually. France has a good potential for hydro-electric power, but this is now being fully exploited. Alter-
native sources of energy still account for only 1.8% of national
consumption.

When it comes to metal ores, the only plentiful resource
is nickel in New Caledonia. Iron ore production is no longer carried out
in Lorraine, having ceased to be cost-effective, and all the other ores
have to be imported.

Distant Lands

In addition to its 96 metropolitan (mainland) departments, France includes a number of outposts and islands scattered all
over the world. These are a legacy of its colonial past and of the journeys made by French explorers. In all, they cover an area of some
120,000 km^2. While they are home to only 2.3 million people, they provide France with a presence in all the oceans and are a source of tropical fruits and drinks, as well as of minerals. They also have exceptional
potential for tourism and greatly extend French waters - the size of
France's exclusive economic zone under the terms of the law of the sea
established by the 1982 Convention makes it the country with the third
largest maritime area in the world (after the United States and the United
Kingdom) covering 10.2 million km^2. It has extremely varied plant and
animal life, as well as mineral and energy resources such as the poly-
metallic nodules covering some parts of the continental plateau around
these islands.

These far-off parts of France consist primarily of four
overseas departments (DOM), all of which are in the tropics. Three of

them – Guadeloupe and Martinique in the West Indies and Réunion in the Indian Ocean – are mountainous islands. Volcanoes, be they extinct like Mount Pelée on Martinique or active like La Soufrière in Guadeloupe and La Fournaise on Réunion, occupy much of their surface area. Little space is left for the plains. Much of the coastline of these islands is very irregular, and is made up of cliffs and beaches of black volcanic sand or white sand in alluvial areas. Some islands are surrounded by coral reefs. The tropical climate in these islands, where the temperature is always above 20°C, typically has two seasons: a wet summer and a dry winter. The slopes which are exposed to the trade winds have high rainfall figures, whilst those downwind, in the lee of the mountains, seem to be drier and more suitable for holiday-makers. In late summer, these islands may be swept by fearsome tropical storms or cyclones which wreak terrible damage.

French Guiana, in South America, is an overseas department dotted with hills less than 600 m. high and almost entirely covered by the dense Amazonian rainforest which flourishes in a climate of constant high temperatures and high rainfall. This forest, which contains a large number of plant species, is still difficult to penetrate and exploit and largely uninhabited. The Kourou space centre, from which the Ariane rockets are launched, towers over the mangrove-bordered coast.

France also has four overseas territories (TOM). Three of them are in the Pacific Ocean. New Caledonia is a long mountainous island surrounded by a coral reef and flanked by the small, low-lying Loyauté islands. The flora in these islands is rich and varied, thanks to the trade wind climate, which also makes them popular with tourists. French Polynesia is made up of over 150 volcanic islands and islets and coral atolls. Wallis and Futuna are also volcanic islands, as are the French Southern Territories in the Antarctic Ocean: the Crozet Islands, Amsterdam, Saint Paul and Kerguelen, which are often buffeted by ferocious storms and mainly used as bases for scientific research. This is also the case for Adélie Land, which is part of the Antarctic ice-cap. To these must be added the territorial units of Mayotte in the Indian Ocean and Saint-Pierre-et-Miquelon in the Atlantic Ocean, off the Canadian coast. The communities in this archipelago earn their living primarily from fishing.

Further reading:

R. Brunet, F. Auriac (editors), *Atlas de France* (14 vol.), vol. 6 : *Milieux et ressources*, Reclus-La Documentation française, 1995.

F. Damette, J. Scheibling, *La France, permanences et mutations*, Hachette, Carré géographie series, 1995.

J. Martin, L. Pernet et al., *Géographie*, Hachette, 1991.

Ph. Pinchemel, *La France*, 2 vol., A. Colin, 1992.

D. Pumain, Th. Saint-Julien, *La France*, Géographie universelle Belin-Reclus, vol. 2, 1990.

Metropolitan France, overseas departments (DOM), overseas territories (TOM) and "territorial collectivities" with special status: lands in every part of the world

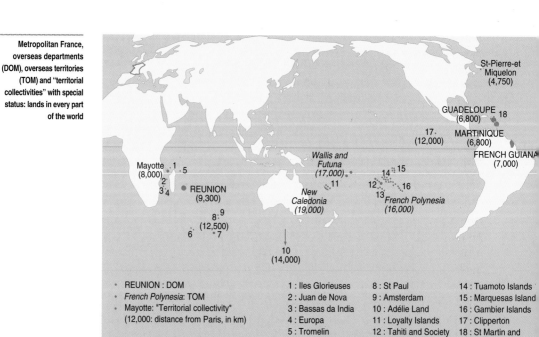

St-Pierre-et Miquelon (4,750)

GUADELOUPE (6,800) 18

17. (12,000) MARTINIQUE (6,800)

FRENCH GUIANA (7,000)

Mayotte 1 (8,000) 2 5 3 4

REUNION (9,300)

8: 9 (12,500) 6 7

Wallis and Futuna (17,000)

14 15 12 16 13 French Polynesia (16,000)

11 New Caledonia (19,000)

10 (14,000)

- REUNION : DOM
- *French Polynesia*: TOM
- Mayotte: "Territorial collectivity" (12,000: distance from Paris, in km)

1 : Iles Glorieuses	8 : St Paul	14 : Tuamoto Islands
2 : Juan de Nova	9 : Amsterdam	15 : Marquesas Island
3 : Bassas da India	10 : Adélie Land	16 : Gambier Islands
4 : Europa	11 : Loyalty Islands	17 : Clipperton
5 : Tromelin	12 : Tahiti and Society	18 : St Martin and
6 : Crozet Islands	Islands	St Barthélemy
7 : Kerguelen Islands	13 : Tubuai Islands	

Environmental Protection

In France, as in most industrialised countries, there has only been an environment policy as such for about twenty-five years. However, France was one of the first countries to set up, on 27 January 1971, a specific ministry for the protection of nature and the environment, which was then responsible simply for coordinating the work of the other ministries. Some earlier measures had demonstrated increasing interest in environmental issues, such as the 1960 law establishing national parks and the 1964 law on water, which was very advanced for its time in that it included financial incentives based on the "polluter pays" principle.

Between 1970 and 1990, French environment policy was largely a matter of laying down regulations and creating specialised bodies to deal with waste recovery and disposal (1976) and to monitor air quality (1981) and manage energy resources (1982). In 1990 these bodies were merged to form ADEME (*Agence de l'environnement et de la maîtrise de l'énergie* - Agency for the Environment and Energy Management). This 20-year period culminated in a national plan for the environment, which was debated in Parliament and approved by the government at the end of 1990.

Rapidly Rising Budget

Today, the Ministry for the Environment and Town and Country Planning has a staff of nearly 2,550 working within the central administration and around the country. Its budget for 1999 is almost 4 billion francs ($666 million) – a remarkable 110% increase on that for 1998. A new appropriation of 500 million francs ($83.3 million) has been allotted to ADEME, which has a brief to give a new boost to French policy on energy management and the development of renewable sources of energy. The environmental protection budget is also benefiting from the introduction of a general tax on activities which cause pollution. However, it does not include appropriations allotted for environmental purposes by other ministries, public corporations and local authorities,

40050385

which today total over 80 billion francs ($13.3 billion). Local authorities are responsible for the major proportion of public spending on the environment (over 65 billion francs), the bulk of which is carried out at the level of the *commune* (smallest administrative subdivision in France), which, together with that of the central government, is the essential one when it comes to managing environmental issues in France. If spending by industry and households is included, France now spends over 150 billion francs ($25 billion) on the environment. Regulation and legislation in this area are now relatively comprehensive. In March 1993 an inter-ministerial committee for the environment was established to promote environmental protection policies within all central government agencies. The existence since 1991 of 26 regional environmental boards (DIREN – *Directions régionales de l'environnement*), including four in the overseas departments, acting as intermediaries in discussions of environmental issues at local level, is another step forward.

The Ministry for the Environment and Town and Country Planning gives preference to dialogue over coercion and places greater emphasis on preventive action than on repairing damage. Local authorities have played a vital role since the 1983 law decentralising responsibility for town planning, which gave the mayor responsibility for the supply of drinking water, sewage treatment, land use, collection and treatment of household waste and traffic. More and more towns have established specialised agencies: over 100 have drawn up a municipal environment plan or an environment charter in order to ensure comprehensive management within a framework of sustainable development. Grass-roots interest in the environment has also increased. In the past 15 years, some 40,000 voluntary organisations have been founded (of which about 1,500 seem to be genuinely active) to defend the physical environment and protect the natural habitat and national heritage. Following the decree of 7 July 1977, recognised voluntary organisations are considered official partners of the state which grants them subsidies. In 20 years, their position has tended to become more flexible. They have moved from a defensive attitude towards a policy of dialogue.

France's Action at International Level

In recent years, protection of the environment has emerged as a necessity transcending national boundaries and sometimes requiring a global response. This has led to many treaties, directives and conventions. France has signed over a hundred European and some thirty international agreements and has often played a driving role in their negotiation. This was in particular the case of the declaration on the protection of the atmosphere signed by 24 states on 11 March 1989 in The Hague, and of a world environment fund set up in 1990 to help poorer countries. France also proposed the designation of the Antarctic as a nature reserve, devoted to science, and the establishment of a whale sanctuary around it. Paris hosted the 15th summit of the industrialised countries, on 16 July 1989, which strongly emphasised environmental questions and played an active part in the second United Nations Conference on Environment and Development held in Rio de Janeiro in June 1992. It ratified

the two conventions, on the climate and on biodiversity, in January and June 1994 respectively and signed the convention on desertification adopted following negotiations held in Paris in October 1994. France has launched a programme to promote renewable energy sources in Africa in order to reduce the impact of deforestation. In March 1998, representatives from 84 countries came to Paris for an international conference on water and sustainable development. During the international summits in Rio (1992), New York (1997) and Kyoto (1997), France committed itself to promoting sustainable development.

To stimulate the international community to improve management of water resources, France organised a Unesco conference on 'Water and Sustainable Development' in Paris in March 1998

Developing a medium- and long-term growth model, which husbands natural resources and protects both the environment and human health, has become an EU common policy (like the Common Agricultural Policy), under the terms of the Treaty of Amsterdam whose article 6 stresses that this is necessary in order to safeguard the future of generations to come.

Protection of the Atmosphere

The tramway in Strasbourg (Bas-Rhin) – a "green" means of public transport

In 1990, as a contribution to the international efforts, France set up an interministerial mission to examine the greenhouse effect. Since France does not

have significant fossil fuel resources, its energy policy is based on a large-scale nuclear power programme which, while presenting it with the problem of disposing of the nuclear waste, enabled it to reduce its carbon dioxide emissions by a third between 1980 and 1988. Since then, the increased volume of traffic has hampered its efforts to continue the reduction process, but with annual per capita emissions of 1.9 tonnes, France is still the industrialised country which releases the least carbon dioxide (CO_2).

As regards protection of the ozone layer, France participated actively in the negotiation of the Montreal Protocol, ratified in January 1989, which initially called for total elimination of chlorofluorocarbons (CFCs) by 1 January 2000. Subsequently, France and its European partners stepped up the pace by deciding to ban CFCs by 1 January 1995.

In terms of local pollution, France has reduced its sulphur dioxide emissions (SO_2) and stabilised lead pollution levels, but there are local increases in the concentration of nitrogen oxides as a result of increased car use. Stricter monitoring of old vehicles, government encouragement of scrapping of the oldest cars by offering owners a scrapyard bonus and the introduction of catalytic converters, which have been mandatory for new cars since 1 January 1993, along with the use of unleaded petrol, have not been enough. This is why research is under way to find less polluting substitute fuels such as natural gas or liquid petroleum gas. In addition, there have been renewed attempts to develop electric car production. In France, approximately 1,500 companies are subject to a special tax based on the quantity of atmospheric pollutants they emit, with the product of this tax used to develop techniques for reducing pollution and waste and to pay for an air quality monitoring system. Indeed, France has set up an imaginative system to monitor air pollution within urban areas. Some 30 networks of automatic measuring devices, run by local partnerships of those involved, have been installed all over the country to give immediate warning if pollution exceeds predetermined safety levels.

Recharging point for electric cars in La Rochelle (Charente-Maritime). In the year 2000, approximately 100,000 electric vehicles will be registered in France

Combating air pollution

Now that factories have been modernised and more and more heating systems use natural gas, air pollution mainly results from vehicle exhaust fumes, and the increased use of motor vehicles is exacerbating the problem. There have been many attempts by the authorities to combat this type of pollution. The law on air quality and rational use of energy of 30 December 1996 laid down a number of measures to ensure that everyone living in France can "breathe air which doesn't harm their health". When the warning threshold is reached, the public must be informed and restrictions applied to traffic and industry in the affected area. These may go so far as banning the use of vehicles without a green disc, for which only the least polluting vehicles – those which run on electricity or LPG or are fitted with a catalytic converter – are eligible. The air monitoring network, now principally covering the main conurbations and modelled on Airparif which has some thirty monitoring points in Paris, will eventually be extended to the whole country.

Water – a Precious Resource

France is privileged in comparison with many other countries in that it has an abundant supply of water; but this is a vulnerable resource, which is unequally distributed within the country. To manage this resource – estimated at 1,000 billion m^3 – an original system of water boards was instituted some 30 years ago. There are six of these public bodies, one for each of the great river basins in France. They are supervised by the Environment and Town and Country Planning Ministry, but are financed independently, through a tax levied on consumers in proportion to the amount of water used or pollution caused. These funds are then redistributed in the form of loans or subsidies, for example to help the building or improvement of a water treatment plant. Although this policy is based on the "polluter-pays" principle, the water boards have always favoured a cooperative approach facilitated by the existence of "basin committees".

The 'Silure', the boat that cleans up the river Seine, in Paris

Within each agency, this body acts as a "water parliament" where all those concerned by decisions can have their say. The 1964 law on water was revised in January 1992 to reinforce the role of local authorities, particularly in maintaining waterways, and underlines a fundamental principle: that water is now considered part of the nation's shared heritage. The aim is to restore the quality of France's 277,000 km of rivers and streams. Thanks to the active role of the water boards real progress has been made: in 20 years, industrial pollution of water has been reduced by over 70%. One of the government's objectives is completely to eliminate toxic wastes from watercourses before the end of the century.

Groundwater has not escaped pollution in regions where there is intensive farming. There is a national programme designed to alert farmers to the problems, including those caused by such practices as the thoughtless use of liquid pig manure and excessive use of fertilisers in their fields. To reduce pollution from household waste, France is committed, under a 1991 European directive, to bringing in systems ensuring the collection and treatment of all liquid waste by 2005. Giving a boost to its water policy is a priority for France and, since 1992, aid and investment have been substantially increased.

Sea-water is of course also affected by pollution, whether it be from farming, centres of population, industry or disasters at sea. Every year, millions of tourists flock to the beaches all along France's 5,500 km of coastline. Bathing water quality is monitored in over 700 seaside *communes* and, throughout the year, over 20,000 samples of sea water are analysed to check whether they

**The Coastal and Lakeside Areas Conservation Agency,
Effective Action**

An underrated jewel of the Environment and Town and Country Planning Ministry, the Coastal and Lakeside Areas Conservation Agency was set up in 1975. In the over 20 years of its existence, this government-run agency has saved 10% of France's coastal areas from urban and industrial development and intensive farming – doing so without treating its 360 protected sites (covering an area of nearly 50,000 hectares along 650 km of coast) as museum pieces. The lakes involved include those of Annecy, Grandlieu, the forest of Orient and Léman (Geneva). Once the agency has bought the land, the sites are managed by the communal or departmental authorities, so that as many people as possible can enjoy them. From its inception, the agency has acted as a real estate agency: its regional representatives scour their areas for suitable sites (either of special ecological interest or of outstanding natural beauty), exercise their pre-emptive right to first refusal on properties and make offers, endeavour to convince local councillors of the importance of conserving the sites and, finally, negotiate with potential sponsors and patrons to balance their budgets.

As an *établissement public* (public institution), the agency can receive gifts and bequests, but is mainly state-funded. Its investment budget is approximately 130 million francs ($28 million), part being used to equip and restore the sites it acquires, by clearing paths, shoring up sand-dunes and replanting woodland. The agency's ultimate goal is to protect 25% of French coastal areas. Earlier generations have left an invaluable mark on France's landscapes, of which twenty or so, Mont-Saint-Michel amongst them, are included in UNESCO's list of world heritage sites.

comply with the standards set by a European directive; each year, the list of top-rated localities is announced at the start of the summer season.

As more waste treatment plants have been set up in coastal towns, the health ratings of the beaches have improved considerably, since water at over 85% of the monitoring points now reaches the required standard.

The Coastal and Lakeside Areas Conservation Agency is responsible for protecting the invaluable natural heritage of the French coastal areas. This government-run body, set up in 1975, acquires land bordering the coast and around large lakes and other stretches of water in order to preserve the natural diversity and integrity of these sites. While it was not considered practicable to prevent development all along the French coast, some special protective measures have been taken. The Coastline Law of 3 January 1986, strengthened in 1989, was designed to slow or prevent development in areas defined as "remarkable" in over 1,100 *communes*.

Protection of Nature and the Landscape

The diversity of its natural environment is reflected in the wealth of flora and fauna and France passed a law on the protection of nature back in 1976. Since 1982 more than 14,000 "natural areas whose flora and fauna are of ecological interest" (*Zones naturelles d'intérêt écologique faunistique et floristique* - ZNIEFF), mostly located in humid areas or forests, have been identified and studied. In response to the European "Habitat directive" of 21 May 1992 on conservation of natural habitats and wild plants and animals, France is completing the first inventory of its resources. By 2004, the "Natura 2000" network will include all the sites of interest to ensure that biodiversity is preserved within Europe.

Certain endangered species require special protective measures. The Atlantic salmon, which had completely disappeared from most rivers, has made a comeback since the waters in which it spawns have been allowed to recover, special dams through which the fish may pass built and alevins reintroduced. In 1994 the Environment Minister and the mayors of the *communes* concerned signed a charter to try to protect the last remaining bears of the Pyrenees and are implementing a plan to reintroduce bears into the area.

The Law of 8 January 1993 on the protection and enhancement of the landscape is allowing the relevant authorities to take a fresh look at the areas surrounding towns, often disfigured by the anarchic proliferation of billboards, factories and supermarkets, in some places order the burying of electricity cables and, in general, take environmental concerns into account.

The most crucial problem for the future is that of the countryside. An increasingly industrialised agricultural sector and continuing flight from the land are having damaging repercussions on the traditional rural landscapes. Solutions must be found quickly to save France's rural heritage.

The brightest jewels in France's system of nature protection are still the national parks, which consist of the park itself, a central uninhabited area, surrounded by a peripheral area in which less stringent regulations apply. There are six in metropolitan France and one in Guadeloupe. Six more, principally in the Mont Blanc area of the Alps, Corsica, Brittany and French Guiana are at the planning stage. The existing parks cover a total of 992,000 hectares, of which 371,000 are within the central uninhabited areas which receive maximum protection. While the national parks (except for the island of Port Cros) are located in mountain areas, the 30-or-so regional natural parks are spread all over the country and include the moorlands of the Monts d'Arrée in Brittany, *ballons* (rounded mountains) of Alsace, Camargue marshes in southern France, lakes of Brenne and lavender fields of Luberon. They cover 5,020,000 hectares and are located in 2,600 *communes* with a total of almost two million inhabitants. More than ten new parks are planned. While one of the main purposes of these parks, governed by less stringent legislation than national parks, is, of course, to protect the environment, they also contribute to the balanced development of the various economic activities.

There are also many nature reserves belonging to the State, *communes* or private owners, some of which are the last refuge for endangered species. There are 132 nature reserves in France today with some 40 more at the planning stage. Amongst the best-known are the Aiguilles Rouges in the Alps and the Banc d'Arguin in the Arcachon basin.

Waste Disposal Policy

The volume of household and industrial waste is constantly rising in all the industrialised countries. Each year France produces over 24 million tonnes of household waste. The total amount has more than doubled in 30 years and now averages 416 kilograms per person every year. Large conurbations produce proportionally much more than rural communities. Most of this waste ends up, usually after compacting, on rubbish tips which, since 1 July 1992, accept only "ultimate" waste which cannot be re-used or recycled at incineration plants: fly ash and the residues left after scrubbing smoke, which contain very large amounts of heavy metals and other pollutants.

An average of 30,000 tonnes a day of household waste is burned in almost 300 incinerators throughout France. In the largest incineration plants, the energy potential is recovered through combined cycle generation, which simultaneously produces heat and power. The aim is to produce fewer waste products to begin with and to use or recycle those that are produced. Sorting rubbish at home is becoming a priority. Many French communes have introduced special rubbish bins or large containers to separate paper and glass, and in some cases aluminium, metal, plastic and used motor oil, from other waste products. Apart from plastics, in France glass recycling has been the most successful. 35% of glass is now recycled, more than double the amount 15 years ago. Since 1 January 1993, businesses have been required to deal with, or contribute to the cost of dealing with the waste resulting from the packaging used with their products. The goal is to recycle 75% of packaging by the year 2002.

The Law of 13 July 1992 stipulating that each department draw up a plan for eliminating household waste by 1996 also covers the around 150 million tonnes of industrial waste. Of this, 100 million tonnes can be used as remblai, hard core, etc., 40 million tonnes is considered harmless and on a par with household waste and the rest contains toxic or hazardous pollutants. There are different elimination procedures for the specific categories of waste: incineration, physico-chemical detoxification and burial (half the waste) in one of the 11 monitored waste disposal sites reserved for this type of product. After 2002, only ultimate waste will be authorised for storage in these dumps. The new rules provide for setting up a local information and monitoring committee (which will include local residents and voluntary groups) at each waste treatment or storage site. Despite these measures, old illegal dumps still exist. The new rules condemn illegal dumping and ban imports of household waste for disposal in France. Cross-border transfer of waste is now much more strictly monitored. On 1 April 1993 a tax on the dumping of household and similar waste was brought in and the Law of 2 February 1995 imposed one on the processing and dumping of special industrial waste.

Each person living in France produces an average of 416 kilos of household waste a year, making sorting, as shown here in Clermont-Ferrand (Puy-de-Dôme), a necessity

Constant Battle against Soil Pollution

Soil pollution is caused by a wide variety of agents, including trace elements – such as metals, metal compounds and organic micro-pollutants –, pesticides, etc. used in agriculture, hydrocarbons and radio-active materials. In the long term, the most dangerous metals are mercury, lead, cadmium, nickel and chromium. Insecticides, herbicides, fungicides and bactericides, all of which are now widely used in farming, also cause serious damage. Soil pollution harms vegetation and leads to a build-up of toxic substances in plants, causing severe problems for human health. Chemicals present in the soil can also lead to corrosion of structures under the ground.

Mining areas, regions in which there is intensive farming, pastures and ploughed fields close to motorways and land on which agro-industrial effluent or urban compost has been spread are amongst the worst affected areas. In 1998, the Ministry for the Environment and Town and Country Planning inventory listed 896 polluted sites. Since 1994, 123 have been treated and another 226 identified. The majority of these sites are found in the industrial heartlands such as the Nord-Pas-de-Calais, Ile-de-France and Rhône-Alpes.

The existence of sites affected by industrial pollution has led to the development of special anti-pollution procedures, one of which is to encase the pollutants in leak-proof containers; this does not eliminate the waste, but it prevents it from contaminating the natural environment. However, genuine cleaning of sites requires the elimination of pollutants, necessitating their treatment on site or in specialised plants. On-site techniques include incineration in the case of hydrocarbons, cleaning the polluted land using mineral substances, volatisation of the waste and biological methods for pollution due to organic products. ADEME, the Agency for the Environment and Energy Management is active in all these fields.

Economy, Research and Development

The role of the environment has recently been integrated into the overall plan to stimulate the French economy. All in all, in 1994 France devoted over 1% of its GDP to environmental protection and firms are having to make environmental concerns part of their overall strategic thinking. But real progress consists not only in reducing the effects of pollution, i.e. installing filters, dust removers or waste processing plants, but in adopting clean technology. ADEME allocated part of its 1.1 billion franc budget to the development and use of clean technology. Products themselves must become "eco-products" which do not pollute during production, when used or when they are destroyed. Introduced in 1991, the "NF Environnement" label signifies that the producer has carried out an ecological audit (ecoaudit) of a product over its whole life cycle, beginning with the raw materials, and that it is therefore environmentally friendly. Annual turnover in the "eco-industries" exceeds 110 billion francs ($18 billion), of which the water and waste product sectors account for the lion's share.

Almost 400,000 people are employed in environmental protection of whom over 60% are engaged in the battle against pollution. The gradual exodus from the French countryside is tending to increase the number of jobs for those who remain: for example, people are needed to maintain streams and footpaths and conserve the nation's natural heritage. Indeed, as part of its campaign to reduce unemployment, the government is helping to create "green jobs".

An effective environmental policy also requires high-level research. France devotes 4.5% of its public research budget to this, funding nearly 4,000 scientists and engineers within world-renowned research teams, notably in the fields of climate, atmosphere, security and hydrogeology. But, unlike some countries, such as the United States and Japan, France does not have one single all-embracing environmental research agency. The work is carried out in several hundred university laboratories and in scientific institutes such as the CNRS (*Centre national de la recherche scientifique* – national centre for scientific research), the National Natural History Museum, INSERM (*Institut national de la santé et de la recherche médicale* – national institute for health and medical research), INRA (*Institut national de la recherche agronomique* – national institute for agronomic research), BRGM (*Bureau de recherches géologiques et minières* – geological and mining research agency), ORSTOM (*Office de recherche scientifique et technique outre-mer* – Overseas Technical and Scientific Research Office) now IRD (*Institut de recherche pour le développement* – Research institute for development), IFREMER (*Institut français de recherche sur la mer* – French research establishment for marine resources), CEMAGREF (*Centre national du machinisme agricole, du génie rural, des eaux et des forêts* – national centre for agricultural mechanisation, rural engineering, water and forestry), *Météo-France* (meteorological office), CNES (*Centre national d'études spatiales* – National Space Research Centre), etc. The only exception to this rule, INERIS (*Institut national de l'environnement industriel et les risques* – national institute for the industrial environment and hazards), specialises in risk analysis and evaluation and the development of less polluting processes and assists in defining standards. IFEN (*Institut français de l'environnement* – French environment institute), established on 18 November 1991, is also an essential tool in environment policy. Working in conjunction with all the other relevant bodies, IFEN is responsible for monitoring the state of the environment and collecting and processing all data relating to it. IFEN is in regular contact with the European Environment Agency which has its headquarters in Copenhagen.

A New Vision

Real progress depends not only on this comprehensive approach, but in fact essentially on the spirit of cooperation which is ever-increasingly governing town and country planning in France. Indeed, the environment and town and country planning are now covered by the same ministry. Proposals for major infrastructure projects such as building motorways and extending the high-speed

(TGV) rail network are now the subject of democratic debate. Of the 6,000 impact studies carried out in France each year, 300 concern infrastructure projects, including those for high-voltage cables. The decree of 25 February 1993 broadened the scope of impact studies and made them more accessible to the public. The public enquiries required before a new road, motorway extension or section of the TGV rail network can be built are also being reformed so that there is more transparency and consultation before decisions are made.

In addition, all manner of initiatives are strengthening a new civic value, "eco-citizenship". For example, over 120,000 young people took part in the operation "1,000 Challenges for my Planet" launched in 1993. Similarly in 1994, 250 young Frenchmen volunteered to do their national service working for the environment. Since 1995, those taking up this option have worked for their employers as civilians. In France, the environment is becoming everyone's business.

Further reading:

Ministère de l'Environnement et de l'Aménagement du territoire, *Données économiques de l'environnement, 1997 edition*, La Documentation française-Économica, 1997.

Ministère de l'Environnement - Institut français de l'environnement, *L'environnement en France*, Dunod, 1994-1995.

Ministère de l'Environnement, *Éthique et environnement*, Actes du colloque du 13 décembre 1996, La Documentation française, 1997.

P.-H. Bourrelier, Commissariat général du Plan, *La prévention des risques naturels: rapport d'évaluation*, La Documentation française, 1997.

R. Brunet, F. Auriac (editors), *Atlas de France*, vol. 6, *Milieux et ressources*, Reclus-La Documentation française, 1995.

3

The Population

On 1 January 1999, metropolitan (mainland) France had a population of 58.7 million – the twenty-first largest population in the world and third largest in the European Union. If the over two million inhabitants of the overseas departments and territories are added to this figure, the population of France is nearly 61 million.

Great Variations in Density

With an average population of 107 inhabitants per km², France is relatively densely populated in global terms. The average population density worldwide is 45 inhabitants per km², and the United States has a population density of only 29 inhabitants per km². But in Europe, France is among the less densely populated countries, coming ninth on the list of EU countries, a long way behind the Netherlands (at 460 inhabitants per km²), the United Kingdom (240 inhabitants per km²), Germany (235 inhabitants

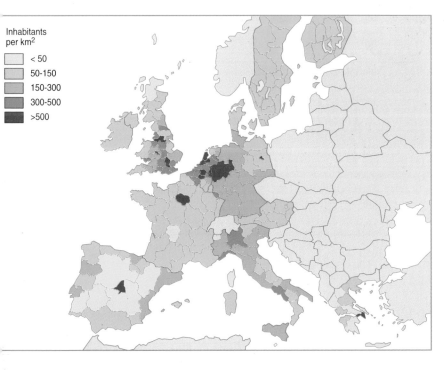

Inhabitants per km²

- < 50
- 50-150
- 150-300
- 300-500
- >500

Population density in Europe. Next to the highly populated European diagonal, France – apart from the Paris region – stands out as an oasis of low population density

per km²) and Italy (195 inhabitants per km²). But average density is not a particularly useful indicator, since population distribution is highly uneven. Half of the population occupy just over 10% of the surface area – the Paris area and lower part of the Seine valley, the Lyon area, the Rhône valley and the Mediterranean coast, the Loire, Garonne and Rhine valleys, the Brittany coast and industrial areas in Lorraine and the north. These areas have the densest populations; it is Paris which holds the record, with 20,000 inhabitants per km². Meanwhile, vast swathes of countryside are sparsely populated – sometimes with fewer than 20 inhabitants per km². Apart from the mountainous zones of the Alps, the Massif Central, the Pyrenees and Corsica, these empty areas contain the great forests – the Landes, Sologne, the eastern part of the Paris basin and the Ardennes. They form a diagonal band stretching from the Pyrenean part of Piedmont to the massif of the Ardennes. In some parts of this deserted swathe, there are districts with fewer than ten inhabitants per km², such as Castellane, Florac and Barcelonnette.

Urbanisation occurred later in France than in some other European countries, such as Britain and Germany. It was only in 1930 that the urban population overtook the rural population. From the 1950s, France started to catch up and in 1996 76.4% of the population were living in the 361 urban areas identified by INSEE, the French national institute of economic and statistical information. At first, there was population growth in both town centres and suburbs, but in the 1970s this trend was reversed and the populations of most city centres and inner suburbs of the larger conurbations decreased in size. At the same time, outer suburbs and rural districts around towns and cities experienced a significant rise in the number of inhabitants. These outlying suburbs now house a total of 9 million people, an increase of nearly 800,000 between the 1982 and 1990 censuses, whilst the populations of town and city centres decreased by a total of over 700,000.

In the past forty years, the French population has grown by almost 15 million, as much as between 1810 and 1959, but the rate of growth is tending to slow down

Population Growth in France

c. 1150	15 million
c. 1680	20 million
1750	25 million
1810	30 million
1841	35 million
1924	40 million
1959	45 million
1968	50 million
1985	55 million
1999	59 million

The largest urban area is Paris, whose conurbation is home to 10.3 million people – over 20% of the total number of city-dwellers in France. The conurbations of northern France (at 3.7 million inhabitants), Marseille and the Lower Rhône (2.8 million) and the Lyon area (also 2.8 million) are much smaller than Paris – the only French city which can really be said to rival metropolises like New York, Tokyo and London. The *Direction de la Population et des Migrations* (office of population and migration)

A land of varying population density

Toulouse and its bridges
over the Garonne
(Haute-Garonne)

Monthélie (Côte-d'Or)
a village in Bourgogne

The boulevard
de Villefontaine
in L'Isle-d'Abeau (Isère)

at the Ministry for Employment and Solidarity estimates that the population of the Ile-de-France (Paris area) will increase by 16% between 1990 and 2020, when it will reach 12 million.

Future population growth will be even greater in the Provence-Alpes-Côtes d'Azur and Languedoc-Roussillon regions, with respective increases of 30 and 37%. During the last two decades, these have been the ones whose populations have grown the fastest, along with Rhône-Alpes, the Centre and Aquitaine. Conversely, regions which were urbanised and industrialised earlier, like the Nord-Pas-de-Calais, Lorraine and Champagne-Ardenne, and essentially rural areas like the Limousin and the Auvergne, are likely to see their population remain stable or even decrease.

Broadly speaking, these figures confirm the redistribution of the population in France which began nearly a quarter of a century ago.

The End of the Population Boom

For a long time now, population trends in France have been rather different from those in neighbouring countries. France was one of the first countries in the world to experience a significant fall in the death rate – in the 18th century – and a phase of rapid population growth. But the boom did not last and, from the early 19th century to the Second World War, population growth was moderate, owing to an early

decrease in the fertility rate. There were 30 million inhabitants in 1800, and only 41 million in 1940. During the same period, the populations of Germany and the United Kingdom approximately quadrupled: if the French population had grown to a similar extent, there would have been 120 million inhabitants in 1940, and perhaps as many as 150 million today. On the other hand, post-war population growth has been greater in France than elsewhere: the number of inhabitants has risen by 18 million, i.e. 44%, in the last 50 years. The fact that France has now caught up with comparable European neighbours can be explained by an increase in the fertility rate throughout the 'baby boom' years (it varied between 2.9 and 2.3 children per woman between 1946 and 1973); the continued fall in the death rate, particularly infant mortality (which was 52 per 1,000 in 1950, compared with fewer than 5 per 1,000 today); and high levels of immigration (which, on average, accounted for a quarter of this growth).

As life expectancy rises yearly, grandparents are able to share hobbies with their grandchildren – in this case, mountain-biking

Population growth in France is currently somewhat healthier than in other European countries. The natural growth rate was 3.3 per

1,000 in 1997. (The birth rate was 9.1 per 1,000 and the death rate 12.4 per 1,000.) This is the third highest rate of growth in the 15 countries of the European Union, topped only by Ireland and Luxembourg. But it is still a very low figure and although France is not yet in the same bracket as Germany, Italy and Spain, where the net natural change is nil or even negative, it is likely to be so in the end. Population figures in France are still being influenced by growth in the past: there are a large number of women of child-bearing age who were born when the birth rate was still high (the average age of women giving birth is now 29); and the death rate remains stable at less than 10 per 1,000, since the population is at present relatively young. But this will change when the generations born in the last twenty years, when fewer babies were born, reach child-bearing age. The annual number of births, which currently stands at 740,000, might then fall to 200,000 if the fertility rate remains at its present level of 1.7 children per woman. At the same time, the number of deaths will not fall and might even rise, since the population as a whole is getting older. People are living longer – average life expectancy is now 74 for men and 82 for women. In combination with the low fertility rate, this inevitably results in an ageing population. If such factors are taken into account, and if immigration does not compensate for these losses, the population of France could start to decline in about twenty-five years' time.

A Long Tradition of Immigration

Immigrants have been settling in France for almost 150 years. During the second half of the 19th century, when most Euro-

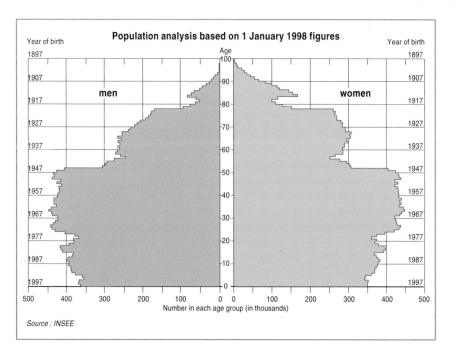

Population analysis based on 1 January 1998 figures

Year of birth — men — Age — women — Year of birth

Number in each age group (in thousands)

Source : INSEE

A falling birthrate narrows the base of the age-pyramid, while increased longevity widens it at the upper levels

pean migrants were leaving the continent to people new lands such as the United States of America, Canada, Argentina, Australia and Brazil, France was the only one of the older nations with a sizeable contingent of foreign inhabitants. A hundred years after the Revolution, in 1889, there were over a million of them, and many were naturalised on the occasion of its centenary. Up to the interwar period, France lacked people and manpower, as a result of the slow rate of population growth; and in addition to immigrants seeking jobs (above all, Italians and Poles), there were refugees – Greeks, Armenians, Russians, Spaniards and so on.

There was a renewed influx of immigrants after the Second World War, especially in the late 1950s: the baby boomers were not yet old enough to work and France was entering the thirty-year period of high growth known as the *Trente Glorieuses*. Immigrants at this time were largely young workers, initially from Italy and Spain, then the Maghreb and Portugal, sub-Saharan Africa and the Middle East and, a little later on, Asia.

From the mid-1970s, the economic crisis combined with baby boomers entering the employment market to generate a swift rise in unemployment. In 1974, measures were brought in to curb economic immigration. There was then a drop in the number of immigrants entering the country: an average 220,000 per year from 1974 to 1982 fell to 100,000 per year from 1982 to 1990, before rising slightly to 120,000 between 1990 and 1995; in 1997, 74,000 immigrants came to France.

One in four French people has some foreign antecedents. Recent immigrants, younger and more likely to be women than formerly, come from a very wide range of countries

The nature of immigration to France has also changed. People are now migrating to France primarily to join members of their family who are already there, and women and children are replacing young men in the immigration statistics. Immigrants now also come from a wider variety of countries, with a significant rise in the numbers arriving from Asia and Latin America and, more recently, from Eastern Europe and Russia. Illegal immigration is a problem in France, as in many EU countries: by its very nature, it cannot be quantified and this gives rise to widely differing estimates. However, in the main, illegal immigrants are known to be young workers attracted by the possibility of finding work in the black economy.

In times of economic crisis, immigration is the subject of heated debate, as it always has been in hard times. But earlier waves of immigrants have always succeeded in becoming integrated into the existing population, although at times not without difficulty. Indeed, recent developments show that second- and third-generation children of immigrants tend to adopt 'French' habits and lifestyles. If we add the number of French people with at least one foreign parent or grandparent to the number of foreigners currently living in France (approximately 4 million), we reach a total figure of over 12 million inhabitants with a relatively recent foreign background. If we take into account immigration figures since the 19th century, it is reasonable to say that one in four French people has some foreign roots. Since natural population growth is tending gradually to decline, it is possible that only migration to France can ensure that the population remains stable or increases.

The Labour Force

France's working population (by which we mean people currently in work, those seeking work and those who have taken early retirement) stood at 26.6 million in 1997, 45.3% of the total population. The labour force has grown rapidly during the last forty years (the 1954 figure was 19.5 million) as a result of the post-war baby boom, increase in immigration, and rise in the number of women with jobs outside the home. The latter has doubled since 1954 and now accounts for 47% of the total working population.

At the same time, the employment structure has altered. There has been a long decline in the number of jobs in agriculture, which now provides employment for only a million people – 4% of the population currently in work, compared with 30% in 1954. In most rural areas today farmers are very much in the minority: only one person in five living in the country belongs to a farming family.

The proportion of jobs in industry and construction has been declining for over 20 years. This sector employed 38% of the labour force in the early 1970s, but only 26% in 1996. The drop in the number of jobs has been accompanied by a significant rise in the level

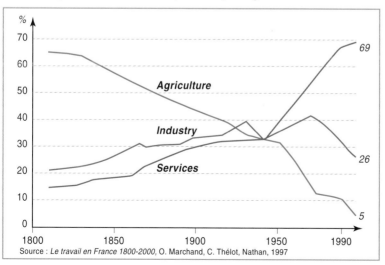

Source : *Le travail en France 1800-2000*, O. Marchand, C. Thélot, Nathan, 1997

Collapsing agricultural employment over the past century, falling industrial employment in the past 25 years and rapidly rising service sector employment reflect profound changes in France's society and economy

of qualifications. The number of unskilled workers fell by almost 2 million between 1975 and 1996, whereas the number of skilled workers and technicians rose by 700,000.

The dominance of the service sector in the economy has been confirmed. Nearly 16 million people are now employed in this sector, i.e. 69% of those in work (compared with 40% in 1954), which has created over 5 million additional jobs since 1970. Here too, the number of unskilled jobs is falling – largely as a result of computerisation. Whilst it is true that sectors like transport, health, tourism and leisure activities and the environment continue to generate employment, others, like small-scale retailing and banking are cutting down on the number of people they employ.

In 1997, 3.1 million people were unemployed (12.4% of the labour force). Until 1974, the rate of unemployment was under 3% and it was only in 1977 that French unemployment exceeded one million for the first time. In the space of twenty years, unemployment has become the chief social problem in France. It has arisen from a combination of long-lasting

Laboratory technicians in the Mirabel centre (Puy-de-Dôme): women make up 47 % of the French workforce

economic crisis and an increase in the number of people in the employment market. The baby boomers are still of working age, the generations coming into the labour market are not yet those affected by the fall in the birth rate and the number of women in employment continues to rise. At the same time, the number of jobs in industry is rapidly falling, and employment in the tertiary sector is not only no longer growing, but may even be declining. Increasingly, the jobs available are for skilled workers and often few in number. 16% of the workforce are now in part-time employment, but an increase in this area will not solve the unemployment problem, which is a severe drain on the public purse: over 300 billion francs ($ 50 billion) are spent every year on unemployment benefit and job creation schemes. Governments have striven to find long-term solutions – one example is the shorter working week of 35 hours instead of 39 – but the problem will genuinely be alleviated from 2006 onwards when the baby boomers start to retire and the generations born since the end of the 'seventies take their place.

Further reading:

R. Brunet, F. Auriac (editors), *Atlas de France* (14 vol.), vol. 6 : *Milieux et ressources*, vol. 2 : *L'espace des villes*, Reclus-La Documentation française, 1995.

F. Damette, J. Scheibling, *La France*, Hachette supérieur, 1989.

D. Noin, *L'espace français*, A. Colin, 1995.

J.-L. Mathieu, *La France en Europe et dans le monde*, Géographie Première, Bordas, 1997.

P. Merienne, *Le petit atlas de la France, départements et territoires d'outre-mer*, Édition Ouest-France, 1997.

L'état de la France 98-99, La Découverte, 1998.

Données sociales 1997, INSEE, 1997.

HISTORY

4

From Ancient Times to the Fifth Republic

France is often used as a typical example of the nation-state, a comparatively rare historical and geographical phenomenon in which the three essential elements in a country's identity – territory, state and people – are melded into a united whole. For a country to reach this point, its citizens have to identify with a geographical area and a sufficiently stable and long-lasting political system – in this case the Republic. These circumstances are the result of a lengthy process of construction culminating with the advent of the Fifth Republic.

Pre-Revolutionary France – a Slow Gestation Period

It is by no means easy to date France's birth as a nation. Was it 496 AD, when King Clovis converted to Christianity, or 987, the coronation of Hugh Capet, founder of the Capetian dynasty which was to reign for nine hundred years, or 1789, the year of the Revolution in which France declared itself to be a nation, as well as a state? Neither historians nor ordinary citizens seem able to agree; and France as a nation has recently celebrated all three occasions – the 1,500th anniversary of Clovis' conversion to Christianity, the 1,000th anniversary of Hugh Capet's coronation and the bicentenary of the Revolution. The wealth of possible "dates of birth" shows, at any rate, that France, like any living entity, developed gradually and absorbed many different influences into its identity.

True, the France inherited from antiquity and the Middle Ages bore little resemblance to the France we know today and, in the late fifteenth century, the Capetian kingdom was more

Life in France in the fifteenth century – harvesting and bathing in August, illustration by Pol de Limbourg in the *Très riches heures du Duc de Berry*, now kept in the Condé museum in Chantilly

like a fragmented archipelago than today's metropolitan France. But these long evolutionary phases were essential, in that they wove the fabric of the French nation and laid the foundations of France's territorial structure, by determining the sites of most towns and communication links. These focal points and axes were to knit the territory together and shape France geographically through wars, annexations, cessions of territory, inheritances and marriages. Some phases were vital to this long process of development – one thinks of the period of Roman domination, which left Gaul fine-meshed with towns and road-links and sowed the seeds of linguistic unity by spreading the use of Latin, or the medieval expansion which saw the rebirth of towns, mushrooming of villages and an increase in contacts with other communities from the eleventh to thirteenth centuries.

It should not be forgotten that during this slow emergence France was host to many different peoples. The prehistoric settlements we know about from the many sites they left behind them were added to by Celtic invaders, then Mediterranean peoples like the Greeks and Romans, warrior nomads from the Steppes such as the Huns, Germanic and Nordic peoples such as the Vandals, Swabians, Burgundians, Alemannians, Visigoths and Franks, and later the Arabs and Vikings. These peoples sometimes determined the core population in certain areas, but most of all, they mixed and intermarried in the melting-pot in which France was cast. It was in this period, too, under the Capetians, that the territory of France was gradually established and the institutions and administrative structures which govern and organise it today were first set up. The choice of Paris as the capital was crucial: the territory and the nascent state were able gradually to unite France around the focal point of the capital.

The Legacy of the Revolution and the Empire

France's status as nation was reinforced by the Revolution in 1789. On 14 July 1790, a year after the fall of the Bastille, delegates from all parts of the country flocked to Paris to celebrate the *Fête de la Fédération* and proclaim their allegiance to a single, common nation. The ideals proclaimed were: individual freedom and mutual respect; the right of peoples to self-determination; and institutions which would protect the welfare of citizens. These aspirations, which were codified in the Declaration of the Rights of Man and the Citizen of 26 August 1789, grew out of the work of Enlightenment philosophers in the eighteenth century and were heavily influenced by the ideas of authors like Montesquieu, who laid down the principle of separation of the legislature, executive and judiciary in his *The Spirit of the Law* of 1748, and Jean-Jacques Rousseau, who developed theories of political equality and the sovereignty of the people in *The Social Contract* (1762). These texts had considerable influence on the writers of the Constitution of the United States of America in 1787. The values propounded in them are seen as universal and may be considered the cornerstone of modern democracy. They had widespread repercussions and provided a model for national liberation movements during the nineteenth century. The United Nations' Universal Declaration of Human Rights of 10 December 1948 also owed much to the Declaration of the Rights of Man and the Citizen.

But these principles did not immediately become law. Many of them were enshrined in the first French Constitution in 1791, and even more in the 1793 constitution; however, only time and numerous political struggles and social conflicts were to see them affirmed as inalienable rights. The First Republic was proclaimed on 22 September 1792, but the democratic Constitution it produced in 1793 was never implemented. Civil war and clashes with the many other European states who banded together against France ended in the Reign of Terror – a far cry from the noble ideals of 1789. After Robespierre's execution in July 1794, the Thermidorian Convention (1794-1795) and the Directory (1795-1797) led to a coup by Napoleon Bonaparte, who took over first as Consul (1799-1804), then as Emperor of the French. The monarchy had been abolished in 1792; it was now superseded by the Empire and, however different the structures and organisation of that Empire might be, the French, who had briefly been citizens, were once more subjects. During the wars of the Revolution and the Empire, France tried to impose its model and institutions on many other European countries; but its initial desire to free "oppressed peoples" was soon replaced by a desire to conquer and annex territories, revealing the "right of peoples to self-determination" as empty words.

In 1748 Montesquieu (1689-1755) published *L'Esprit des lois*, a major political work defining the principles of a democratic state and the separation of the executive, legislative and judicial authorities

France ceased to be an empire in 1815, but freedom and democracy were not reinstated. The monarchy was restored with the accession of Louis XVIII. He was succeeded by Charles X in 1824 and, following the 1830 Revolution in July of that year, Louis-Philippe reigned for 18 years. The 1848 Revolution instituted the Second Republic which, like the First, ended in a coup d'état, this time by Louis-Napoleon Bonaparte in 1851. The Second Empire he created lasted from 1852 to 1870.

Under these various regimes, citizens had scarcely any say in political matters. Until 1848, only those who paid the poll tax voted, which effectively restricted the vote to a minority of citizens, and the political feelings of the masses were chiefly expressed through isolated incidents of revolt which were swiftly quelled.

Nonetheless, under the surface of political instability, fundamental changes were taking place, which laid the foundations of modern France. They concerned principally the territorial and administrative structure of the country. In 1789, France was not governed in the same way in different parts of the country. Instead, it was divided into different constituencies (baileys, governorships, generalities, provincial states and countries) which had evolved at different stages and now overlapped with each other. With such a complicated system, there were often delays and conflicts over areas of responsibility, making it difficult to govern the country efficiently. In this respect, the Revolution and the Empire were to complete the process of centralisation begun under the Ancien Regime. In 1790, the territory was divided into *départements* (counties), which in turn were divided into *cantons* made up of *communes* (municipalities or districts). These are still the administrative units to which power is devolved locally in France. Napoleon completed the system, rationalising it and making it more efficient through the Law of 28 Pluviôse Year VIII (17 February 1800) which created the posts of prefect and mayor, although mayors at that time were appointed, rather than elected as they are today. Administrative authorities were thus standardised on a basis of equality and staff were thenceforward recruited by competitive examination, substituting a meritocratic system for the old system of privilege.

The Revolutionary regime and Empire also saw the birth of genuine public services and the strengthening of the role of the state in national and regional development, the creation of infrastructures and town planning. The will to unite the French people also resulted in the creation of norms and standards which would be valid all over France, as exemplified not only by the institution of a Civil Code, but also by the systematic registration of property and the decision to opt for a metric system of weights and measures. The metric system is now universally used in France and widely used in the rest of the world.

The period from the Revolution to the Second Empire was also characterised by profound economic and social transformations. Whilst it is true that the political upheavals which took place in France from 1789 to 1815 had afforded England a certain economic advantage, France too had entered the industrial age of coal, steam, modern foundries, large-scale textile factories and railways. With hindsight, the Second Empire appears to have been a crucial period, particularly from 1860 onwards. The people had been deprived of democracy, racketeering was rife and the colonial adventure begun in 1830 with the conquest of Algeria was continuing; but, at the same time, the country was undergoing the rapid yet profound changes that were to turn it into a modern power – industrial development, the creation of banks and the department stores which heralded modern retailing, the transformation of towns and cities, substantial extension of the rail network, a reforestation policy and measures against soil erosion. But whilst the economic boom was undeniable, social progress lagged behind and, during this first half of the nineteenth century, living conditions were tough and the working classes endured acute poverty and overcrowding in the industrial towns.

1870-1914: France as a Republic – Crises and Consolidation

After France's defeat by Germany in 1870, the Third Republic came to be seen as a period of stability and consolidation, despite domestic unrest and the terrible damage done to the country by the First World War. The Third Republic was proclaimed on 4 September

1870 and Adolphe Thiers became its first President on 31 August 1871, after the Paris Commune uprising was brutally crushed towards the end of May 1871. This regime had a difficult start, but it was to prove the most long-lasting since the Revolution, surviving right up until 1940. Thiers began as a monarchist, but he was gradually won over to republicanism. The laws defining the organisation and operating procedures of government were passed between February and July 1875; but it was only with the elections of 14 and 28 October 1877, which resulted in a republican majority in the Chamber of Deputies, that the new regime was fully recognised.

Before the First World War, the Third Republic had to weather two serious political crises, which threatened its very existence. The first of these was the Boulangist movement (1886-1889), which became a focus for a number of causes of discontent and rocked the foundations of parliamentary democracy. The second was the Dreyfus Affair (1894-1899), which revealed the extent of anti-Semitism in France and deep social and political divisions. These crises were especially dangerous for the Republic in that they happened against a backdrop of bitter social and political conflict – industrial disputes, violent acts by political leagues and factions, and the clashes between clerical and anti-clerical groups which led, in 1905, to the separation of church and state. Political and financial scandals and acts of terrorism, such as the assassination of President Sadi Carnot in 1894, exacerbated these tensions.

The 'Triumph of the Republic', an allegorical work sculpted by Jules Dalou between 1879 and 1899, and erected in the Place de la Nation in Paris

However, there was significant institutional and social progress during this period, as well as improvements in the sphere of civil liberties. The laws of 1882 and 1885 made primary education free and compulsory, whilst 1881 saw a new law on freedom of the Press; in 1884 freedom to belong to a trade union became enshrined in law; working conditions for women and children were regulated from 1892 onwards; and in 1901 there was the law on the right of association. Modernisation of the economy continued despite fluctuations and France produced many of the scientific and technical innovations behind the second industrial revolution. During the *Belle Epoque*, just before the Great War, France enjoyed considerable international prestige: it had

The Third Republic made universal education one of its priorities by introducing free, compulsory primary schooling; this photograph shows the primary-school canteen at Bellevue (Orne) in 1889

the second largest colonial empire in the world, played a leading role in international diplomacy and was at the forefront in the realms of art and culture.

1914-1945: Between the Wars

In the first years of the new century, international tensions within Europe began to mount: political, commercial and colonial rivalries between the great powers were played out against a backdrop of growing nationalism, fomented by regional crises such as those in Morocco and the Balkans. France formed a Triple Entente with Russia (agreements of 1893) - which was itself allied to Serbia - and Britain (through the Entente Cordiale signed in 1904). Ranged against them were the Central Powers of the Triple Alliance (dating back to 1882) of Germany, the Austro-Hungarian Empire and Italy – with support from the Ottoman Empire. The assassination of the heir to the Austro-Hungarian throne on 28 June 1914 by a Bosnian Serb in Sarajevo, then under Austrian domination, was the spark. The system of alliances which had been so patiently constructed came into play and led to the outbreak of the First World War.

On 3 August 1914 France went to war against Germany and the Austro-Hungarian Empire, joining forces with England and Russia; these allies were later joined by Italy and the United States. The French emerged victorious from the four-year conflict but, like all the European countries which took part in the Great War, France had been dealt a heavy blow. The North and East of the country had been laid waste; the war effort had drained the public purse and the national economy and temporarily halted social advances. Worst of all, the war had inflicted human loss on a terrible scale: almost 1.5 million young men were killed and almost three million wounded; and the birth-rate was falling to disastrous levels, in a country whose population growth was already very low.

The War had rallied political parties to the defence of the nation, leading to the formation of the Union Sacrée, symbolised by the strong personality of Clemenceau, the "Father of Victory". He remained in power until January 1920.

Political life in the 1920s was dominated from then on by right-wing coalitions, except for the period (1924-1926) when the *Cartel des Gauches* (an alliance between Socialists and Radicals) was in power. Since December 1920, when the French Communist Party was formed, the Socialist Left had been divided. The Depression in the Thirties, financial and social problems and the worsening international situation, with the rise of Fascism in

One of the important social measures brought in by the *Front populaire*, in 1936, was the introduction of paid annual holidays
Photo by Willy Ronis

Italy and Nazism in Germany, deepened the divisions in France and fostered the rise of many nationalist conservative or extreme right-wing anti-parliamentary movements ("Leagues"). These held an increasing number of violent demonstrations, including the one on 6 February 1934 which prompted the Left to form an anti-fascist alliance of Socialists, Radicals and Communists – the Popular Front.

The reunited Left won the 1936 parliamentary elections and the Popular Front government, headed by Léon Blum, implemented major reforms: the 40-hour working week, collective bargaining, paid holidays, the first nationalisations and a change in the status of the Bank of France. However, internal divisions had not disappeared, and external difficulties still less so. The new premier, Edouard Daladier, initially believed that concessions to Hitler at Munich in 1938 would make it possible to avoid hostilities, but on 3 September 1939 he committed France to the Second World War, alongside the British.

The war was to leave France doubly scarred – not only by the shock of swift defeat by the German forces, but also by the Vichy government's policy of collaboration with the enemy. The rout of the French army by the Nazi invasion in May 1940 forced many civilians to flee their homes and travel long distances across France. Under the terms of the armistice signed in 1940, France was divided into two zones, one occupied and the other free. The Third Republic collapsed. On 10 July 1940 Parliament gave full powers to Pétain, a hero of the First World War, who set up a new regime, the "French State", with Vichy as its provisional capital. This regime was personal, authoritarian, corporatist and discriminated against Jews, who were subject to a special statute from 1941 onwards. Collaboration with Nazi Germany began on 24 October 1940 with a meeting between Pétain and Hitler in the village of Montoire. It was to lead the Vichy government to support the war effort of their conquerors by hunting down opponents of Nazism and assisting in the deportation of Jews. The Legion of French Volunteers against Bolshevism fought alongside German divisions on the Eastern Front.

However, the Resistance which had sprung up in the earliest days of the Occupation was to pave the way for a new postwar France. The Resistance may be said to have been born on 18 June 1940, when General Charles de Gaulle, speaking from London, issued a call to the French to continue the fight alongside the Allies. He became the focus of a resistance movement outside France, comprising the Free French Forces (FFL) and a French National Committee, to which colonial territories rallied. Within France, the Resistance was at first very limited, but gradually gained strength and became more structured, developing into networks which, besides the ope-

De Gaulle's appeal of 18 June 1940: "*I hoped that the heads of government departments, the Church and chiefs of staff would rally to me. Instead it was the rank-and-file, seamen from Dunkirk and fishermen from the Ile-de-Sein who came. Ultimately it was with them – with the people – that I was able to build Free France.*" Charles de Gaulle, *Mémoires de Guerre*, Volume 1, Plon

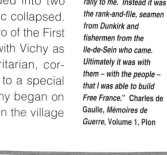

A TOUS LES FRANÇAIS

La France a perdu une bataille!
Mais la France n'a pas perdu la guerre!

Des gouvernants de rencontre ont pu capituler, cédant à la panique, oubliant l'honneur, livrant le pays à la servitude. Cependant, rien n'est perdu!

Rien n'est perdu, parce que cette guerre est une guerre mondiale. Dans l'univers libre, des forces immenses n'ont pas encore donné. Un jour, ces forces écraseront l'ennemi. Il faut que la France, ce jour-là, soit présente à la victoire. Alors, elle retrouvera sa liberté et sa grandeur. Tel est mon but, mon seul but!

Voilà pourquoi je convie tous les Français, où qu'ils se trouvent, à s'unir à moi dans l'action, dans le sacrifice et dans l'espérance.

Notre patrie est en péril de mort.
Luttons tous pour la sauver!

VIVE LA FRANCE !

18 JUIN 1940

GENERAL DE GAULLE

rations carried out in France itself, were to provide vital assistance to the Allies in the form of intelligence and military support during the Normandy landings. Meanwhile, in North Africa, which had been liberated by the Allies in November 1942, a new French army had formed and joined in the fighting. In the spring of 1943 Jean Moulin, General de Gaulle's delegate in Occupied France, was instrumental in uniting the main resistance organisations into the National Resistance Council (CNR). At the same time, de Gaulle, now based in Algiers, set up a provisional government of the French Republic whose members were drawn from the ranks of the CNR.

Whilst the role of the Resistance was not a deciding factor in the Allied victory over Nazism, it was crucial for France in that it convinced British, American and Soviet politicians that France should be considered one of the victorious Allies, rather than an enemy whose territory should be occupied. France was thus able to participate fully in the victory and was present at the signing of Germany's capitulation on 8 May 1945. In this sense, it is fair to say that it was the Resistance, personified by de Gaulle, which allowed France to hold on to its international position despite having suffered a military defeat.

Reconstruction (1945-1958)

France had been subjected to the ordeal of two wars in thirty years. Fewer lives were lost in the Second World War (about 600,000 dead) than in the Great War, but material losses were far greater. Fighting and bombing destroyed cities, factories, bridges, railway lines and stations. The devastation was compounded by the fact that the occupying power had intensively exploited the French economy. Nonetheless, there was a remarkable growth period as the country recovered: times were hard, but peace had restored confidence in the future – as the upsurge in population growth known as the "baby boom" bears witness – and Marshall Aid made it possible to attend to the most pressing needs.

From 1945, despite the tough circumstances, emergency measures were taken. Key sectors of the economy were nationalised (energy, air transport, savings banks and insurance) along with major companies (such as Renault) and a Social Security (welfare) system was set up, as were works committees and economic planning under the guidance of Jean Monnet.

However, the political forces that had emerged from the Resistance – Communists, Christian Democrats and Socialists – and had supported the provisional government of General de Gaulle soon disagreed as to what institutions the new France should have and what direction the economy should take. The former leader of Free France left the government in January 1946 and in 1947 founded a new political party, the RPF, the Rassemblement du peuple français ("Rallying of the French People").

Two constituent assemblies elected by universal suffrage (women got the vote in 1944) and three referenda were required before the adoption of the Constitution of the Fourth Republic (promulgated on 27 October 1946), which established an all-powerful National Assembly and a President with limited powers. In January 1947, Parliament elected Vincent Auriol President of the Republic.

Divisions resulting from the Cold War and decolonisation were soon added to these internal political divisions. Despite Communist opposition, France confirmed its Atlantic sympathies and placed itself firmly in the Western camp. France joined the European Organisation for Economic Cooperation (EOEC), set up in April 1948 to distribute American aid and became a member of the Atlantic Alliance (NATO) in April 1949. In addition, after Germany was divided, France opted for a policy of entente with West Germany which was to lay the foundations of the European Community. Jean Monnet and Robert Schuman and Chancellor Konrad Adenauer were instrumental in bringing the two countries closer together – a strategy which resulted, in 1951, in the creation of the European Coal and Steel Community (ECSC), a first milestone on the road to a united Europe. France rejected the idea of a European defence community (EDC), both the Communists and the Gaullists being opposed to a proposal which they felt implied loss of national sovereignty. France did, however, play an active role in setting up the European Economic Community (EEC) or Common Market instituted by the Treaty of Rome signed on 25 March 1957.

By this time decolonisation had led to a serious crisis for the Fourth Republic. Decolonisation had started in Indochina, from which France had to retreat after eight years of a difficult war. The Prime Minister, Pierre Mendès France, ended the conflict with the adoption of the Geneva Accords of 20 July 1954. Morocco and Tunisia became independent in 1956, while in sub-Saharan Africa a peaceful process of decolonisation had begun. But in Algeria, decolonisation took place following a conflict which lasted from 1954 until 1962 and was to bring down the Fourth Republic.

Jean Monnet (1888-1979) was a great advocate of closer links between European countries. He was Commissioner-General of the National Planning Board in 1946 and instigator of the declaration of 9 May 1950 which laid the foundations of the European Coal and Steel Community (ECSC). He was first president of the ECSC's High Authority from 1952-1955

Further reading:

Histoire de la France in 3 volumes (Ed. G. Duby), Larousse, 1971.

Histoire de France in 5 volumes, Hachette, 1990.

C. Ambrosi, A. Ambrosi, B. Galloux, *La France de 1870 à nos jours*, A. Colin, U series, 1997.

J.-C. Caron, *La nation, l'État et la démocratie en France de 1789 à 1914*, A. Colin, U series, 1995.

X. de Planhol, *Géographie historique de la France*, Fayard, 1988.

5

France since 1958

France under General de Gaulle

Rioting in Algiers by the French population of Algeria on 13 May 1958 led to the fall of the last government of the Fourth Republic, led by Pierre Pflimlin. General de Gaulle was called out of retirement at Colombey-les-Deux-Eglises by President René Coty. On 1 June 1958, the National Assembly voted him full powers for six months and he initiated the drafting of a new Constitution, which was to lay down the future modus operandi of the French institutions. On 28 September 1958, the Constitution of the Fifth Republic was adopted by referendum. It gave the President of the Republic much broader authority. On 21 December 1958, de Gaulle was elected President by a college of deputies, senators and local elected representatives.

General de Gaulle visiting Villefranche-de-Rouergue (Aveyron), September 1961

From 1960 onwards, the countries of French Africa gradually gained independence, whilst maintaining special links with France. But the thorniest problem inherited from the Fourth Republic was the continuing war in Algeria. Serious disturbances both in mainland France and in Algeria, and a putsch by generals in Algiers on 22 April 1961, led to an acceleration of the negotiations with the provisional government of the Algerian Republic which culminated in the Evian agreements, overwhelmingly approved by referendum on 8 April 1962. Algeria gained independence and a million French inhabitants had to return to mainland France and a new life. On 28 October 1962, de Gaulle called a referendum which approved election of the head of state by direct universal suffrage. He was himself elected president by this system in the second round of voting on 19 December 1965, beating the left-wing candidate François Mitterrand.

The majority (first-past-the-post) system ensured the dominant political force a lasting majority thus providing France with greater political and parliamentary stability than had been seen for a long time. A thriving economy and rehabilitated currency, symbolised by the introduction of the new franc in 1960, allowed de Gaulle to conduct an energetic foreign policy. His goal was to assert France's independence and its role on the world stage. In support of this policy, he relied on the deterrent capability France had had since acquiring nuclear weapons. On 13 February 1960, France tested its first atomic bomb at the Reggane base in the Sahara and subsequently acquired thermonuclear weapons (first test in 1968) and the whole range of modern delivery vehicles: ground missiles, strategic air force bombers and missile-launching submarines. France thus became the third largest nuclear power, surpassed only by the USA and USSR (whose strike capability was, however, far greater). To signal this newly-won independence, de Gaulle decided to withdraw France from NATO's integrated military command, although it remained a member of the Atlantic Alliance.

The Building of Europe and Transformation of France

There were two strands to France's European policy: on the one hand, development of what de Gaulle called "détente, understanding and cooperation" with the Eastern bloc countries in order to end the Cold War and pave the way for a Europe stretching from the Atlantic to the Urals and, on the other, implementation of the Treaty of Rome whilst vigorously defending the sovereignty and fundamental interests of the member states. For this reason, deeming the European Commission to have exceeded its powers, France refused for six months (in 1965) to participate in the European Community institutions ("empty chair" policy). This crisis led to the Luxembourg compromise: when a member state believes its fundamental interests to be under threat, a decision in the matter must be reached unanimously. This period also saw the failure of France's proposals for political union (Fouchet Plan) and de Gaulle twice oppose British entry into the EEC, which he considered premature.

However, the most important legacy of these years remains the close cooperation between France and Germany, brought about by the personal rapport between Chancellor Adenauer and General de Gaulle. The Chancellor's official visit to France and the General's to Germany, the founding of the Franco-German Youth Office and the signature of the Elysée Treaty in 1963 crowned this rapprochement. The Franco-German tandem became, and remains to this day, one of the driving forces behind the European enterprise.

This was also a time of large-scale economic projects, encouraged by the technical and demographic dynamism of the Fifth

Republic - launch of the liner *France* in January 1962, maiden flight of the prototype of the supersonic plane *Concorde* in 1969, beginning of space exploration in 1965 and active support for technological innovation and the high-tech aeronautics, information technology and telecommunications industries - and carried out within the framework of an active town and country planning policy. However, during the 1960s, the profound changes in the French economy, coinciding with major developments on the social front linked to fact that the population was getting younger and the continuous rise in living standards, aroused concern and led to new social aspirations. The increasing impact of the media (transistor radios and development of television) helped take these demands nationwide and the events of May-June 1968 brought them to a head.

Watershed of 1968 and the Post-de Gaulle Era

Many industrialised countries were hit by student revolts in the spring of 1968, but in France the workers joined in and the movement spread to provincial towns, finally bringing the whole country to a standstill. By the last week in May, a month which saw open rebellion against the established order, approximately nine million workers were on strike. But, after two weeks of temporising, the deep divisions within the protest movement and the fear of party and trade union leaders that matters might escalate beyond their control allowed the authorities to regain control of the situation. After a firm speech by de Gaulle, his supporters rallied and, following dissolution of the National Assembly and new elections, calm was restored in France in June 1968. Less than a year later, however, on 28 April 1969, de Gaulle left office permanently following the nation's rejection in a referendum of proposals on regionalisation and reform of the Senate. He died on 9 November 1970. One of de Gaulle's former Prime Ministers, Georges Pompidou, succeeded him as President after the elections of 15 June 1969 and, following Pompidou's premature death, Valéry Giscard d'Estaing, his finance minister, was elected President on 19 May 1974.

At the end of May 1968, nine million workers were on strike in France; the CGT (*Confédération Générale du travail*) trade union demonstration in Paris on 24 May 1968

After de Gaulle's departure there was no sudden and sharp change in the way France was governed, but rather some gradual shifts in policy. By and large, under Georges Pompidou the Gaullist tradition and broad lines of both domestic and foreign policy were maintained. The "new society" project drawn up by Prime Minister Jacques

Chaban-Delmas (1969-1972) brought some significant social progress, with legislation on vocational training and welfare cover for the poorest citizens and the elderly. In the European arena, a decisive step forward was taken: France lifted its veto on Britain's entry into the EEC, which was also opened to Ireland and Denmark; the three countries joined in 1973, bringing its membership to nine.

President Valéry Giscard d'Estaing's seven-year term saw the clearer emergence of a determination to establish a modern free market economy ("the advanced liberal society") and modernise employer/employee relations, especially in the light of his programme of radical economic reform. In fact, in the mid-seventies, the 30 year postwar boom (the *Trente glorieuses*) came to an end and France entered a prolonged crisis. Nonetheless, there were some major reforms, including the lowering of the age of majority to eighteen, legalisation of abortion, and ending of censorship of films and broadcasting. President Valéry Giscard d'Estaing also initiated the G7 meetings of the seven most industrialised countries and, together with the German Chancellor Helmut Schmidt, was instrumental in setting up the European Monetary System and the election of Members of the European Parliament by universal suffrage.

With the election of François Mitterrand as President of the Republic on 10 May 1981, the Left came to power for the first time under the Fifth Republic; the investiture ceremony at the Panthéon in Paris on 21 May 1981

The Left Comes to Power

In the seventies, against a background of increasing dissension within the right-wing majority, with a widening gulf between the centre-right and Giscardian *Union pour la démocratie française* (UDF, Union for French Democracy) and the "Gaullist" *Rassemblement pour la République* movement (Rally for the Republic, RPR) founded by Jacques Chirac in December 1976, the left-wing opposition, led by François Mitterrand, succeeded in putting together a strategy to bring it to power. The Socialist Party, revitalised and restructured at the Epinay Congress in June 1971, Communist Party and *Radicaux de gauche* (Radicals of the Left) formed the *Union de la Gauche* (Union of the Left) before the 1973 general election and agreed a common government programme. Despite an undercurrent of tension, temporary splits and then the abandonment of the Common Programme in 1978, the Union was resuscitated for the second ballot of the presidential election of April-May 1981, in which François Mitterrand defeated Valéry Giscard d'Estaing, the outgoing President. For the first time in the history of the Fifth Republic, the Left had come to power. This changeover of political power demonstrated that the 1958 Constitution, which some said had been tailor-made for General de Gaulle, allows a democratic change of political majority while guaranteeing the stability of the institutions.

The government formed by Prime Minister Pierre Mauroy (June 1981) included four Communist ministers and decided on a major programme of reforms. These included retirement at 60, a 39-hour working week, a fifth week of paid holidays, increased recruitment of civil servants, nationalisation of banks and industrial groups, a wealth tax, decentralisation of powers to local authorities, abolition of the death penalty and an end to the state monopoly on radio and then on television. But the trade deficit grew dangerously, the national debt worsened, inflation persisted and the franc lost value against the other major currencies. The government found itself up against severe constraints and, after three successive devaluations, austerity measures were brought in, which reflected what was a more realistic policy, given the existence of a market economy, and were made inevitable by France's commitment to Europe. The architect of these measures was Finance Minister Jacques Delors. He ended the practice of indexing wages to prices and embarked on a policy of controlling public deficits, fighting inflation and defending the currency. The appointment of Laurent Fabius as Prime Minister in July 1984 and departure of the Communist ministers from the government confirmed the dominance within the Left of the advocates of realism, promoting what were increasingly openly social-democratic policies.

Three "Cohabitations" (1986-1998)

Cohabitation is, without doubt, the great new political development of recent years. It occurs when the President of the Republic and the government formed from the parliamentary majority come from the opposing sides of France's political spectrum, traditionally known as "Left" and "Right" – although the classification is over-simplistic nowadays. Nobody had really anticipated such a situation – neither the authors of the Constitution, nor General de Gaulle. Indeed, for a long time, the electorate voted in presidents and governments of the same political colour, a tradition confirmed after the dissolutions by de Gaulle and Mitterrand of the National Assembly in 1968 and 1981 respectively, when the ensuing general elections gave the presidents' respective parties comfortable majorities.

Things changed in 1986, when the general election resulted in a parliamentary majority for the two main right-wing parties, the RPR and the UDF; this first cohabitation, with François Mitterrand as President and Jacques Chirac as Prime Minister, lasted until 1988. President Mitterrand's re-election in 1988 for a second seven-year term marked the end of the first cohabitation because the President then dissolved the National Assembly and a Socialist majority returned to power in June 1988; Michel Rocard became Prime Minister, followed by Edith Cresson (May 1991) and then Pierre Bérégovoy (April 1992).

The second cohabitation began in 1993 when President Mitterrand chose Edouard Balladur as Prime Minister after the March 1993 general election had given the RPR-UDF alliance a strong majority. This cohabitation ended with Jacques Chirac's election as President in 1995. Executive and legislative powers were once more in the hands of a single political movement and Alain Juppé was appointed Prime Minister.

The third cohabitation began in June 1997, when the general election which followed Jacques Chirac's April dissolution of the National Assembly resulted in a left-wing majority and the President appointed Lionel Jospin, the Socialist party leader, Prime Minister. The roles of Left and Right were reversed, compared with the two previous cohabitations, but this new modus operandi clearly seems increasingly to satisfy what has become a volatile electorate. All in all, the three cohabitations have shown that the institutions of the Fifth Republic work satisfactorily and guarantee a measure of political stability in France.

Cohabitation in action in foreign policy: President Jacques Chirac and Prime Minister Lionel Jospin with British Prime Minister Tony Blair at the Franco-British Summit in London on 6 November 1997

Constants in Domestic and Foreign Policy

The frequency of the changes in the political coalitions over the past few years might give the impression of a lack of continuity in French policies. True, successive governments have their own political orientations, reflected in specific policy choices. The RPR-UDF coalition set about privatising large public-sector companies such as Saint-Gobain, the *Société Générale* bank, the television channel TF1 and the pharmaceuticals firm Rhône-Poulenc. Right-wing governments argue for reduced state intervention and, when in power, have cut taxes and compulsory social security contributions. Conversely, Socialist and left-wing coalitions have opted for the *status quo* with regard to nationalisation and privatisation, stepped up civil service recruitment and, as far as possible, maintained government and State controls on the economy.

However, there are some fundamental constants, regardless of the government's political colour. These include employment policy and measures to combat unemployment and social exclusion: unemployment benefit, guaranteed minimum incomes for the poorest (RMI "minimum integration income", which is a form of income support, and a minimum state pension), policies to develop vocational training programmes and encourage integration into the world of work

(work-placements, state-subsidised "employment-solidarity" contracts, youth employment programmes). Another constant in French policy is France's commitment to building Europe, a goal which all the presidents and prime ministers of this period have unwaveringly pursued, mobilising their governments in support of it. Indeed, divisions over Europe have not been along traditional Left-Right lines and the referendum on the Treaty of Maastricht on 20 September 1992 saw campaigners on both Left and Right split into "yes" and "no" camps – as did France as a whole, since the ratification was approved by a majority of only 51%. Since then, the ranks of the pro-Europeans have swelled and there is greater consensus on the single currency, even though bitter opposition persists in some quarters. Lastly, the successive governments all strove to maintain the competitiveness of French industry in world markets by providing support for sectors in difficulty (such as fishing, iron and steel and textiles) and encouraging the development of new sectors (such as aerospace, telecommunications, biotechnology and environment-related activities).

So, all in all, while the structures and organisations which have shaped France's political life since the 1960s have been evolving only slowly, its people's attitudes and ideologies have radically changed. A genuine consensus has emerged on the way forward and France is moving towards a model similar to that of the social democracies of northern Europe.

Further reading:

J.-J. Becker, *Crises et alternances 1974-1995*, Le Seuil, Points histoire series, Nouvelle histoire de la France contemporaine, 1998.

D. Borne, *Histoire de la société française depuis 1945*, A. Colin, Cursus series, 1992.

D. Chagnollaud et J.-L. Quermonne, *Le gouvernement de la France sous la Ve République*, new edition, Fayard, 1996.

J.-F. Sirinelli, *Dictionnaire historique de la vie politique française au XXe siècle*, PUF, 1995.

C. Ysmal, *Les partis politiques sous la Ve République*, Montchrestien, Domat politique, 1989.

The Presidents of the French Republic

L.-N. Bonaparte (1848-1852) - A. Thiers (1871-1873) - Mac-Mahon (1873-1879) - J. Grévy (1879-1887) - S. Carnot (1887-1894)
J. Casimir-Périer (1894-1895) - F. Faure (1895-1899) - É. Loubet (1899-1906) - A. Fallières (1906-1913) - R. Poincaré (1913-1920)
P. Deschanel (1920-1920) - A. Millerand (1920-1924) - G. Doumergue (1924-1931) - P. Doumer (1931-1932) - A. Lebrun (1932-1940)
V. Auriol (1947-1953) - R. Coty (1953-1959) - C. de Gaulle (1959-1969) - G. Pompidou (1969-1974) - V. Giscard d'Estaing (1974-1981)
F. Mitterrand (1981-1995) - J. Chirac (1995-...)

THE STATE
AND
POLITICAL LIFE

Institutional structure established by the 1958 Constitution

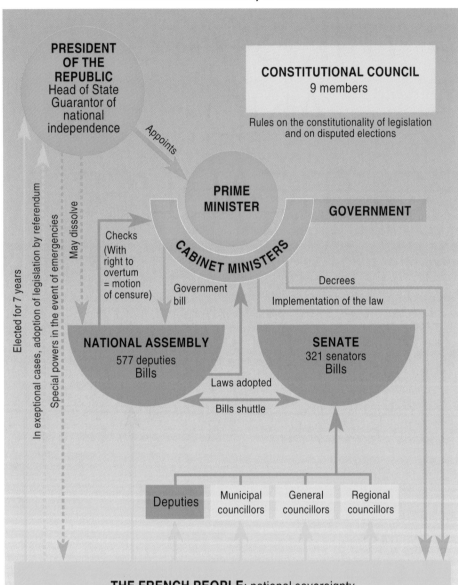

PRESIDENT OF THE REPUBLIC
Head of State
Guarantor of national independence

CONSTITUTIONAL COUNCIL
9 members

Rules on the constitutionality of legislation and on disputed elections

Appoints

PRIME MINISTER

GOVERNMENT

CABINET MINISTERS

Checks (With right to overtum = motion of censure)

Government bill

Decrees

Implementation of the law

Elected for 7 years

In exeptional cases, adoption of legislation by referendum

Special powers in the event of emergencies

May dissolve

NATIONAL ASSEMBLY
577 deputies
Bills

SENATE
321 senators
Bills

Laws adopted

Bills shuttle

Deputies

Municipal councillors

General councillors

Regional councillors

THE FRENCH PEOPLE: national sovereignty
Universal suffrage: all citizens over the age of 18 may vote

Legislative branch   Executive branch

6

The Institutions

A Strong Executive Power

The Fifth Republic, established by the Constitution of 1958, strengthened the power of the executive (the President of the Republic and the government) and ensured that each legislature had a clear political majority, thus putting an end to the instability of the previous regimes. Despite vehement initial opposition from the left, the 1958 Constitution eventually gained fairly wide acceptance, very probably largely because it has allowed changeovers of political power and "cohabitation" between a president and government from different sides of the political spectrum. The satisfactory operation of the institutions perhaps stems from the fact that Gaullism, whose principles inspired the Constitution, is less an ideology than a method of action based on a few clear principles: the greatness of France, the central role of the state and the primacy of the national interest over ideologies, and the need for the head of state to be "above the parties" and derive his/her legitimacy from the sovereignty of the people. It was this last point which led General de Gaulle to propose a key reform of the 1958 Constitution: election of the President of the Republic by direct universal suffrage, which was introduced by constitutional amendment in 1962.

The Élysée Palace in the rue du Faubourg-Saint-Honoré in Paris has been the official residence of the President of the Republic and housed the office of the Presidency since 1873

Predominant Role of the President of the Republic

The Constitution of 4 October 1958 had provided for the election of the President of the Republic by indirect universal suffrage by an electoral college comprising the members of Parliament and various representatives of local elected officials. General de Gaulle was elected president under this system in 1958 before being re-elected by direct universal suffrage in 1965. The new procedure

made the President the cornerstone of the new institutions and broke with the tradition of the Third and Fourth Republics, in which the elected Parliament was the supreme organ of government and had the responsibility of choosing the President. Moreover, constitutional practice, which was dominated by General de Gaulle's strong personality, was to strengthen the supremacy of the executive.

The Constitution defines the President's powers as follows:

• The President is elected for seven years — the longest term in any parliamentary system — and may be re-elected an indefinite number of times.

• The President is commander-in-chief of the armed forces (article 15) and the guarantor of national independence, territorial integrity and observance of treaties (article 5). He thus plays a key role in foreign policy, while sharing responsibility with the government in this area.

• The President "shall see that the Constitution is observed. He shall ensure, by his arbitration, the proper functioning of the public authorities and the continuity of the state" (article 5). He appoints the prime minister and "presides over the Council of Ministers".

• The President promulgates Acts of Parliament (article 10) and "signs the ordinances and decrees deliberated upon by the Council of Ministers" (article 13).

• The President is "the guarantor of the independence of the judicial authority" (article 64) and presides over the High Council of the Judiciary, which makes proposals and advises on the appointment of judges.

• The President makes appointments to the highest civilian and military posts (article 13). He has the right to grant pardon (article 17) and may be invested with special emergency powers (article 16). On the proposal of the government or the assemblies he may call a referendum on certain bills. After consulting the government and the presidents of the assemblies he may dissolve the National Assembly. He may refer legislation to the Constitutional Council for review of its constitutionality before it is promulgated (see below).

The Constitution specifies the powers that are exercised personally by the President and those which he shares with the Prime Minister, which has enabled France's institutions to function successfully during periods of "cohabitation".

The Prime Minister and the Government

The government determines and conducts the policy of the nation. For this purpose, it has at its disposal the civil service and the armed forces. It is responsible to Parliament (article 20). The Prime Minister, who is appointed by the President of the Republic, directs the operation of the government. He or she is responsible for national defence and "shall ensure implementation of legislation" (article 21). Within the limits imposed by the Constitution, the Prime Minister has power to make regulations (article 21). This is a fundamental point: whilst statutes are passed by Parliament, regulations (decrees and ministerial orders) emanate from the government, i.e. the Prime Minister and ministers. In this respect, the 1958 Constitution introduces an important innovation by making a clear distinction between the "ambit of statute", defined within strict limits in article 34, and the domain of government regulations which includes all other matters (article 37). In exceptional circumstances, regulatory power may be expanded, if Parliament authorises the government "for a limited period, to take measures by ordinance that are normally a matter for statute" (article 38).

Apart from its regulatory power, and in common with every other parliamentary system, the government shares with members of Parliament the power to initiate legislation. But the government enjoys an unquestionable advantage over Parliament since it sets the agendas of the assemblies (article 48) and may call for a vote *bloqué* [1]. Last but not least, the Prime Minister can decide to make the government's programme, a statement of general policy, or the passing of a bill (article 49, paragraph 3) an issue of its responsibility before the National Assembly. The text is then considered adopted unless a motion of censure is introduced in the National Assembly and wins a majority of the deputies' votes. If this happens, the Prime Minister must tender the government's resignation to the President of the Republic. Thanks to this procedure, unique in Western Europe, the government's action cannot systematically be obstructed by Parliament.

First Council of Ministers of Lionel Jospin's government, in June 1997, chaired by M. Jacques Chirac. Council of Ministers' meetings are held every Wednesday in the Élysée Palace

As head of the government, the Prime Minister's authority is greater than the other ministers and he/she also has special administrative facilities such as the *Secrétariat général du gouvernement*, the permanent staff of his/her office. The ministers and ministers of state, the number of whom varies according to each government's priorities and the political balance sought, participate in meetings of government bodies and have to countersign government acts in their areas of competence. They are also required to defend the policies of their ministries before Parliament. Lastly, they are responsible for ensuring that the administrative services under their direction implement government decisions effectively. Members of the government may not sit in Parliament or be employed either in the civil service or the private sector. However, they may hold local electoral mandates. An unusual characteristic of the French system is that ministers choose the members of their private office (*cabinet ministériel*), who are usually drawn from the ranks of senior civil servants. In carrying out their duties, they use the central administration and the decentralised services of the state in the department and regions and sometimes abroad.

---

[1] Procedure whereby the government may require Parliament to decide by a single vote on the whole or part of a Bill under consideration.

Members of the government are individually answerable to the Prime Minister and the President of the Republic. Resignation may be spontaneous (for personal reasons), automatic (in the case of collective resignation of the government) or provoked (by disagreement with the Prime Minister or the President). Under the terms of the constitutional law of 27 July 1993 (title X of the Constitution), members of the government are "criminally liable for acts performed in the exercise of their office and classified as serious crimes or other major offences at the time they were committed. They shall be tried by the Court of Justice of the Republic."

Legislature: Parliament's Powers

The National Assembly (known as the Chamber of Deputies during previous Republics), which sits in the Palais Bourbon, and the Senate, which meets in the Palais du Luxembourg, together constitute Parliament.

The 1958 Constitution assigns an important role to Parliament in its dual capacity as a legislative body and a check on government. Article 34 of the Constitution defines this role, which includes passing annual finance bills (the budget) and the so-called "programme Acts", which enable the government to schedule measures involving expenditure covering several financial years in the areas of economic and social policy and defence of the state. Before adopting statutes, Parliament may consult the Economic and Social Council; this body, comprising the whole range of the country's economic and social forces, is regularly entrusted with studies on the major economic and social issues affecting the life of the nation.

Statutes may be initiated by government (*projets de loi* - government bills); after consultation with the *Conseil d'Etat* these are discussed by the Council of Ministers before going to one of the two assemblies for debate. They may also be introduced by members of Parliament (*propositions de loi* - members' bills). Both government and members' bills are debated by the two assemblies, shuttling back and forth between them, the aim being to have an identical text passed by both. If this proves impossible, there are special procedures for trying to resolve the differences. If these fail, the National Assembly has the last word (article 45). In practice, during recent legislatures, fewer than one in five of the statutes passed started off as members' bills, a fact which is fuelling a continual debate on the real role of Parliament.

National Assembly

The National Assembly is made up of 577 deputies elected by direct universal suffrage with a two-ballot uninominal (single candidate) majority (first-past-the-post) polling system; they have constituencies of varying sizes, with one deputy representing approximately

100,000 inhabitants. Each parliament is elected for a period of five years which may be curtailed if the President of the Republic decides to dissolve the Assembly, as happened on 21 April 1997, for the fifth time since the Fifth Republic was established. Since the adoption of the Constitutional amendment of August 1995, the National Assembly has had a single session each year, beginning on the first working day of October and ending on the last working day of June. The President may also call extraordinary sessions which he/she opens and closes by decree. Most sessions are open to the public and are reported in the press with debates published in full in the *Journal officiel*. Once a week, on Wednesdays, there is a televised session during which deputies may put questions to members of the government.

Prime Minister Lionel Jospin addressing the National Assembly, June 1997

Deputies usually belong to one of the Assembly's political groups, but this is not compulsory. Each deputy is also a member and participates in the work of one of the National Assembly's six standing committees: Cultural, Family and Social Affairs; Foreign Affairs; Defence and Armed Forces; Finance, General Economic Affairs and Planning; Constitutional Laws, Legislation and General Administration of the Republic; and Manufacturing and Trade.

Unlike the Senate, the National Assembly has the power to force the government to resign by passing a motion of censure. Another distinction between the two houses is that finance and social security finance bills must be submitted to the National Assembly first (article 39).

Senate

The Senate's 321 members are elected for a nine-year term by indirect universal suffrage by an electoral college made up in each department of deputies, regional councillors, general councillors and representatives of the municipal councils. One third of senators are elected every three years; the Senate contains a high proportion of local elected representatives.

Like the deputies, senators are first and foremost legislators. However, their legislative power is essentially expressed through the right to make amendments. Bills are debated in the Senate just as they are in the National Assembly, i.e. initially in one of the six standing committees (Cultural Affairs; Economic Affairs and Planning; Foreign Affairs, Defence and Armed Forces; Social Affairs; Finance, Budgetary Supervision and National Economic Accounts; Constitutional Laws, Legislation, Universal Suffrage and Procedure and General Administration) and then in public session.

Except for the possibility of bringing down the government by passing a censure motion, when it comes to providing a check on the government, senators have identical powers to those of deputies. They may submit written questions to the ministers (from 5,000 to 6,000 each year), debate general policy statements, carry out fact-finding missions and form committees of enquiry. In addition to passing legislation and keeping a check on the government, the 1958 Constitution calls on the Senate to represent France's local authorities, i.e., the *communes*, departments, regions and overseas territories. French citizens living abroad are also represented in the Senate.

The method of election, the senators' long term of office and the fact that the Senate cannot be dissolved ensures great political stability in the French upper house. This is why the Constitution entrusts its president with the task of temporarily standing in for the President of the Republic if the office falls vacant or if the elected President is incapacitated. This has happened twice: in 1969 after General de Gaulle resigned and in 1974 when President Pompidou died in office. The Senate has thus come to be seen as the institution which ensures continuity in government operations and hence of the state as a whole.

Constitutional Council, Guardian of the Constitution

The Constitutional Council is a court formed of nine members chosen for a nine-year non-renewable term, during which they may not be removed; one third of its members are replaced every three years. Three of the Council members are appointed by the President of the Republic, three by the president of the National Assembly and three by the president of the Senate. In addition, former Presidents of the Republic are ex officio members, although none have actually sat on the Council. The President of the Constitutional Council is appointed by the President of the Republic and casts the deciding vote in the event of a tie.

The Council's powers are strictly defined by the Constitution (articles 58 to 61) and its decisions are not subject to appeal (article 62). The Council has two main functions: it hands down decisions in election disputes and rules on the constitutionality of statutes. In addition it formally establishes incapacitation of the President and must be consulted before the President is invested with emergency powers under the terms of article 16.

With regard to elections, the Constitutional Council has jurisdiction over presidential, general and senate elections, along with referendums; it monitors candidates' eligibility and their compliance with the laws on incompatibility of offices. When a referendum is held the Council has a dual function: consultative before the vote is held and judicial afterwards, since it is responsible for considering any complaints about the conduct of the poll. The Constitutional Council's other function is to rule on constitutionality. Such a ruling is mandatory with respect to the rules of procedure of the two assemblies and institutional Acts, but optional in the case of ordinary statutes and international treaties and obligations. The President, Prime Minister, Presidents of the National Assembly and the Senate and, since 1974, any group of 60 deputies or 60 senators may submit statutes and treaties to the Council. This last provision allows opposition parties to refer statutes adopted by the parliamentary majority to the Constitutional Council.

The Constitutional Council and the *Conseil d'État* sit in the Palais-Royal in Paris

In 1971, the Constitutional Council took an important decision concerning its power to rule on constitutionality. Since that date the Council has ruled on whether statutes are in line with not only the 1958 Constitution itself, but also with the texts to which it refers, i.e. the Preamble to the 1946 Constitution and the 1789 Declaration of the Rights of Man and of the Citizen, and with the fundamental principles recognised by the laws of the Republic. With this decision the Constitutional Council took on the responsibility of protecting the rights and fundamental liberties of citizens. An abundant body of detailed and rigorous jurisprudence has resulted.

Judiciary

In France, a basic distinction is made between administrative courts and civil and criminal courts.

Administrative Courts

In contrast to American and British tradition, in France the law applying to citizens and private businesses is not the same as that governing public administrations and local authorities when they are acting as public-law corporations. The latter come under the jurisdiction of administrative law, which has its own rules and courts. Matters to do with conditions of employment in the public sector, town planning, public contracts and, in fact, all disputes regarding the public sector are dealt with by administrative courts. The supreme court of the administrative hierarchy is the *Conseil d'Etat* (Council of State), the independence of whose 200 or so members is guaranteed by statute. The *Conseil d'Etat* functions both as a court and a consultative body.

As a court, the *Conseil d'Etat* – which considers points of both law and fact – rules directly on the legality of the most important administrative acts. It also acts as a court of appeal for decisions of the administrative courts and administrative appellate courts. In this capacity, the *Conseil d'Etat* is the court of final appeal in disputes involving the state and public entities. It may also review and annul regulations signed by the President of the Republic or the Prime Minister, thus providing citizens with recourse against any arbitrary use of power by the state.

As a consultative body, the *Conseil d'Etat* serves as the government's legal advisor, examining bills before they are discussed at the Council of Ministers (article 39) and certain draft decrees. The government may seek its opinion on a variety of legal questions.

Government services are also subject to budgetary checks by the 250 members of the Auditor-General's Department or Audit Court (*Cour des comptes*), which is assisted by the regional audit courts. This Court, which, like the *Conseil d'Etat*, has a reputation for independence, audits the accounts of all the public accountants. It supervises the management of administrative authorities and officials in the public sector, which includes the large state-owned enterprises. It issues a public annual report on its activities.

Plenary assembly of the *Cour de Cassation*. As France's supreme judicial authority, the *Cour de Cassation* exercises ultimate supervision on questions of law and can quash verdicts delivered by lower courts

Civil and Criminal Courts

As in all democratic regimes, French civil and criminal courts have a supreme authority, the *Cour de cassation* (Court of Cassation, literally a quashing court), which decides appeals on points of law and procedure made against the decisions of the 27 appellate courts. Upon appeal, the appellate courts review points of law and fact in decisions handed down by the lowest-level courts, which are themselves divided into two distinct branches, civil and criminal courts.

Civil actions are judged by the *tribunaux de grande instance* (lower civil courts) or *tribunaux d'instance* (lowest civil courts), and criminal offences by the *tribunaux correctionnels* (courts hearing intermediate criminal offences, e.g. theft and fraud) and *tribunaux de police* (petty offences). All these courts have professional judges. Disputes on commercial matters are heard in the *tribunaux de commerce* (commercial courts) which have judges (*juges consulaires*) who are not career judges, but are business people elected by an electoral college of representatives themselves elected by the local business community. Labour disputes are heard by the *conseils des prud'hommes* (industrial conciliation tribunals), composed of an equal number of employers' and employees' representatives. Cases of serious crime are tried by the Assize Courts (*cours d'assise*) which differ from other French courts in that they are composed of a presiding judge and two other judges coming from either that court or the *tribunal de grande instance* sitting with nine jurors – ordinary citizens whose names are drawn by lot from the electoral rolls. Another peculiarity of the Assize Courts is that there exists no right of appeal for a person convicted before them; up until now the only possibility of overturning a decision is by appealing to the *Cour de Cassation* on a point of law.

French Law and European Law

Since France is a member of both the European Union and the Council of Europe, French law and its application have been significantly modified over the past 20 years. Indeed, the Constitution of 1958 stipulates that international law "shall prevail over" French law (article 55).

European Community law is based on treaties (EEC, ECSC, Euratom, EU, etc.) and on subordinate legislation brought in by the European institutions and taking the form of regulations, directives and decisions. The legality of this whole body of legislation is guaranteed by the Court of Justice of the European Communities which sits in Luxembourg. This court has founded its case law on two basic principles: direct applicability and the preeminence of Community law. The principle of direct applicability (decree of 1963) enables any individual to invoke Community law in cases before a national judge. The principle of primacy (decree of 1964) means that Community rules take precedence over national ones. Thus in France, the *Cour de Cassation* (since 1975) and the *Conseil d'Etat* (since 1989) have applied the principle of the primacy of the rule of Community law over any subsequent national law not compatible with them.

In addition, in 1974 France ratified the European Convention on Human Rights. Respect for human rights is ensured by the new permanent (since November 1998) European Court of Human Rights in Strasbourg. The European Convention on Human Rights guarantees any individual residing in a member state of the Council of Europe a complete and highly developed body of rights. Applicable by French judges under the primacy rule, use of the Convention has become increasingly frequent since 1981, when France ratified article

Departments and regions

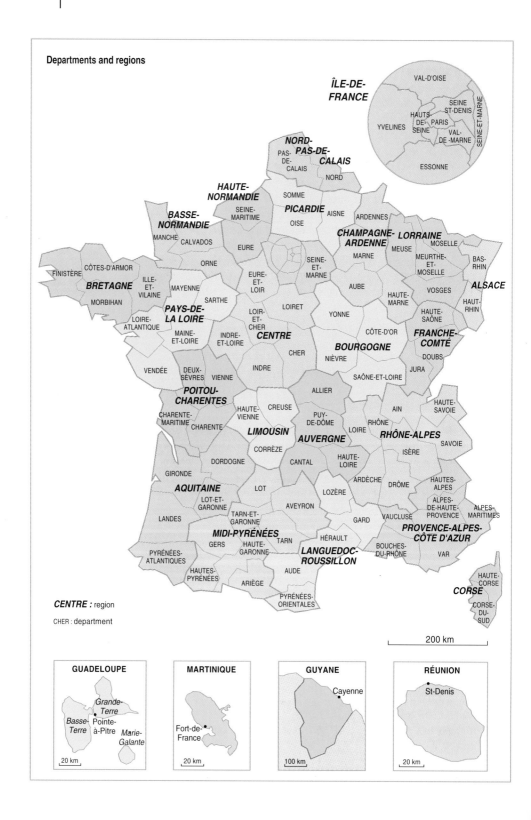

ÎLE-DE-FRANCE

VAL-D'OISE

SEINE-ST-DENIS

HAUTS-DE-SEINE

PARIS

YVELINES

VAL-DE-MARNE

SEINE-ET-MARNE

ESSONNE

NORD-PAS-DE-CALAIS

PAS-DE-CALAIS

NORD

HAUTE-NORMANDIE

SOMME

SEINE-MARITIME

PICARDIE

AISNE

ARDENNES

BASSE-NORMANDIE

OISE

CHAMPAGNE-ARDENNE

LORRAINE

MOSELLE

MANCHE

CALVADOS

EURE

MARNE

MEUSE

MEURTHE-ET-MOSELLE

BAS-RHIN

ORNE

SEINE-ET-MARNE

AUBE

VOSGES

CÔTES-D'ARMOR

EURE-ET-LOIR

HAUT-RHIN

FINISTÈRE

ALSACE

BRETAGNE

ILLE-ET-VILAINE

MAYENNE

SARTHE

LOIRET

HAUTE-MARNE

HAUTE-SAÔNE

MORBIHAN

PAYS-DE-LA LOIRE

LOIR-ET-CHER

YONNE

FRANCHE-COMTÉ

LOIRE-ATLANTIQUE

MAINE-ET-LOIRE

INDRE-ET-LOIRE

CENTRE

CÔTE-D'OR

DOUBS

BOURGOGNE

CHER

NIÈVRE

JURA

VENDÉE

DEUX-SÈVRES

VIENNE

INDRE

SAÔNE-ET-LOIRE

POITOU-CHARENTES

ALLIER

HAUTE-SAVOIE

CHARENTE-MARITIME

HAUTE-VIENNE

CREUSE

PUY-DE-DÔME

AIN

CHARENTE

LIMOUSIN

AUVERGNE

RHÔNE

LOIRE

RHÔNE-ALPES

SAVOIE

CORRÈZE

ISÈRE

DORDOGNE

CANTAL

HAUTE-LOIRE

GIRONDE

ARDÈCHE

DRÔME

HAUTES-ALPES

AQUITAINE

LOT

LOZÈRE

LOT-ET-GARONNE

AVEYRON

ALPES-DE-HAUTE-PROVENCE

ALPES-MARITIMES

LANDES

TARN-ET-GARONNE

GARD

VAUCLUSE

MIDI-PYRÉNÉES

TARN

HÉRAULT

PROVENCE-ALPES-CÔTE D'AZUR

GERS

HAUTE-GARONNE

BOUCHES-DU-RHÔNE

VAR

PYRÉNÉES-ATLANTIQUES

LANGUEDOC-ROUSSILLON

HAUTES-PYRÉNÉES

ARIÈGE

AUDE

HAUTE-CORSE

CORSE

PYRÉNÉES-ORIENTALES

CORSE-DU-SUD

CENTRE : region

CHER : department

200 km

GUADELOUPE

Grande-Terre

Basse-Terre

Pointe-à-Pitre

Marie-Galante

20 km

MARTINIQUE

Fort-de-France

20 km

GUYANE

Cayenne

100 km

RÉUNION

St-Denis

20 km

25 on the right of individual petition. From that date, any natural or legal person has had the right to turn to the European Court of Human Rights provided all domestic remedies have been exhausted. The proliferation of links between France and the organs of the Council of Europe confirms the great importance France attaches to its founding principles and to continued improvement in the way its procedures are applied.

Local government structure

While local government in France has a long history of centralisation, the past 20 years have brought some radical changes. At first sight, the system may seem complex: France is one of the few states in the European Union with four tiers of government – the state or central government, region, department and *commune*.

The decentralisation law of 2 March 1982 and the legislation completing it marked the Paris government's desire to alter the balance of power between the state and local authorities (regions, departments and *communes*). It gave far greater autonomy in decision-making by sharing administrative and budgetary tasks between central and local authorities.

Three Tiers of Local Administration

In France there are three main tiers of local administration: the *commune*, department and region. These are both districts in which administrative decisions made at national level are carried out and local authorities with powers of their own. Legally speaking, a local authority is a public-law corporation with its own name, territory, budget, employees, etc. and specific powers and a certain degree of autonomy vis-à-vis central government.

In addition, there are France's overseas territories and regional bodies (*collectivités territoriales*) with special status (Paris, Marseille, Lyon, Corsica, Mayotte and Saint-Pierre-et-Miquelon).

■ Commune

The *commune*, which dates from 1789, is the lowest tier of the French administrative hierarchy. There are nearly 37,000 *communes*, many more than are found in the other countries of the European Union, because in France the term *commune* is applied to all municipalities whatever their size – 80% of them have fewer than 1,000 residents. This situation has led the government to encourage smaller *communes* to merge to form urban communities (*communautés urbaines*) or group together in associations of several *communes* (*syndicats intercommunaux*). In addition, the law of 6 February 1992 suggested new forms of cooperation to rationalise municipal administration by taking common interests into consideration. In reality, the closer links often go no further than pooling a few services and mergers are extremely rare, as both residents and local councillors often retain a strong sense of identity with their *communes*.

Like the department and region, the *commune* has a deliberative or decision-making body (the municipal council) and an executive (the mayor), elected by the municipal council. The number of municipal councillors is proportional to the population. Elected for six years by direct universal suffrage, municipal councillors lay down guidelines for municipal policy, adopt the budget, manage municipal assets, notably primary school buildings and equipment, and decide how the municipal administration is to operate.

The town halls of Conches and Savigny-le-Temple (Seine-et-Marne)

The mayor has two hats, since he or she is both the *commune*'s elected authority and the state's representative in it. As the *commune*'s chief executive, the mayor carries out the decisions of the municipal council, is the municipality's legal representative, proposes and implements the budget, ensures the conservation and management of the *commune*'s natural environment and built heritage and issues building permits. Mayors also have powers in their own right, being responsible for security and public health and having at their disposal the municipal administration, which they head. As the state's representative, the mayor is the registrar of births, marriages (at which he officiates) and deaths and is an officer of the *police judiciaire* and so entitled to exercise special powers in connection with the repression of crime under the authority of the public prosecutor. Finally, he/she is responsible for various administrative tasks including publicising laws and regulations and drawing up the electoral register. Mayoral acts are unilateral administrative acts, generally orders, whose legality is subject to a posteriori control by the courts when they are issued by the mayor as the *commune*'s chief executive and to the approval of the prefect (see below) to whom the mayor is subordinate when acting in the capacity of the state's representative.

So the *commune*'s own powers cover activities which affect its inhabitants' daily lives. Its economic and social brief, long limited to granting aid for job creation and helping needy families, has been broadened to enable it to play an important role in combating unemployment and social exclusion and engage actively in economic restructuring and development of new activities.

Department

There are 100 departments in France, 96 in metropolitan France and four overseas (Martinique, Guadeloupe, Réunion and French Guiana). Established in 1789, the department has developed from a partially decentralised local authority to one with full powers of its own (since 1982). It has played a prominent role in the country's administrative and geographical organisation. The department essentially has competence in health and social services, rural capital works, departmental roads, and the capital expenditure and running costs of *collèges* (cf. chapter 13).

The *Hôtel du département*, where the general council meets in Avignon (Vaucluse)

Prefect

For almost 200 years (1800 to 1982), the prefect held the executive power in the department, but the law of March 1982 modified his/her powers. Appointed by the government, the prefect is still the sole person empowered to act on the state's behalf in the department: he/she represents the Prime Minister and all the members of the government, has authority over the state's external services in the department and ensures the administrative supervision of the department's local authorities.

However, the law of 2 March 1982 conferred executive authority for the department on the chairman of the general council. The general council is the department's decision-making organ. It is made up of general councillors elected for a six-year term in a two-ballot uninominal majority poll. Each department is divided into *cantons* (France has 3,500 *cantons*) which serve as the constituencies for the election. Elected by the councillors for a six-year term, the chairman prepares the council's debates and implements its decisions, including on budgetary matters. He/she represents the department at the legal level, heads the department's staff and services and, finally, as the person in charge of running the department, he/she exercises certain police powers in the areas of conservation and departmental highways (without prejudice to the powers of the mayors and prefect in these areas).

Region

France has 26 regions, 22 in metropolitan France and four overseas. The latter have a special status, being at the same time departments and regions. Created in 1955 to provide a framework for regional town and country planning, the region became a local authority in 1982. Its main spheres of competence are planning, regional town and country planning, economic development, vocational training, and the building, equipment and running costs of *lycées* (cf. chapter 13).

The decision-making organ is the regional council whose members are elected for six-years. They are assisted by an economic and social committee, which is a consultative assembly made up of representatives of businesses, the professions, trade unions and other employees' organisations, regional voluntary organisations, etc.. This committee must be consulted on the preparation and implementation of national plans, the establishment of the regional development plan and the major guidelines for the regional budget. The committee is also free to comment on any regional matter or, at the initiative of the regional council's chairman, any economic, social or cultural proposal. The regional council chairman, elected by the councillors, is the region's executive authority. His/her responsibilities are identical to those of the general council chairman in the areas within the region's sphere of competence.

Permanency and Change in French Local Authority Administration

Article 72 of the Constitution stipulates that the Republic's local authorities ("territorial units") "... shall be self-governing through elected councils", and the 1982 reforms did not change this. The principles of independent administration by local authorities and the election of the members of their decision-making bodies remain the fundamentals of French local government.

So while basic principles and structures have not changed and there is a clear distinction between the spheres of competence of the different tiers, the decentralisation legislation did bring in some innovations, especially regarding supervision. Some degree of ex post facto monitoring of local government action is necessary in order to reconcile the fact that the authorities are self-governing with the need for coordinated action within a unitary state and ensure that the principle of equality of all citizens does not override the general interests of the nation as a whole.

The March 1982 law also made several changes concerning financing. Any transfer of state competence to a local authority must be accompanied by a transfer of resources (chiefly fiscal). In practice, local taxes have tended to rise. The reform also extended the responsibilities of the communal, departmental and regional accountants, giving them the status of chief accountant directly responsible to the Treasury. Lastly, it assigned to a new court, the regional audit chamber, responsibility for a posteriori auditing of local authority accounts.

The process of decentralisation has profoundly altered local government in France. The new system is indisputably more costly than the old for the public purse and has led to some fragmentation of tasks and objectives, as local authorities act primarily in their own rather than the national interest. However, decentralisation is helping to ensure that tasks are carried out at the most appropriate level of responsibility in all sectors of public life, so bringing greater democracy to the country's administration and management.

Pays-de-la-Loire regional council meets in Nantes (Loire-Atlantique)

Further reading:

On the institutions of the Fifth Republic:

Le Président de la Vᵉ République, La Documentation française, Documents d'études series, N° 1.06, 1995.

Constitution française du 4 octobre 1958, La Documentation française, Documents d'études series, N° 1.04, 1998.

D. Maus, *Les grands textes de la pratique institutionnelle de la Vᵉ République*, La Documentation française, Retour aux textes series, 1998.

B. Tricot, R. Hadas-Lebel, D. Kessler, *Les institutions politiques françaises*, Presses de la FNSP-Dalloz, Amphithéâtre series, 1995.

P. Ardant, *Les institutions de la Vᵉ République*, Hachette, 1995.

O. Duhamel, *Le pouvoir politique en France*, Le Seuil, 1995.

J.-L. Sauron, *L'application du droit de l'Union européenne en France*, La Documentation française, Réflexe Europe series, 1995.

Institutions et vie politique en France, La Documentation française, Les Notices series, 1997.

On local government in France:

J.-P. Lebreton, *L'administration territoriale : le système général*, La Documentation française, Documents d'études series, N° 2.02, 1996.

Les collectivités locales en France, La Documentation française-CNFPT, Les Notices series, 1996.

P. Duran, J.-C. Thoenig, " L'État et la gestion publique territoriale ", *Revue française de sciences politiques*, vol. 43, N° 4, 1996.

Ministère de l'Intérieur, *Les collectivités locales en chiffres*, 1996 edition, La Documentation française, 1997.

7

Politics

The French traditionally take an active interest in public life. The Revolution saw the rapid development of newspapers, clubs and circles, reflecting an interest in politics on the part of a large sector of the population which had hitherto been confined to a narrow circle around the throne. The introduction of direct universal male suffrage in 1848 made possible the expression of political opinions through the ballot box, but it was essentially during the Third Republic (1875-1940) that a political consciousness was forged in France thanks to the establishment of genuine political parties, the rapid growth of the trade-union movement and the heightened role of the press. The press contributed to the spread of existing ideologies and new ideas, allowing ordinary citizens to play a greater part in the great debates of the time, such as the separation of Church and state and the Dreyfus affair. However, institutions, political parties and the media are not the only components of political life, to which all French citizens can contribute.

Historical and Constitutional Foundations of the French Political System

The roots of political life in France reach deep into the past and for this reason political debate there makes constant reference to history.

Historical Foundations

The introduction of universal suffrage in 1848 under the Second Republic generated a vigorous and rich political life. The people's right to exercise sovereignty meant that each Frenchman felt himself to be a fully-fledged citizen, a member of society and an active participant in political decision-making. The Constituent Assembly elected in 1848 enacted other measures which also encouraged citizens' involvement, such as abolishing the death penalty for political offences and affirming the freedom of the press and freedom to hold public meetings.

Subsequently, the Third Republic played an essential role by gradually increasing French citizens' commitment to the concept of the republic. The longevity of the Third Republic was an important factor in this process, because counter-revolutionary sympathisers gradually ceased to see this form of government as a source of unrest and a threat to civil order. The parliamentary republic, whose legitimacy stems from the democratic principle of universal suffrage, gradually became the poli-

tical system supported by the majority of citizens. The Third Republic conveyed certain values in which the French people came to believe fervently: faith in education, democracy and the nation became the republican credo.

Until 1905 the Third Republic was a genuine citizens' republic, but thereafter it increasingly became a parliamentarians' republic. The fact that governments did not really reflect the opinions of a coherent majority and the constant forming and reforming of alliances and coalitions began to distance ordinary citizens from the exercise of power, whilst the role of the parties and political groups increased.

Jean Jaurès speaks at Pré-Saint-Gervais, on 25 May 1913, at a demonstration against the law bringing in a three-year period of military service

Not really existing as such in France before 1900, political parties began to become structured at the beginning of the twentieth century, but remained modest in scale, in comparison with similar organisations in other Western democracies. However, after the First World War, their role became more established and political debate spread from the clubs, reading and educational societies, public meetings and republican banquets to cafés and workplaces. Cafés were the scene of lively discussion prompted by newspaper articles on political themes, contributing to exchanges of ideas. The workplace, especially factories, also played a part in developing social and political awareness among citizens through trade union activities, which spread political ideas, notably Marxism, amongst the working classes.

After the Second World War, the Fourth Republic (1945-1958) was a period of great instability. The Liberation, women's suffrage and General de Gaulle's condemnation of the Third Republic's regime of parties raised high hopes: these were modernized political parties with new ideologies, capable of raising moral standards in public life, and the majority of them were led by Resistance heroes. However, these hopes were dashed. There were too many parties, some too bureaucratic and others lacking any structure at all and they were divided and destabilised by internal quarrels between individuals or factions. In short, they did not prove equal to the situation, resulting in the failure of the Fourth Republic and the weakening of the authority of the state.

Institutional Foundations

The Constitution of the Fifth Republic sought to restore that weakened authority by strengthening the executive vis-à-vis the legislature. The role of the President of the Republic, head of state, pivot of this new system, was and is that of a national arbiter standing above party politics and responsible for ensuring that the institutions function properly. Since 1962, the President has been elected by direct universal suffrage in a two-ballot majority poll, i.e. to win in the first ballot a candidate must have an absolute majority of the votes cast, with the result of the second, a run-off between the two leading candidates, decided on a first-past-the-post basis. One might imagine that, in these circumstances, a public which had grown indifferent to, if not suspicious of political parties widely discredited by the way they had exercised power under the Fourth Republic would put their trust in the charismatic leadership of one individual. However, in the main this has not been the case. The Constitution of the Fifth Republic was in fact the first in French history to acknowledge that the political parties had a role, and went so far as to define it in article 4:

The 1962 referendum: despite an active "no" campaign, the proposal to elect Presidents of the Republic by direct universal suffrage was approved by 61.7%

"Political parties and groups shall contribute to the exercise of suffrage. They shall be formed and carry on their activities freely. They must respect the principles of national sovereignty and democracy." Although from a legal point of view parties are classed merely as associations (Law of 1901), in practice they mediate between the general public and the state. Tuned in to citizens' concerns and problems, they draw up programmes addressing these and campaign on specific platforms at election time. The Constitution of the Fifth Republic thus institutionalised the role of political parties. These are represented in both houses of Parliament, where they form parliamentary groups on the basis of which debates are organised and bills proposed and voted on. Thanks to this system, the volatility inherent in multi-party politics is counterbalanced by stable institutions allowing changeovers of governments of different colours and even "cohabitation" between a President and government on opposite sides of the political spectrum. Indeed, since the President is elected by direct universal suffrage and thus must receive an absolute majority of the votes cast, no candidate can rely solely on the supporters of one party, but must attract additional voters by building a coalition of parties on the basis of a joint programme or common government platform. Consequently, once elected, the President of the Republic emerges as an impartial arbiter standing above the parties, including those of the coalition which had backed him in the election. According to Gaullist tradition, the President is accountable only to the people of France, who have elected him.

Landmarks in Political Life – Elections and Referenda

Elections are major events in the political life of the country. Except for Senate elections, voting is by direct universal suffrage and there are just over 40 million electors (out of a total population of 58 million). Electors must have reached their majority (i.e. be at least 18 years old), be of French nationality, except for municipal and European Parliament elections, be on the electoral role in their commune of residence and be in full possession of their civic rights - convictions for certain serious crimes may lead to loss of civic rights for a specified length of time. The conditions candidates must fulfil are the same for all elections except as regards the minimum age, which varies according to the mandate sought (they must be 18 to run for municipal councillor, 21 for regional councillor, 23 for National Assembly deputy or President of the Republic and 35 for Senator).

Polling station at Arradon, Morbihan, during the first ballot of the general election, 25 May 1997

French electors vote not only to choose their representatives at communal, departmental, regional or national level, but also on occasion in referenda. Indeed, in response to a proposal by the government or Parliament, the President of the Republic may submit a bill or major decision to them for approval in a referendum. This has happened twice in the past ten years: the first, on 6 November 1988, was on the status of New Caledonia, and the second, on 20 September 1992, on the ratification of the Treaty on European Union. A reform of the Constitution in August 1995 broadened the scope of referenda to include bills on "reforms relating to the economic or social policy of the Nation and to the public services contributing thereto".

Local Elections

In their commune, French citizens and (from 2001) residents who are nationals of other European Union states elect municipal councillors for a six-year term by direct universal suffrage; the councillors then elect the mayor. The number of municipal councillors depends on the size of the population, as do some aspects of the voting system, which in both cases is a two-ballot majority list poll. However:

- in communes with fewer than 3,500 inhabitants, voting for candidates on different lists (vote-splitting) and deletion of names (preference voting) are allowed and votes are counted by candidate;

- while in those with more than 3,500 inhabitants, the ballot paper must not be altered by the voter and any vote for a list on which names have been deleted is considered invalid, votes are counted by list and some seats are allocated proportionally.

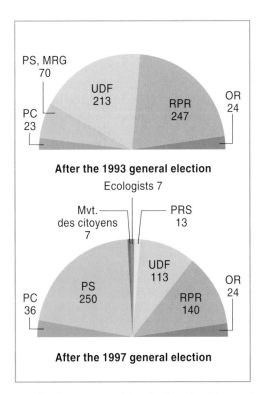

After the 1993 general election

After the 1997 general election

Composition of the National Assembly after the 1993 and 1997 general elections
PC: *Parti Communiste* (Communist Party)
PS: *Parti Socialiste* (Socialist Party)
MRG: *Mouvement des Radicaux de Gauche* (Radical Left Movement)
PRS: *Parti Radical Socialiste* (Radical Socialist Party)
UDF: *Union pour la Démocratie Française* (Union for French Democracy)
RPR: *Rassemblement Pour la République* (Rally for the Republic)
OR: Other Right

At departmental level, French citizens vote in what are known as "cantonal elections" for members of the General Council for a six-year term. These are two ballot majority uninominal (single candi-

After September 1998 Senatorial Elections (situation on 6th October 1998)	
Groupe Rassemblement pour la République	99 Senators
Groupe socialiste	78 Senators
Groupe communiste, républicain et citoyen	16 Senators
Groupe de l'Union centriste	52 Senators
Groupe des Républicains et indépendants	49 Senators
Groupe Rassemblement démocratique et social européen	21 Senators

date) polls, with one councillor elected for each constituency (canton). Half the councillors come up for election every three years.

In 1982 the decentralisation legislation made the region a new tier of local government in France. Members of the regional council are elected for six years. Electors vote for a departmental list of candidates, with proportional representation and distribution of the remaining seats using the highest averages system, a polling method that allows minorities and small parties to be represented.

National Elections

General or legislative elections are held to choose the 577 deputies who sit in the National Assembly; they are elected for a five-year term by direct universal suffrage on the two-ballot, uninominal majority system. Each deputy represents a constituency which may vary in size, but has on average 100,000 inhabitants. First-past-the-post voting was introduced by General de Gaulle as an antidote to the instability which had plagued the governments of the Fourth Republic and which had been largely due to proportional representation. The proportional system was brought back for the 1986 general election by the Socialist government - which was seeking better representation for small political groups - but the first-past-the-post system was reinstated for the 1988 elections and has been retained ever since.

In senatorial elections, the 321 members of the Senate are elected by indirect universal suffrage by an electoral college in each department made up of deputies, general councillors, regional councillors and representatives of the municipal councils. Senators are elected for a nine-year term, with one third of their number replaced every three years.

The presidential election is, of course, a major event in French political life, in which the people make a sort of moral pact with a leader. The President is chosen by direct universal suffrage for a seven-year renewable term in a two-ballot majority poll. Candidates must be sponsored by at least 500 national and/or local elected representatives.

Finally, European elections are held to elect the 87 French MEPs for a five-year term by direct universal suffrage with voting by proportional representation for national lists. Under the terms of the Treaty on European Union, citizens of other European Union states resident in France may vote for one of the French lists of candidates.

Each election or referendum is preceded by an election campaign during which there is an increase in political activity and debate. This is the time when candidates meet the voters and present their programmes and proposals. They have various ways of doing this: they can meet them in markets, shopping centres or even the street and use the media (press, radio and television), a platform widely available to them during election campaigns. However, to ensure that candidates receive equal treatment, the *Conseil supérieur de l'audiovisuel* (Higher Council for the Audiovisual Sector - CSA), the public body which regulates the broadcast media, sees that each candidate or political party is allotted an equivalent amount of time by each radio station and television channel, on which political advertising is prohibited. Finally, in the weeks preceding an election, each voter receives an electoral envelope containing all the candidates' statements and manifestos. In order to avoid the election outcome being influenced by public opinion polls, which have become increasingly important in French politics, their findings may not be published during the week before a ballot.

Under the laws of 22 December 1990 and 19 January 1995 on the funding of political parties and election campaigns, parties and committees formed to support the various candidates are required to publish their campaign accounts – which must balance – and must include in their reports all expenditure on political communications. For a period of one year preceding the date of the election, the current spending limit in presidential elections is 90 million francs ($16 million) and for candidates present in the second round 120 million francs ($21 million). A ban on political advertising on commercial hoardings commences four months before the official campaign opens. Restrictions have also been placed on the funding of political parties: first, stringent ceilings were imposed on

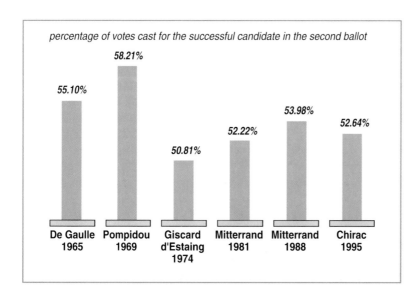

percentage of votes cast for the successful candidate in the second ballot

De Gaulle 1965	Pompidou 1969	Giscard d'Estaing 1974	Mitterrand 1981	Mitterrand 1988	Chirac 1995
55.10%	58.21%	50.81%	52.22%	53.98%	52.64%

Results of presidential elections during the Fifth Republic: since the election of V. Giscard d'Estaing, votes have been fairly evenly split between right and left-wing candidates

Ageing Electorate

In 1995, a year which saw presidential and municipal elections, INED, the National Institute of Demographic Studies, published figures showing that the average age of voters in France had risen: 19.6% of the electorate were over 65, i.e. almost one in five voters, which is considerably higher than the proportion of over-65s in the population as a whole (only 15%) and 1.5% more than at the 1988 presidential election. The same study put the 18-24 age-group at only 13.1% of the total electorate, compared with 14.4% in 1988. In a 1991 survey on the influence of age on voting decisions, the tendency of elderly people to be more conservative was attributed to the fact that they belong to "groups in which there was an over-representation of individuals likely to prefer right-wing to left-wing policies, notably women, the self-employed, practising Catholics and owners of assets or property". INED thus identified a paradox: an older electorate is now having to decide how best to deal with the problems experienced by the young.

the resources parties may hold, together with an obligation to declare funds provided by businesses, industrial groups and private donors, subsequently all funding of political parties by businesses became illegal. The state reimburses a proportion of campaign expenses depending on the results obtained in the election (one million francs - $180,000) for any presidential candidate, plus 8% of the spending limit for these candidates and 36% for those winning more than 5% of the votes in the first ballot). These provisions are designed to make politics fairer by limiting expenditure and waste and guaranteeing a degree of equity between the candidates.

5 March 1998 at the Zénith (Paris): leading figures in the left-wing coalition during the regional election campaign. Front row: R. Hue, D. Voynet, L. Jospin, M.-G. Buffet and D. Strauss-Kahn

Current Political Scene

Political parties play the essential role of mediator between ordinary people and politics. In France, they change quite frequently, with the result that their stances on issues and their alliances with one another are more complex than in the United States, United Kingdom or Germany, where the party structure seems more stable. French political parties have seen a significant decline in their membership for over a decade, as have the trade union confederations. The fact that people have been turning their backs

on these organizations reflects a degree of suspicion towards bodies whose methods of obtaining funding have at times led to court convictions. In the hope of restoring citizens' faith in public life, the successive governments of the last ten years have endeavoured to clarify the rules of party funding, bring in younger leaders and give women greater responsibilities.

The victory of the left in the 1997 general election led to the Fifth Republic's third right/left cohabitation, following those between 1986-1988 and 1992-1995. But this time the situation was reversed, with a right-wing President and a left-wing government. While the situation has little effect on the country's stance on international issues, as the President and Prime Minister speak with one voice at major conferences, the opposition between left and right is as strong as ever on the domestic front.

The defeat of the right in the general election, followed by losses in the 1998 regional elections, contributed to its fragmentation, with splits accentuated by the personal ambitions of a number of party leaders. Its two main components, the RPR (*Rassemblement pour la République* - Rally for the Republic) and the UDF (*Union pour la Démocratie française* - Union for French Democracy), are being affected by centrifugal forces. Although since May 1998 there has been a formal Alliance of the elements which make up the "Republican opposition", i.e. the RPR, UDF and *Démocratie libérale*, this is chiefly an alliance between the parties' leaderships with little support on the ground and it has not eliminated the divisions between different groups on the right.

In 1998 there was a split between free marketeers and other centre-right politicians, who had waged common cause since 1978 under the banner of the UDF, founded by former President Valéry Giscard d'Estaing. Some free marketeers now belong to *Démocratie libérale*, which succeeded the former *Parti républicain* and is led by Alain Madelin. Others have remained in the UDF, aligning themselves with the Republican, independent and free-market wing of the movement. The centre-right, now in the majority in the UDF, have now regrouped around François Bayrou's *Force démocrate*. Since 1995, *Force démocrate* has combined the former CDS (*Centre des Démocrates-sociaux*) and PSD (*Parti social-démocrate*). Other parties established by former members of the UDF include Jean-Pierre Soisson's *Mouvement des Réformateurs*, Charles Millon's *La Droite* and Philippe de Villiers' *Mouvement pour la France*.

The leaders of the *Alliance pour la France* at a rally on 27 June 1998 at Port-Marly (Yvelines): N. Sarkozy, A. Madelin, P. Séguin and F. Bayrou

The RPR itself, while retaining outward unity, despite the aftermath of rivalry between Jacques Chirac and Edouard Balladur in the 1995 presidential elections, brings together several different strands of political opinion, as Charles Pasqua's new movement, *Demain la France*, demonstrates.

Today's divisions within the Republican right stem in large part from differing attitudes towards the *Front national* (FN). Some right-wing politicians have moved closer to the extreme right party, with whom they share the leadership of some regional councils; others, on the other hand, are opposed to any concession to it. The FN, benefiting from the unrest in society and the disillusionment of some voters with the Republican parties, is gaining a foothold in several regions. It champions an anti-European brand of nationalism, coupled with condemnation of the main political parties.

The left is also divided. However, the *Parti socialiste* remains by far the most powerful component in the ruling left-wing coalition known as the *gauche plurielle* (multi-party left). Its internal conflicts, widely reported during the 1980s because of the infighting, have become less pronounced since the victory in the last general election, although there is at times some criticism of the government. To the left of the *Parti socialiste* is the *Mouvement des Citoyens* (Citizens' Movement) led by Jean-Pierre Chevènement.

After losing in the past two decades a large proportion of its activists and supporters, some of them to the *Parti socialiste*, the *Parti communiste* has in the past few years succeeded in maintaining a 9-10% share of the electorate. Now adopting a more pragmatic approach, the PC is seeking to update its image, but there is conflict between the leadership and the "reformists", some of whom have remained party members while others are active from the outside.

The *Parti Radical socialiste*, strongest in the south-west, is struggling to make its voice heard by its socialist ally.

1995 Presidential Elections

First Round: (main candidates)

Lionel Jospin (PS)	23.2 %
Jacques Chirac (RPR)	20.4 %
Édouard Balladur (RPR)	18.5 %
Jean-Marie Le Pen (FN)	15.2 %
Robert Hue (PCF)	8.7 %

Second Round:

Jacques Chirac	52.7 %
(elected President of the Republic)	
Lionel Jospin	47.3 %

The ecologists, who first appeared on France's political scene in 1974, are divided into rival factions of which one, *Les Verts* (the Greens), are represented in the government. Another, Brice Lalonde's *Génération Ecologie* has moved closer to the RPR and UDF.

Finally, the 1997 general election confirmed the rise of the extreme left, in which the most important group appears to be *Lutte ouvrière* (Workers' Struggle) headed by Arlette Laguiller, followed by the *Ligue communiste révolutionnaire*. Contesting some of the government's measures, the extreme left is gaining support amongst the movements of unemployed people and defenders of the rights of illegal immigrants.

Main Political Groups

▓ Parti socialiste (PS) – Socialist Party

Historically, the *Parti socialiste* was the successor of the SFIO (French Section of the Workers International) founded in the early twentieth century by Jules Guesde and Jean Jaurès and later led by Léon Blum. The reformed PS was founded by François Mitterrand in 1971 at the Epinay congress. In the space of ten years it became one of France's leading political parties, and in 1981 its First Secretary was elected President of the Republic. The current First Secretary, François Hollande, succeeded Lionel Jospin when the latter was appointed Prime Minister following the left's victory in the 1997 general election.

▓ Parti communiste français (PCF) – French Communist Party

At the Tours Congress of the SFIO in 1920, the majority of those present, who accepted the "21 conditions" set out in the Communist Charter, founded the SFIC (French Section of the Communist International), later to become the PCF. It formed an alliance with the *Parti socialiste* after François Mitterrand was elected President of the Republic, enabling it to take part in the 1981-1984 left-wing government. The *Parti communiste* has two ministers and a minister of state in the government which Prime Minister Lionel Jospin formed in 1997.

▓ Rassemblement pour la République (RPR) – Rally for the Republic

Founded in 1976 by Jacques Chirac, the RPR succeeded the UDR (*Union des démocrates pour la République*) and claims the legacy of Gaullism, as the latest embodiment of the *Rassemblement du Peuple Français* (RPF) movement established by General de Gaulle in 1947.

▨ Union pour la démocratie française (UDF) – Union for French Democracy

Founded on 1 February 1978 on the initiative of Valéry Giscard d'Estaing, the *Union pour la démocratie française* was a confederation of parties until November 1998, when its national party council decided to make it a unified party. Its components are: *Force démocrate*, the *Parti populaire pour la démocratie française*, the *Parti radical*, and the *Pôle républicain, indépendant et libéral*, as well as direct supporters of the UDF.

▨ Front national (FN) – National Front

Founded in 1972 by Jean-Marie Le Pen, the *Front national* defines itself as a party of the nationalist and popular right. It gained little electoral support between 1972 and 1982, but since 1983 the FN has increased its electorate. In 1999 wrangles over party leadership led to the creation of a breakaway faction, the *Front national-Mouvement national* (National Front-National Movement) led by Bruno Mégret.

Further reading:

J.-J. Becker, *Histoire politique de la France depuis 1945*, A. Colin, "Cursus" series, 1996.

P. Bréchon, *La France aux urnes, cinquante ans d'histoire électorale*, La Documentation française, "Les Études" series, 1998.

CEVIPOF, *L'électeur a ses raisons*, Presses de sciences po, 1997.

D. Chagnollaud (Ed.), *La vie politique en France*, Le Seuil, "Points Essais" series, 1993.

Institutions et vie politique, La Documentation française, "Les Notices" series, 1997.

J. Massot, *Alternances et cohabitation sous la Ve République*, La Documentation française, "Les Études" series, 1997.

Y. Mény, *Le système politique français*, Montchrestien, Clefs politiques series, 1996, available in English in the Getting to know French Administration series, La Documentation Française - IIAP, 1998.

J.-F. Sirinelli (Ed.), *Dictionnaire historique de la vie politique française au XXe siècle*, PUF, 1995.

C. Ysmal, *Les partis politiques sous la Ve République*, Montchrestien, Domat politique, 1989.

FRANCE
IN
THE WORLD

8

French Foreign Policy

As one of the oldest European nations, the country in which the ideals of the Universal Declaration of Human Rights originated and a permanent member of the Security Council, France has always claimed the right to influence international affairs and done so.

After the Second World War, the determination to bring to an end the rivalries that had long torn Europe apart led France, together with its European neighbours, to build the European Community which subsequently became the European Union. Further afield, France has continued to develop its special relations with African, Middle-Eastern and Asian countries and has campaigned for development in the Southern hemisphere, especially in the Least Developed Countries. A shared history has forged close ties with the Americas, which it continues to maintain. France remains faithful to the ideals of the 1789 Revolution: Liberty, Equality, Fraternity for all of humanity. France's activity in support of democracy and peace all over the world is proof of its commitment to these ideals.

Principles

The aims of French foreign policy are unchanging. The type of influence exerted has of course evolved since the end of the Second World War, but French policy has always been based on respect for certain principles.

France values its independence highly, a principle which guided General de Gaulle's foreign policy during the 1960s and underpinned his decision that France should develop a credible independent defence capability based on nuclear deterrence. The same spirit lay behind some spectacular diplomatic initiatives, notably in the Middle East and Asia which showed that France remained wholly in control when it came to analysing situations and deciding its foreign policy options. The determination to continue along this path did not weaken over the subsequent decades.

However, France's commitment to independence does not preclude efforts to develop solidarity with others. Throughout the Cold War, France reaffirmed through words and deeds that it was a part of the free world. It fulfils the responsibilities devolving from its international status as a permanent member of the United Nations Security Council and a member of various alliances and is guided by the ambition to see that the values it has inspired - values enshrined in solemn documents by international institutions - prevail throughout the world.

These principles and ambitions have lost none of their validity now that the Cold War has ended. They continue to shape France's major foreign policy goals, which are to pursue European integration in order to guarantee stability and prosperity on the continent, and to encourage progress towards peace, democracy and development within the international community.

France and the Building of Europe

Since 1945, building Europe has been central to French foreign policy. Three considerations have made this ambitious design a priority: the determination to end the conflicts that twice in the space of 30 years tore the continent apart and weakened France; the need, in the Cold War context, to ensure stability and guarantee the security of the democratic nations west of the Iron Curtain; and finally the desire to build a unified economic area adapted to modern production conditions, guaranteeing the prosperity of the European peoples.

Two French politicians were instrumental in launching the building of Europe: Robert Schuman and Jean Monnet. Believing in the need to bring the nations of Europe together into a single organisation, they set up a framework of economic cooperation with a view to speeding up the establishment of closer political ties. This was the context in which the European Coal and Steel Community (ECSC) was founded on 18 April 1951 and its institutions were to serve as a model for subsequent stages in European integration. On 25 March 1957, the six member states of the ECSC (Belgium, France, Germany, Italy, Luxembourg and the Netherlands) signed the Treaty of Rome setting up the European Economic Community (EEC). The six countries pledged to link their economic future by abolishing all customs barriers between them and establishing a Common Agricultural Policy (CAP).

When General de Gaulle became President of France in 1958, he expressed his determination to go further in this direction, as have his successors. And so, in the three decades since the Treaty of Rome was signed, France actively contributed to the steady progress of the process of building Europe. Under Georges Pompidou's presidency, on 1 January 1973, the customs union was followed by a first enlargement of the Community to include three new members: the United Kingdom, Denmark and Ireland. The 1970s saw important political reforms such as the establishment of the European Council (bringing together heads of state or government), the election of members of the European Parliament by universal suffrage and the development of the European Monetary System (EMS) at the instigation of President Valéry Giscard d'Estaing and Chancellor Helmut Schmidt of Germany. Soon afterwards, the desire to help the democratic states of southern Europe led to a further enlargement: Greece joined the Community in 1981, Spain and Portugal in 1986. Finally, at the instigation of François Mitterrand, Helmut Kohl and Jacques Delors (then President of the European Commission) the Single European Act was adopted in February 1986. Its aim is to create a genuine single European market guaranteeing freedom of movement for people, goods and capital, as well as freedom to provide services anywhere in the Community. By and large, this was achieved by 1993.

The European Union today

Together with its partners, France has been applying itself to the next phase of European integration: implementation of the Treaty on European Union, signed on 7 February 1992 in the Dutch town of Maastricht.

This document extends the Community's powers in several important areas: the environment, consumer protection, education and vocational training and social policy. It modifies certain institutional mechanisms to enhance the role of the European Parliament and codifies the principle of subsidiarity, under which the European Union should deal only with questions which cannot be settled at a national level. It also gives EU citizens the right to vote in local and European elections in their country of residence, whichever EU country they come from.

The Treaty introduces two new pillars of European construction: the common foreign and security policy (CFSP), one of whose aims is the establishment of a common defence, and cooperation in the sphere of justice and home affairs.

The increasing integration of EU member states has sometimes encountered resistance at national level. France has chosen its path: after much debate, the ratification of the Treaty of Maastricht was finally approved by referendum on 20 September 1992. This further strengthened France's commitment to Europe.

At the end of the nineties, the most important step towards deepening the EU has been the single currency – the euro.

The euro was born on 1 January 1999. Eleven of the fifteen member states of the European Union — France, Germany, Italy, Benelux, Ireland, Spain, Portugal, Austria and Finland — are already taking part in this bold enterprise.

For France, the euro is a crucial stage in European integration. It confirms France's commitment to an economic and financial policy coordinated with its European partners. The EU now has an independent monetary authority in the shape of the European Central Bank which is responsible for managing the euro and whose decisions apply equally to all the participating States. The euro is consolidating the EU's role as an influential international player, particularly vis-à-vis the dollar, and is contributing to promoting a political Europe, going beyond economic integration. Finally, the single currency will help efforts to encourage economic growth and generate employment.

Enlarging Europe

Enlargement is an accepted principle of the EU and 1 January 1995 saw the accession of three EFTA (European Free Trade Association) countries, Austria, Finland and Sweden.

French Foreign Minister Hubert Védrine signs the Treaty of Amsterdam on 2 October 1997

The new democracies of Central and Eastern Europe (Bulgaria, Czech Republic, Hungary, Poland, Romania and Slovakia) and the Baltic States (Estonia, Latvia and Lithuania) are also natural candidates for EU membership. In eastern and southern parts of the continent, other states are also attracted by the prospect. France has maintained a friendly and supportive relationship with them and now intends to encourage their integration into an enlarged Europe: the European Union has adopted measures designed to help these countries complete the reforms needed to consolidate the rule of law and make the transition to a free market economy.

Sizeable aid and technical cooperation programmes have been set up to help these countries modernise their infrastructures, provide training and set up new institutions. The European Union provides more than 60% of the overall funding for this assistance to the Baltic and Central and East European states provided by the group of 24 industrialized countries.

In addition, to facilitate the development of trade and flow of direct investment, Europe Agreements have been signed between these countries and the EU providing for the establishment of political dialogue, commercial arrangements leading gradually to a free-trade area for industrial products, and wide-ranging cooperation. As a result, the EU is now the leading customer and supplier and chief source of investment for the Central and East European countries.

In June 1993, at the Copenhagen European Council, the twelve EU heads of state and government agreed that the Baltic States and associated countries of Central and Eastern Europe which wished to do so could join the EU as soon as they were ready. With this goal in mind, they decided right away to involve the countries concerned in the CFSP.

Since 1990, France has launched many initiatives with the aim of creating institutions able to guarantee security and stability in Europe. Skilled in the art of preventive diplomacy, it was instrumental in setting up a European Court of Conciliation and Arbitration under the aegis of the CSCE (Conference on Security and Cooperation in Europe). France also supported the UN Secretary-General Boutros Boutros-Ghali's efforts to create an international criminal tribunal, which was established in The Hague in November 1993, to try those responsible for war crimes in the former Yugoslavia. In the same year, the Prime Minister, Edouard Balladur, presented France's EU partners with a plan for a pact on stability in Europe, to pre-empt potential conflicts arising from historic enmities. This initiative gave the Baltic and Central and East European countries a framework in which to negotiate "good neighbour" agreements, confirming borders and ensuring respect for the rights of national minorities. The European Union welcomed the adoption of the plan by the Inaugural Conference in Paris in May 1994 and the Pact itself was signed, also in the French capital, in March 1995. The EU offered economic and political help in achieving this goal, and entrusted to the OSCE (Organization for Security and Cooperation in Europe — the successor to the CSCE) the monitoring of the bilateral agreements and arrangements included in the Pact. France also proposed the adoption of a security charter bringing together all the members of the OSCE.

The Agreement on Partnership and Cooperation signed with Russia during the Corfu European summit (June 1994) is another example of European efforts to increase stability and prosperity in the continent as a whole.

Links between NATO and Russia were strengthened by the signature on 27 June 1997 of the Founding Act. The Atlantic Summit in Madrid on 8 July 1997 agreed on the principle of the accession to NATO of Poland, the Czech Republic and Hungary and opened the prospect of membership to Romania and Slovenia.

In December 1997, the Luxembourg European Council began the process of eastward enlargement. On 30 March 1998, accession negotiations opened with Cyprus, Hungary, Poland, Estonia, the Czech Republic and Slovenia. At the same time, a process to help prepare for accession was initiated with Romania, Slovakia and Bulgaria. In addition, all the applicant states and those wishing to join the European Union, including Turkey, were invited to take part in a European Conference.

Clearly, EU institutions designed for cooperation between a small number of states will have to be adapted to take account of the new accessions. France is preparing for this by exploring, together with its EU partners, possible ways of achieving four fundamental objectives: to maintain the efficacy of the EU, make its institutions more representative, clearly define the concept of subsidiarity and bring Europe closer to its citizens.

As provided for in the Treaty of Maastricht, an Intergovernmental Conference (IGC) was held from March 1996 to June 1997 to decide how to adapt the EU institutions. The conference produced, although not without difficulty, the Treaty of Amsterdam, which was signed on 2 October 1997. This Treaty only partially addresses French concerns. Admittedly, it allows states which wish to go further and faster to do so by means of a very laborious procedure (enhanced cooperation mechanism). But no genuine institutional reform has been achieved, and "big" and "small" member states disagree both regarding the reduction of the number of Commissioners and the "re-weighting" of votes in the Council of Ministers for decisions by qualified majority.

Several countries, including France, are keen to see institutional reform before any future enlargement.

Ensuring Stability on the European Continent

The end of the Cold War created a new situation which led European countries to set themselves new security objectives. Indeed, the resurgence of longstanding claims, ethnic and nationalist passions and political disorder threaten the stability of the European continent. The war which has been raging in the former Yugoslavia demonstrates the seriousness of the risks and the need to address them collectively. This has implications for several institutions.

The oldest, the Council of Europe, was created in 1949 on the initiative of French minister Georges Bidault. It has its headquarters in Strasbourg and brings together nations committed to democracy and a multi-party political system. The new democracies in Central and Eastern Europe and the Baltic States have gradually started participating in its work.

The Organization for Security and Cooperation in Europe - OSCE (known as the Conference on Security and Cooperation - CSCE - in Europe until December 1994) has 52 member countries, including the United States and Canada and all the former Soviet republics. The role of this organisation, created in 1975 in the context of East-West détente by the Helsinki Final Act, has substantially increased since the end of the Cold War.

At its Paris summit in November 1990, the CSCE issued the Charter for a New Europe, which, inter alia, provided for the creation of a new Security Forum and a Conflict Prevention Centre. The summit also saw the signature of a major agreement on conventional disarmament (Treaty on Conventional Armed Forces in Europe), by 22 member states of the Atlantic Alliance and Warsaw Pact.

SOMMET O.T.A.N. - RUSSIE
Paris, 27 mai 1997

Finally, the military organisations, NATO (North Atlantic Treaty Organization) and WEU (Western European Union), are also having to evolve: the Treaty of Maastricht gave WEU new ambitions, while NATO instigated the creation of the North Atlantic Cooperation Council (NACC) to provide a framework for dialogue between NATO and 9 Central and East European countries and the Baltic States, which led to the establishment of the "Partnership for Peace" at the NATO summit of 11 January 1994.

The Founding Act on Mutual Relations, Cooperation and Security between NATO and the Russian Federation is signed on 27 June 1997 in Paris

The Franco-German Tandem

France and Germany have played the leading roles in each new phase of European integration. As General de Gaulle and Chancellor Adenauer well understood, Europe could not be built without reconciliation between France and Germany. As early as 1958, the former Free French leader invited the West German Chancellor, founder of the Federal Republic, to France, before going himself to West Germany. Their combined efforts brought France and Germany closer together and on 23 January 1963 the Elysée Treaty was signed. The Treaty provided for two Franco-German summits per year, quarterly round tables between foreign affairs ministers and regular meetings on defence, education and youth affairs. A few months later, the Franco-German Youth Office (OFAJ) was founded. It enables tens of thousands of young people from the two countries to meet one another and study or work together.

Thirty years of this special relationship have led to more than close ties between the successive leaders of the two countries. Nowadays, the regular Franco-German summits, meetings on harmonisation and joint preparation of European issues has generated relationships at every level of government and resulted in a degree of convergence between the two countries unique in the world.

Bilateral Commissions operate in almost every sphere of public activity. The Monetary Committee brings together the President of the Bundesbank, Governor of the Bank of France and the two finance ministers. The Defence Commission achieved concrete results with the creation of the Franco-German Brigade in 1987, the embryo of a European force, the Eurocorps, created in 1993 which also includes Belgium, Luxembourg and Spain. Finally, the Franco-German cultural television channel, Arte, based in Strasbourg, has since 1992 been broadcasting jointly devised programmes not only for French and German viewers, but also for Belgians, Swiss and Austrians. Arte is open to any other interested European states.

French President Jacques Chirac and Chancellor Gerhard Schröder of the Federal Republic of Germany meet on 1 October 1998 in Paris

A joint Franco-German project – the television channel Arte, which grew out of the Treaty signed by the two countries on 2 October 1990, is intended to be truly European

French Participation in UN Action

Since the United Nations was created on 26 June 1945, France has been a permanent member of its highest body, the Security Council, along with the United States, Britain, Russia and China. Since then, France has stated that it is in favour of enlarging the Security Council, in particular to include Germany and Japan, and has stressed that representatives from developing countries should not be left on the sidelines in the proposed future reform. French is one of the six official languages of the UN and one of its two working languages. Paris is home to UNESCO, the United Nations Educational, Scientific and Cultural Organization.

CONFERENCE DE PAIX SUR L'EX-YOUGOSLAVIE
PARIS

On 14 December 1995, the Dayton Agreement was signed in Paris, following a peace conference on the former Yugoslavia. American President Bill Clinton, French President Jacques Chirac and Chancellor Helmut Kohl of the Federal Republic of Germany were present

France is the fourth largest contributor to the UN budget. In 1998 its share amounted to 6.49%, while in 1996 its share of world wealth had been approximately 3.5%. In 1997 France paid 930 million francs ($155 million) of assessed contributions to UN institutions.

French Contributions to the Budget of the Principal UN Organisations in 1998

Beneficiaries	Contribution in the currency in which assessments are denominated (in millions)	Contribution (in millions of francs)
UN	US$ 68.37	410.2
WHO (World Health Organization)	US$ 27	162
UNESCO	US$ 8.8 + FF 79.9	132.9
ILO (International Labour Organization)	Swiss francs 21.4	88.8
FAO (Food and Agriculture Organization)	US$ 21.9	131.3

To this should be added 416 million francs ($69.3 million) of contributions to peacekeeping operations. The previous year, 1997, France's share was 7.96% of the total, i.e. 472 million francs ($80.6 million). These costs are lower since some of the peacekeeping operations have ended or been considerably reduced in scale, in particular in former Yugoslavia. On 31 May 1998, France was the ninth largest contributor of troops and equipment and the largest amongst countries with a permanent seat on the Security Council.

This prominent role places important responsibilities on France. It shoulders these by taking an active part in the revitalisation of the UN, which has had new tasks since the end of the Cold War: ending regional conflicts which are a legacy of that period and ensuring respect for international law. France attaches particular importance to the role of the UN, which is the only organisation open to all countries and which, as a result, is the only one with a mandate to authorise recourse to force, in circumstances other than that of legitimate defence.

The Minister for European Affairs, Pierre Moscovici, at a joint press conference with his Estonian counterpart, Toomas-Hendrik Ilves, in Tallinn, in December 1997

The first major international crisis of the 1990s, Iraq's invasion of Kuwait, is an example of this. The Security Council, no longer paralysed by the rivalry between the United States and the Soviet Union, had no difficulty in adopting resolutions condemning the invasion of the Emirate by Saddam Hussein's troops and demanding their withdrawal and subsequently authorising the intervention by the international coalition. A French contingent of 12,000 men took part in the operations which led to the liberation of Kuwait.

Seven years after the Gulf War, France is actively working for the total fulfilment by Iraq of its disarmament obligations, which will pave the way for lifting the economic sanctions. During the most recent Iraqi crisis, France played an important role in the successful quest for a political solution to the disagreements between Iraq and the Security Council.

In the Middle East, Africa and Asia, countries with which France has long had friendly relations are involved in regional conflicts. Because of these past ties, it is taking an active part in international efforts to find fair solutions.

In the Middle East in particular, France has always tried to mitigate the conflicts tearing the region apart. In 1967, following the Six-Day War, it supported Security Council Resolution (SCR) 242 demanding Israel's immediate withdrawal from the Occupied Territories and since then has consistently reiterated this position: France recognises both Israel's right to exist within secure and recognised borders and the right of Palestinians to a state of their own. It has worked to promote direct dialogue between the Jewish state and the Palestine Liberation Organisation (PLO), which has had an office in Paris since 1975. France welcomed the Oslo peace accord signed in Washington on 19 September 1993 and decided, with its European Union partners, to give immediate support to the peace process by allocating 500 million ECU ($560 million) for reconstruction in the Occupied Territories. Going beyond the Israeli-PLO agreement, France is actively encouraging the search for a comprehensive peace settlement in the Middle East. In the 1996 conflict in Lebanon, it played a major role in achieving a ceasefire agreement supervised by a monitoring committee chaired jointly by France and the United States.

Africa, where most of the crises occur, is a priority for France's foreign policy. France enjoys special relations with many African states: annual summits of heads of state from Africa and France provide an important forum for this fundamental dialogue. France is unstinting in its diplomatic efforts to resolve the conflicts and political crises affecting these countries, both within the UN and by liaising directly with some of the region's states. For example, it supported the international community's efforts to get South Africa to abolish apartheid and draw up a democratic constitution. It participated in UN operations to restore peace and ensure the availability of food in Somalia. In summer 1994, it went to the aid of threatened Rwandans, sending forces to establish a "safe zone". Thanks to Operation Turquoise, authorised by SCR 929, thousands of Rwandans were protected from the fighting and the international community was spurred to action. In the Central African Republic in 1997, France gave logistical and financial support to the MISAB (*Mission interafricaine de surveillance des accords de Bangui*, Inter-African Mission to Monitor the Implementation of the Bangui Agreements) whose creation was approved by SCR 1125. France then supported the setting-up of a peacekeeping mission (MINURCA - *Mission interafricaine des Nations unies en République Centrafricaine*) to take over from MISAB in 1998. France has provided considerable financial aid and manpower (200 "blue berets" are taking part) to launch this operation.

In the area of conflict prevention and rapid deployment of forces, France, the USA and the UK were behind an initiative to strengthen the capacity of African armed forces to participate in peacekeeping operations, under the auspices of the UN. France makes the largest bilateral contribution to this mechanism.

Nor has France forgotten its ties with the countries of the Indochinese peninsular. In 1991 it helped bring about the signing of the Paris Accords designed to set in train a process of national reconciliation in Cambodia. France, which, along with

Indonesia, was the architect of this reconciliation, had a predominant role on the ground throughout the transitional phase. The 1,500 French "blue berets" made up the main contingent assigned to the UN Transitional Authority in Cambodia (UNTAC) whose task was to disarm the contending parties, ensure compliance with the ceasefire and prepare for the restoration of democracy. President Mitterrand's visit to Phnom Penh in February 1993 symbolised the role played by France in the process which ultimately led to free elections in May 1993, and then the return of King Sihanouk to the throne of Cambodia.

France also took part in the military operations which, backed by a UN mandate, the Atlantic Alliance conducted in former Yugoslavia and deployed a Rapid Reaction Force there to protect UN peacekeepers. With the USA, Russia, the UK and Germany, it is a member of the Contact Group which has striven, on behalf of the international community, to get the warring parties to accept a comprehensive peace plan. These efforts led to the signature, in Paris on 14 December 1995, of the Peace Agreement negotiated in Dayton, USA: its implementation is being ensured by a NATO force, SFOR (Stabilisation Force) and a UN police force (the GIP) including over 120 French *gendarmes*.

For a long time the leading contributor of UN troops and equipment, because of its participation in UNPROFOR (former Yugoslavia), France is now the ninth largest contributor to UN peacekeeping operations. There are French "blue berets" in Lebanon, the Western Sahara, Haiti, Georgia, Angola, on the Iran-Iraq border, in Jerusalem, in the former Yugoslavia and in the Central African Republic

Prime Minister Lionel Jospin is welcomed on his official visit to China by the Chinese Prime Minister, Zhu Rongji, outside the People's Palace in Tiananmen Square, Beijing, in September 1998

On a more general note, France encourages all reforms designed to improve the effectiveness of UN peacekeeping operations. It initiated the system of standby forces, which has helped significantly speed up the deployment of "blue berets".

France has spared no effort within the UN and especially the Security Council to secure the establishment of an international judicial system: together with other countries, it instigated the Security Council resolutions setting up the international criminal tribunals for the former Yugoslavia (1993) and Rwanda (1995). Since then, France has fully supported these two international courts, which try persons accused of serious violations of universal humanitarian law. France took an active role in the negotiations which led to the creation, in 1998, of the international criminal court.

Human Rights

Whilst human rights are today universally recognised and defended, they have especial historical significance for France. France's commitment to human rights goes back to the eighteenth century, the age of Enlightenment, and it was one of the first nations to draw up a declaration proclaiming them: the Declaration of the Rights of Man and the Citizen of 26 August 1789. Moreover, it was in Paris that the Universal Declaration of Human Rights was adopted in 1948 by the UN General Assembly, at the Palais de Chaillot. One of its chief architects was the great French jurist, René Cassin, who was later to become president of the European Court of Human Rights and be awarded the Nobel Peace Prize.

La liberté d'expression est née sur les murs.

1ᵉʳ DÉCEMBRE 1998, 50ᵐᵉ ANNIVERSAIRE DE LA DÉCLARATION UNIVERSELLE DES DROITS DE L'HOMME.

LES DROITS DE L'HOMME, C'EST PLUS QU'UNE DÉCLARATION

Les afficheurs vous offrent la possibilité de vous exprimer.

True to its tradition, France today is actively involved in the area of human rights. It considers that concern for them should underpin the work of all the international organisations insofar as they are able, in their differing spheres, to advance their cause. France believes that economic growth and improvements in living conditions world-wide will be conducive to the enhancement of respect for human rights.

Commemorative poster celebrating the 50th anniversary of the Universal Declaration of Human Rights

France is today party to almost every international agreement promoting human rights, and there are several French independent experts in the treaty-monitoring bodies. It has also been a member of the UN Commission on Human Rights almost without interruption since this body was set up in 1946. Within this key forum, France applies its constructive approach to human rights. Without brooking any compromising of the basic principles of respect for human rights whose violation may elicit strong condemnation from the international community, or even lead to it issuing injunctions, France stresses the need to develop cooperation between states rather than adopt a confrontational approach. For example, it is promoting dialogue between China and the international community, which was probably a factor in the Chinese authorities' decision to become a party to the UN International Covenant on Economic, Social and Cultural Rights, and will perhaps encourage them to adhere to the International Covenant on Civil and Political Rights.

In recent years, France has supported the setting-up of two international tribunals to try those responsible for crimes against humanity and acts of genocide committed in the former

Yugoslavia or Rwanda. France had already played a leading role in the international efforts to ensure respect for human rights in these countries. It also backed the concept of establishing a permanent international criminal court empowered to punish serious human rights violations.

At the European level, France is home to the Council of Europe, whose headquarters, since its foundation in 1949, has been in the capital of Alsace, Strasbourg, symbolising Franco-German reconciliation. The aim of the Council of Europe is to achieve ever greater unity between European states, based on their common respect for pluralist democracy, human rights and the rule of law. The European human rights' capital, Strasbourg is also the seat of the European Court of Human Rights which ensures compliance with the 1950 European Convention for the Protection of Human Rights and Fundamental Freedoms. France has ratified the Convention and accepted the right of individual petition by any person, non-governmental organisation or group of individuals claiming to be the victim of a violation of human rights. Protocol No. 11, which came into effect on 1 November 1998, strengthened the Court's legal system by giving individuals the right to appeal against decisions.

France also plays an important role in protecting human rights in the framework of the OSCE (Organization for Security and Cooperation in Europe). In 1990, Paris saw the adoption of the Charter for a New Europe, in which the assembled European states affirmed their commitment to the principles of democracy, human rights and the rule of law, emphasising that these form the basis of economic and social prosperity and are vital to the promotion of peace. The pact on stability in Europe adopted in Paris in 1995 was also the result of a French initiative, and one of its most important tenets is respect for those belonging to minorities.

France carries out many bilateral cooperation initiatives abroad to promote and defend human rights in areas as varied as children's rights, women's rights and the fight against slavery. France also organizes education programmes all over the world promoting international recognition and observance of human rights.

At national level, the Preamble to the current Constitution of 4 October 1958 specifically refers to the Declaration of the Rights of Man and the Citizen and the Preamble to the Constitution of 1946, which confirmed and complemented it. The international agreements promoting human rights have primacy over national laws and, in many cases, may be directly invoked by individuals before the appropriate courts or tribunals. The wealth of national legislation on human rights also bears witness to the fundamental importance France attaches to them.

In 1947, the French government established a National Consultative Committee on Human Rights, the CNCDH, founded by René Cassin. The Committee's powers cover all human rights-related issues. One of its annual tasks is to present a report to the government on the fight against racism and xenophobia. Another is to award the Human Rights Prize of the French Republic which honours those making a special contribution in the sphere. It was to the CNCDH that the Prime Minister announced, in April 1998, the fiftieth anniversary year of the Universal Declaration, his decision to make human rights a "great national cause" of 1998.

The CNCDH endeavours to promote the creation of similar institutions abroad. There are now about forty national institutions of this type and in 1991 their status and powers were set out in the "Paris Principles". The UN General Assembly adopted the text of the Paris Principles in 1993.

All in all, France is very active internationally in the area of human rights. While historically it has played a primordial role in the recognition of human rights, it is today resolutely looking to the future and to the new ones that will have to be defined with the development of the modern world. Indeed, in the late seventies, France was one of the first states to protect the rights of the individual in a computerised society. More recently, the French government has argued for recognition by states of a humanitarian right, of the international community's "duty of humanitarian assistance", which has since been applied on several occasions. Finally, following the adoption in 1997 of the European Convention on Human Rights and Biomedicine, the French government was one of those behind an initiative leading to the conclusion of a protocol banning human cloning in Paris in 1998.

Development Aid

Committed to democracy and human rights, France has always been convinced that this objective is inseparable from the fight for development. Long-established relations with many countries in the Southern hemisphere and the special solidarity between them have led France to define an ambitious cooperation policy.

Since 1958, every French president has stressed France's commitment to development assistance, which is shared across the political spectrum and is reflected by its efforts in this field. In 1997, France was the second largest donor in the world, providing official development aid of 37 billion francs ($6.35 billion) – behind Japan, but ahead of both the US and Germany – i.e. 0.45% of its GNP (average for rich countries: 0.22%). This places France first among the seven members of the G7 group of most industrialised countries and sixth among the member states of the Development Assistance Committee of the OECD (Organization for Economic Cooperation and Development).

In international organisations, France has consistently pleaded the cause of developing countries, so as to make it easier for them to manage their debt. In 1992, it went so far as to cancel the debts owed to it by the least developed countries. It has taken a number of measures to help stabilise the price of the raw materials on which the export earnings of southern developing countries depend. In Francophone Africa, in 1994 France took specific aid measures to limit the effects on the people of the devaluation of the CFA franc (a currency supported by the Bank of France), which enabled the countries concerned to resume working with international financial institutions. A year later, the economies of these countries were able to get off the ground again and their development projects could resume.

A geographical breakdown of France's bilateral aid reveals a heavy concentration on sub-Saharan Africa, which in 1996 received 42.4% of net payments, i.e. 12.4 billion francs ($2.06 billion). The special historical ties between France and Africa explain this high percentage, but there is nevertheless a growing diversification of the geographical distribution of the aid.

In addition to its own cooperation policy, France supports European Union programmes. In 1963, the Yaoundé Convention linked to the European Community eighteen states of Africa and Madagascar, granting them preferential trading arrangements. This agreement, which has been renewed five times and re-named the Lomé Convention, now provides for a more ambitious policy of cooperation involving seventy ACP (African, Caribbean and Pacific) states.

Table of official development aid flows from DAC (Development Assistance Committee) countries in 1997. France is second only to Japan in terms of ODA

	in millions of dollars	% GNP
Australia	1,076	0.28
Austria	531	0.26
Belgium	764	0.31
Canada	2,146	0.36
Denmark	1,635	0.97
Finland	379	0.33
France	**6,348**	**0.45**
Germany	5,913	0.28
Ireland	187	0.31
Italy	1,231	0.11
Japan	9,358	0.22
Luxembourg	87	0.50
The Netherlands	2,946	0.81
New Zealand	145	0.25
Norway	1,306	0.86
Portugal	251	0.25
Spain	1,227	0.23
Sweden	1,672	0.76
Switzerland	839	0.32
United Kingdom	3,371	0.26
United States	6,168	0.08
Total for DAC countries	**47,580**	**0.22**
Total for EU members	26,542	0.33

Source : OECD.

With experience, this aid has become more effective. Like its EU partners, France is helping encourage efforts to step up regional integration and back the macro-economic adjustment programmes carried out under the auspices of the international bodies. Finally, in 1990, at the La Baule Franco-African Summit, France announced its intention to link the level of its bilateral cooperation to the progress made by each country in the areas of democracy and human rights.

Humanitarian Action

French humanitarian action is based on the principle that there is a moral obligation to help civilian communities suffering physical or mental distress wherever they are. To do this, French humanitarian action gives technical and financial support, on a partnership basis, to operations by NGOs and French state agencies – *Sécurité civile* (emergency services dealing with national disasters, bomb disposal, etc.), *SAMU Mondial* (mobile emergency medical service - international branch) and armed forces health services - and also contributes to the programmes of international humanitarian organisations.

France plays a significant role in the European Communities Humanitarian Office (ECHO) to which it contributes 18% of the budget. ECHO is principally working in the Great Lakes region in Africa, Central Europe and the Caucasus.

Humanitarian demining and the fight against antipersonnel landmines are among France's priorities. Its commitment to demining and assistance for landmine victims goes back over twenty years. Since 1994, it has devoted over 50 million francs ($8.3 million), including 28 million francs ($4.6 million) in 1997 alone, to humanitarian demining operations, in the framework of bilateral or UN programmes. On top of this, France contributes to European Union mine-clearance programmes. In 1996-1997, the EU committed over 50 million ecus (about 320 million francs or $53 million dollars), of which France's share was 68 million francs ($11 million), to such programmes. Furthermore, since 1978, the French armed forces, which have considerable experience in this area, have carried out some twenty demining operations abroad, and have above all provided training for demining personnel, particularly in

The Ottawa Convention banning the use of anti-personnel landmines was signed on 3 December 1997 by the Minister for Cooperation and the Francophony, Charles Josselin

A Global Ban on Landmines

Interdiction complète des mines terrestres

Ottawa, Canada 1997

Lebanon, Chad and Cambodia. On 1 July 1998, France ratified the Ottawa Convention totally banning antipersonnel landmines. It has made a declaration announcing its intention to destroy its stocks before the date laid down in the Convention.

Francophony – Exchanges and Solidarity

Today, 105 million people have French as their first language and 55 million use it from time to time. In terms of the number of people who speak it, French is the ninth language in the world. It is taught in education systems throughout the world. Supported not only by France but also by other French-speaking countries, the Francophone community has become a genuine forum of cooperation, not only in linguistic and cultural matters, but also political and economic matters. Several institutions bring the Francophone family of nations together. The Agency for Francophony (ACCT - Agency for Cultural and Technical Cooperation), based in Paris, carries out programmes in a wide range of fields such as education and training, the environment and sustainable development, culture and communications and cooperation on legal and judicial matters. Efforts by the Association of Partially or Wholly French-language Universities (AUPELF) led in 1987 to the creation of the University of French-language Networks (UREF). These two organisations were merged to form the Francophone Agency for Higher Education and Research. In addition, the French-language television channel TV5, launched in Europe in 1984, has gradually expanded to include North America (TV5 Quebec-Canada, 1988) and Africa and Latin America (1992). Seven Francophone Summits have been held at Versailles (1986), Quebec (1987), Dakar (1989), Paris (1991), Port-Louis (1993), Cotonou (1995) and Hanoi (1997). The Hanoi Summit brought together 52 states and created the post of Secretary-General for Francophony, to which the Egyptian, Boutros Boutros-Ghali, former UN Secretary-General, was appointed.

Concurrently, France actively promotes cultural, scientific and technical exchanges all over the world. France's action in this sphere now (1999) takes two main forms:

1. Cooperation in the widest possible variety of sectors (agriculture, health, the environment, public administration, town planning, energy, etc.) involving some 120 developing, emerging and transition countries;

2. A network linking 300 schools and their 150,000 pupils, of whom 60,000 are French. France's cultural presence is also reinforced by approximately 130 cultural organisations in 56 countries, which give French lessons to 140,000 adults and teenagers.

In addition, the *Alliance française* has 1,060 centres which teach French to 318,000 students in 140 countries.

All in all, these 1,500 or so institutions, together with 25 social sciences and humanities research institutes in 20 countries and 203 archaeological digs, contribute to France's presence abroad. Furthermore, in 1998 almost 150,000 foreign students were studying in France, of whom 18,000 had received grants from the French government.

This vast network, which receives substantial state aid, is evidence of the importance France attaches to fostering cultural exchanges as part of its foreign policy.

The French Cultural Centre library and resource centre in Oslo, Norway, demonstrates one of the many ways in which people all over the world can enjoy French culture

Further reading:

L'Union politique de l'Europe. Jalons et textes, documents collected by P. Gerbert, F. de La Serre and G. Nafilyan, foreword by J. Delors, La Documentation française (Retour aux textes), 1998.

Y. Doutriaux, C. Lequesne, *Les institutions de l'Union européenne*, new revised edition, La Documentation française (Réflexe Europe), 1998.

Une politique pour le français, Ministry of Foreign Affairs, DGRCST (Department of Cultural, Scientific and Technical Relations).

La Direction générale des relations culturelles, scientifiques et techniques, Ministère des Affaires étrangères, 1998.

J. Dalloz, *La France et le monde depuis 1945*, Armand Colin (Cursus), 1993.

J. Doise et M. Vaisse, *Diplomatie et outil militaire ; politique étrangère de la France 1871-1991*, Le Seuil (Points), 1992.

A. Grosser, *Affaires extérieures : la politique étrangère de la France 1944-1989*, Flammarion Champs, 1989.

P.-M. de La Gorce et A.-D. Schor, *La politique étrangère de la Vᵉ République*, PUF (Que sais-je ?),1992.

Ph. Moreau Defarges, *La France dans le monde du XXᵉ siècle*, Hachette (Les fondamentaux), 1994.

Politique étrangère de la France, a bi-monthly collection of official foreign policy statements edited by the French Foreign Ministry, Department for Communication and Information. Published and distributed by La Documentation française.

Ministry of Foreign Affairs Website:
http ://www.france.diplomatie.gouv.fr

9

Defence Policy

Because of its history, geographical position, economic potential and international responsibilities, France pays particularly close attention to defence policy. Whilst remaining committed to the principle of national independence and mindful of the need both to defend its interests in the world and uphold democratic values, France has constantly adapted its defence and disarmament policy to the changing international context. Publication in 1994 of a government White Paper on defence, the reform of the armed forces decided on in 1996 and the adoption of a pluriannual sectorial estimates law for 1997-2002 (known in France as the military programme law) enabled France to update the goals of this policy and the means by which it is implemented, so as to take into account the upheavals which have affected international relations and strategy in the past few years.

The French Concept

The French concept of defence as defined in the ordinance of 7 January 1959 is a comprehensive one, setting three goals for the country's defence:

1) To defend France's vital interests, which are defined by the President of the Republic and include, notably, its people, its territory and the freedom to exercise its sovereignty. In this regard, the 1958 Constitution assigns the role of guarantor of territorial integrity to the President of the Republic (article 5) and makes him commander-in-chief of the armed forces (art. 15). At the same time, France must also protect its strategic interests at the international level whilst contributing to conflict prevention, keeping and restoring peace and ensuring respect for international law and democratic values in the world. In these areas, France's status as a permanent member of the United Nations Security Council gives it both prerogatives and responsibilities.

2) To work for the development of the European enterprise and the stability of the European continent. France opted for this

policy at the end of World War II by choosing to participate actively in Western European Union (WEU), the North Atlantic Treaty Organization (NATO) and the Conference on Security and Cooperation in Europe (CSCE), which in December 1994 became the Organization for Security and Cooperation in Europe (OSCE).

3) To implement a comprehensive concept of defence which is not limited to military concerns. Indeed, a country's security and stability are dependent not only on its armed forces and police, but also on its social organisation, education system and social cohesion. The concept of defence is, *de facto*, indissociably linked with that of nation. The *sécurité civile* (emergency services dealing with national disasters, bomb disposal, etc.) protect the population and maintain public order and thus the continuity of the state. They are also responsible for preventing and dealing with major natural and technological hazards and the security of sensitive installations and networks. Lastly, they ensure the proper distribution of resources in times of crisis.

Bastille Day parade along the Champs-Elysées, Paris, 14 July 1998

A New Strategic Environment

Since the fall of the Berlin Wall, the dissolution of the Warsaw Pact and the Soviet Union and the start of genuine conventional and nuclear disarmament by the principal military power on the European continent, France has no longer been faced with a direct military threat to its borders. In addition, the Intermediate-Range Nuclear Forces Treaty (INF), concluded in 1987 between the United States and the Soviet Union, resulted in the elimination of all intermediate-range nuclear missiles deployed on the ground in Europe by these two powers.

The START (Strategic Arms Reduction Talks) Treaties of 1991 and 1993 will by 2007 cut the American and Soviet strategic arsenals to 3,000 and 3,500 warheads respectively (down from more than 12,000 and 11,000 in 1990). The Treaty on Conventional Armed Forces in Europe (CFE), signed in Paris on 19 November 1990 within the framework of the CSCE by 22 member states of the Atlantic Alliance and the former Warsaw Pact, imposed on signatories limits on the amount of heavy military equipment (Army and Air Force). It compelled the former Warsaw Pact forces to destroy almost 34,000 pieces of such equipment.

In 1997, strategic stability was further reinforced by the signing in Paris of the Founding Act between NATO and Russia, and then by the decision, at the NATO Madrid Summit, to admit Hungary, the Czech Republic and Poland.

Alongside these positive factors which put an end to the East-West confrontation, the disappearance of the Eastern bloc coincided with the emergence of new tensions arising from border conflicts or the presence of ethnic minorities. Such tensions are a real threat to the stability of the continent, which for the first time since 1945 has witnessed a resurgence of armed conflicts. This instability is aggravated by the fact that certain countries in Central and Eastern Europe, the Balkans and the former USSR have had difficulties in implementing the reforms to their political, economic and social structures needed for their integration into the international community. These countries still have sizeable capabilities in conventional weapons. Moreover, the proliferation of non-conventional weapons (nuclear, bacteriological and chemical) and their delivery vehicles, ballistic and cruise missiles, remains a source of concern to the international community. Furthermore, terrorism continues to threaten not only civilian populations, but also communications networks and industrial installations. Finally, organised drug trafficking poses a threat not only to public health, but also to international security, particularly by providing financial aid to guerrillas. These new factors risk destabilising states and even generating conflicts.

A Strategy Adapted to the New International Context

France has adapted its strategy to respond to these twin developments in the international context.

At political and diplomatic level, France has sought to promote stability and peace on the European continent, particularly through its support for a Pact on Stability signed between the members of the European Union and the Central and East European and Baltic States, and for association agreements between these countries and WEU. The Partnership for Peace with the former Eastern bloc countries has been developed by the Atlantic Alliance since 1994.

At the military level, France has reaffirmed that its security rests on deterrence, which implies keeping its forces at a sufficiently high level to maintain credibility. Today, conventional weapons have a strategic role of their own and are no longer regarded merely as back-up for the nuclear deterrent forces.

Citizens of various countries are escorted to Brazzaville airport by French soldiers before being evacuated in French military aircraft to Libreville in Gabon, June 1997

According to the White Paper on defence, France now has to be capable of dealing with crises of limited scope and managing and forestalling crises that are long, of variable intensity and whose theatres of operation may be far from France's national territory. Some of these conflicts do not directly challenge France's vital interests, but transgress principles it is committed to defending as a permanent member of the United Nations Security Council, such as respect for international law and the sovereignty of states. Thus France participates in conflict prevention and peacekeeping operations, in cooperation with its partners and allies, in a multilateral framework. In this new environment, France has set itself the goal of obtaining more accurate forecasts and assessments of situations (by improving its intelligence system) and of grasping the complexity of conflicts with both political and military dimensions taking place in regional theatres. This requires greater strategic mobility for French forces. However, French strategy is still based on nuclear deterrence. This doctrine relies on the perception by any potential adversary that the risks of aggression against France or France's vital interests would be unacceptable – i.e. that the risks are disproportionate to what is at stake in the conflict. France continues to make a clear distinction between deterrence and the use of nuclear forces.

Decisions on the use of conventional capabilities are taken in the light of their ability to contribute to the prevention, containment or settlement by force of regional crises and conflicts. To carry out these tasks effectively, France stresses the need for intelligence capabilities, which, through the information they gather (in particular from observation satellites), enable it to intervene in a crisis at any stage, including preventively. France also has pre-positioned forces outside its borders which can be activated where necessary.

Non-proliferation and Disarmament Contribute to Security

Another of France's defence policy objectives is to promote controlled disarmament and fight the proliferation of weapons of mass destruction in order to strengthen international security.

Since France's own nuclear forces are, as has been said, maintained at a level of strict sufficiency, it has for a long time been calling on the two principal powers to reduce their excessive nuclear arms capabilities. France itself immediately responded to the change in the strategic context by unilaterally reducing its own

forces. In 1992, it took its Pluton missiles out of service and dismantled them. On 22 April 1996, President Chirac announced the closure of the French nuclear test centre in the Pacific and his decision
definitively to withdraw the Hadès and strategic ground-to-ground
missiles based on the Albion plateau from service and have them
dismantled. The decision was also taken definitively to close and
dismantle the plants producing fissile material
for nuclear weapons (plutonium at Marcoule and
highly enriched uranium at Pierrelatte).

As regards nuclear tests, on 2
April 1992 France unilaterally suspended its
underground tests in French Polynesia. Then in
1993 it joined the international community consensus in favour of the negotiation of a comprehensive nuclear test ban treaty - within the
framework of the Geneva Conference on Disarmament - provided the treaty were universal and
internationally verifiable.

France was the first nuclear
power to come out in favour, in 1995, of the
"zero option", i.e. the prohibition of any nuclear weapon test or any
other nuclear explosion, regardless of its level. Opened for signature on 24 September 1996, France signed the Comprehensive Test
Ban Treaty on that very day.

Hervé de Charette, the
French Foreign Minister,
signs the treaty
prohibiting nuclear tests
(CTBT) at UN
headquarters in New York,
24 September 1996

Although it did not sign the Nuclear Non-Proliferation
Treaty (NPT) when it came into force in 1970, France always
respected its principles. In 1991, it decided that it would no longer
export nuclear technology and nuclear materials for civilian use to
any state which had not placed all its nuclear installations under the
control of the International Atomic Energy Agency (IAEA). That
same year, because of the new strategic context created by the
break-up of the Soviet Union and the mounting risks associated with
the proliferation of nuclear weapons, France decided to announce
that it would sign the NPT. It formally ratified the Treaty in 1992,
joining the other nuclear powers and leading a large number of
other countries to follow its example.

France also supports efforts to improve regional
security by creating nuclear weapon free zones. Having already
signed the protocols of the Tlatelolco Treaty creating such a zone in
Latin America, in 1996 it ratified the protocols of the treaties creating nuclear free zones in Oceania (the Treaty of Rarotonga) and
Africa (the Treaty of Pelindaba).

In the area of chemical weapons, France was already the depository state of the 1925 Geneva Protocol, which prohibited the use of such weapons in war but not their manufacture. It galvanised the international community, particularly after the Iran-Iraq war, into resuming negotiations, in January 1989 at the Geneva Disarmament Conference, on a treaty banning not only the use but also the development, production and stockpiling of chemical arms. The treaty was signed in Paris in January 1993 by more than 130 states and by the end of 1997 had 165 signatories. It came into force on 29 April 1994, after ratification by the 65th country. Today, over 100 states have ratified it, including the five permanent members of the Security Council. As France had wished, its application is subject to strict verification, carried out by international inspectors.

Three French soldiers from the multinational Brigade in former Yugoslavia, autumn 1995

Moreover, in 1984, France also signed the 1972 Biological Weapons Convention, which bans bacteriological weapons, and since 1991 has sought to provide this international instrument with the verification mechanism it lacks. In 1993, on France's initiative, experts began work on devising the requisite system and this is scheduled to be followed by the drawing up of a Protocol to the Convention.

Finally, as regards conventional weapons, France is participating in the adaptation of the CFE treaty to the new geostrategic political context whilst ensuring it remains a vital security instrument.

With its partners, France is updating the confidence-building and security measures (Vienna Document, 1994), so as to take into account the new geostrategic context: end of the bloc-to-bloc confrontation, but emergence of regional tensions. France's aim is to increase transparency in military activities, which should soon be the case, following ratification of the 1992 "Open Skies" Treaty which permits overflights of national territory on a reciprocal basis.

Within the United Nations organisation, France was behind the setting-up of a Register of Conventional Arms, which should play a role in deterring arms transfers that might introduce or reinforce regional imbalances.

Finally, France was one of the very first countries to take action with a view to ending the use of anti-personnel landmines, which inflict terrible damage on civilian populations in many regions. At national level, France announced moratoriums on the export, production and use of these weapons. Internationally, France was instrumental in the revision of the 1980 Convention governing the use of certain conventional weapons, which resulted in the strengthening of Protocol II which relates to use and transfer of landmines. France also actively contributed to the process leading to the signature on 3 December 1997 of the Ottawa Convention, which totally bans landmines. France will go on working in all the international fora, to make the fight against antipersonnel landmines one of the international community's top priorities.

France's Defence Capabilities

Given the above factors, France's defence policy has to be backed up by adequate military structures and capabilities.

How France's Defence is Organised

The President of the Republic is commander-in-chief of the armed forces (article 15 of the Constitution) and, by virtue of this title, is empowered to commit the nation's nuclear forces, should the need arise. The Prime Minister is responsible for national defence (art. 21) and the Minister of Defence for organising and mobilising the forces.

Special forces are
winched up
by a Puma helicopter

On 22 February 1996, President Chirac announced that France's armed forces would become fully professional as of 31 December 2002. The Law of 28 October 1997 reforming national service suspended conscription into the armed forces for young men born after 31 December 1978, whilst leaving open the option of reinstating it at any time. It also organises the transition to fully professional armed forces.

France is now engaged (1996-2002) in a radical reform of its armed forces, moving from a strength of 548,000 (including conscripts) to one of 440,000 totally professional forces able to meet the new defence requirements. During the transitional phase, young men born before 1 January 1979 will complete their national service under existing conditions.

The new national service will be brought in for young men born after 31 December 1978 and young women born after 31 December 1982. It involves:

- compulsory registration for which the age will gradually be lowered to sixteen;

- from September 1998, compulsory education in the principles and organisation of defence in France as part of the curriculum in the first few years after primary school;

- compulsory participation in a "day of introduction to military service" between the young person's day of registration and his/her eighteenth birthday;

- the subsequent opportunity to spend a year in the forces with the possibility of annually extending this period up to a maximum of five years, or to join the reserves either in the armed forces or in the national *gendarmerie*.

1997-2002 Military Programme Law

The armed forces' new structure announced by the President on 22 February 1996 represents the most radical innovation in this area since the beginning of the Fifth Republic. The 1997-2002 Military Programme Law is a transitional one, marking the first phase of the move towards this new structure. It involves a genuine break with the past and provides for large-scale investment in the structural reform of France's defence machinery. Its key objective is to enable completion of the move to fully professional forces.

The frigate Lafayette

For the first time, these estimates cover total defence spending (investment and operating) and both pluriannual and cash limit appropriations on capital spending. The annual allocation, excluding pensions, totals 185 billion francs in 1995 inflation adjusted terms ($30.8 billion), of which 99 billion francs ($16.5 billion) is for running costs and 86 billion francs ($14.3 billion) for investment, 18% down compared with the previous programme law. In 1997, this accounted for 2.3% of France's GDP.

The government's decision in 1997 to prioritise welfare spending and cut the government deficit in order to meet the criteria for joining the European single currency led to a fall in the Defence Ministry's budget for the first two years of the military programme law, down to 84.9 billion francs ($14.15 billion) for 1997 and 81 billion francs ($13.5 billion) for 1998. The desire to restore coherence to financial planning, led to an inter-ministerial spending review at the end of 1997, resulting in the stabilisation of the Defence Ministry's annual investment budget at 85 billion francs in 1998 inflation adjusted francs ($14 billion) for the four remaining years of the programme law, from 1999 to 2002, and a number of modifications and adjustments to some of its programmes, while maintaining the major ones intact.

Leclerc tank
on an exercise

The 1997-2002 military programme law sets three priorities, confirmed by subsequent spending reviews:

1 • Move to fully professional armed forces by 2002

Between 1996 and 2002, military manpower will be cut from 499,300 to 356,000, whilst civilian personnel will be increased from 73,750 to 81,820. Compulsory military service will disappear by the end of 2002, to be replaced by voluntary national service which, it is estimated, could well attract about 27,000 young people into the armed forces every year.

The move to fully professional armed forces implies a radical reform of the reserves. Fewer in number (set to total 100,000, including 50,000 for the *gendarmerie*), fully-trained and readily available for action, the reservists are now being more closely integrated into professional units. About 30% of these men and women will, if need be, be available at very short notice to supplement these units. In 1998, a specific law laid down the status and employment conditions of reservists, particularly with regard to what are generally referred to as civil-military actions, such as helping to restore war-devastated economies to normality.

2 • Continuing modernisation of defence equipment

In line with the decisions announced by President Chirac, since 1996, France has had a new deterrent posture, with a reduced capability but one which is maintained at a level of strict sufficiency vis-à-vis the new geopolitical context thanks to the acquisition of simulation technology.

The programme provides for the modernisation of the two remaining components of France's deterrent forces - the oceanic strategic and airborne forces. "Triomphant" new-generation nuclear ballistic submarines will gradually be brought into service and the development of an improved intermediate-range air-to-ground missile (ASMP) will be launched.

The task of modernising conventional forces will be pursued in order to improve prevention and projection capabilities.

The development of space-based observation and communication systems such as Hélios 2 will therefore be continued, in cooperation with other European countries, and the interoperability of command systems enhanced.

This law is less ambitious than its predecessor, both in terms of delivery dates and the quantity of equipment to be acquired. Nevertheless, the period it covers will see the bringing into service of the first Rafales, the aircraft carrier Charles de Gaulle, a landing platform dock (LPD) and 33 Leclerc tanks per year, as well as the development of the Horizon frigates and Tiger and NH 90 helicopters.

3 • Restructuring the defence industry

It is essential to restructure France's defence industry, a vital component in French defence policy, in order to adapt it to the new environment. Four main goals are being pursued:

- reduction of costs:

The Délégation générale pour l'armement (weapons procurement agency) has been set a target of a 30% reduction in costs over the period covered by the programme law. To attain it, more use will be made of dual technologies and there will be closer cooperation with the competitive sectors.

- creation of major industrial centres:

Since June 1997, the French government has shown its European partners the way forward by setting up a defence electronics centre, made up of Thomson (the hub), Alcatel, Aérospatiale and Dassault Electronique, and by accelerating a similar arrangement in the aerospace field, by transferring state-owned shares in Dassault to Aérospatiale. In the electromechanical engineering sector, Giat Industries, in line with the programme law objectives, is continuing to refocus its activities on its main areas of expertise and the Direction des constructions navales has been set the challenge of improving productivity through diversifying and opening up procurement to private shipyards.

- constitution of a European industrial defence base made up of competitive, efficient entities geared to the new strategic environment.

The successful establishment of such a base, reduction of existing over-capacity and creation of real complementarity between the partner countries necessitates the implementation of concrete coop-

FRENCH ARMED FORCES

Strength of service and civilian personnel, 1999:

219,538 Army

76,405 Air Force

62,641 Navy

95,956 *Gendarmerie*

27,111 in the other services (responsible for medical services, fuel supplies division, central administration, etc.).

Composition of Nuclear Forces

Since February 1996, the French nuclear deterrent force has had two components: the oceanic strategic force equipped with nuclear ballistic-missile submarines (SSBN), and an air component consisting of Air Force Mirage 2000Ns (re-fuelled by Air Force KC 135 FRs) and carrier-borne Navy Super Etendards equipped with intermediate-range air-to-ground missiles.

Composition of Combat Forces

Since 1 July 1998, the Army's forces have been concentrated under a single command, the Land Combat Command (CFAT), which is to be linked to the Land Logistics Command (CFLT).

1. - Subordinate to the CFAT are 4 Forces Headquarters (EMF) which are tasked with operational planning. They are capable of setting up a multinational NATO-type divisional HQ.

These HQs may be given responsibility for some of 9 brigades for specific contingency operations.

2. - The Land Logistics Command (CFLT) has responsibility for 2 Logistic Brigades.

Altogether the Army is made up of 85 regiments.

The Air Force has about 40 bases and a fleet essentially made up of 380 fighter aircraft (Mirage 2000s, Mirage F1s and Jaguars), about a hundred tactical and logistical transport planes, 14 tanker planes and detection and communication systems including four Awacs.

Naval combat forces (FAN), the maritime component of French projectible forces, consist of 20 battleships, including an aircraft-carrier and amphibious vessels manned by a total of 5,600 men.

The Anti-Submarine Action Group (GASM), the Minewarfare Force and support forces which can, if need be, supplement the naval projectible forces, had 89 vessels on 1 January 1998.

Between them, these various forces have 123 navy aircraft.

The Gendarmerie, whose contribution to security is essential, has around 180 armoured vehicles and some 50 aircraft.

In addition, France has forces stationed overseas, composed of land, naval and air elements, pre-positioned at many points on the globe. Their 20,000 or so men and equipment are permanently stationed in the overseas departments and territories.

There are also nearly 8,000 troops stationed in several African states with which France has defence agreements. This presence is to be reduced to slightly over 5,000 men by 2001, as forces are redeployed to increase their mobility. France is also taking part in the RECAMP operation to strengthen African peacekeeping capabilities.

Finally, France has an ongoing policy of providing sizeable contingents of "blue helmets" for United Nations peacekeeping and humanitarian operations.

In 1995, 13,500 men were engaged in operations outside French territory, including 8,600 in the former Yugoslavia. By 1997, this figure had dropped to 9,000, largely because operations in the former Yugoslavia had been scaled down to the 3,800 men involved in SFOR.

erative projects. In late 1997, France, Germany, Italy, Spain and the United Kingdom agreed to give a major boost to the regrouping of aviation and aerospace industries.

- search for new markets:

This is absolutely essential if French defence firms are to become less dependent on the defence budget.

Further reading:

APHG et SIRPA, *Éléments de géostratégie et défense de la France*, La Documentation française, 1995.

G. Ayade et A. Demant, *Armements et désarmement depuis 1945*, Complexe, 1991.

M. Long (editor), *Livre blanc sur la défense*, La Documentation française, Rapports officiels series, 1994.

Mémento défense-armement : L'Europe et la sécurité internationale, Groupe de recherche et d'information sur la paix (GRIP), 1997.

H. Prévost, *La France, économie et sécurité*, Hachette, Pluriel series, 1994.

J.-P. Hébert, *Production d'armement. Mutation du système français*, La Documentation française, Les Études de la DF series, 1995.

Textes législatifs et réglementaires, Secrétariat général de la Défense nationale, Organisation générale de la Défense nationale, *Journal officiel*.

"La France et sa défense", *Cahiers français* series, N° 283, La Documentation française, October-December 1997.

"Les jeunes et la défense. Opinion publique et service militaire", *Les Champs de mars*, Cahiers du centre d'études en sciences sociales de la défense, N° 2, 1997.

P. Buffolot, "La réforme du service national", *Problèmes politiques et sociaux* series, N° 769, La Documentation française.

L'année stratégique 2000, P. Boniface, Michalon series, 1999.

P. Buffolot, *La défense en Europe. Les adaptations de l'après-guerre froide*, La Documentation française, Les Études de la DF series, 1997.

Periodicals

Armées d'aujourd'hui, monthly journal of the armed forces (DICOD).

Défense nationale (monthly).

10

Foreign Trade

By becoming more open to the rest of the world since 1945 and casting aside its traditional protectionist attitudes, France has remained one of the most important players in the world economy. It is today fully engaged in globalisation and its economy is growing increasingly international, a factor reflected by the substantial growth in trade. France accounts for over 5% of world GDP, making it the country with the fourth largest GDP, behind the USA, Japan and Germany. It is now responsible for 6% of world trade, second only to the USA for services and agricultural exports and the fourth largest exporter of industrial products. France is also one of the leading countries for outward investment and the third largest destination for inward investment.

Trade Surplus

After recording a deficit for fifteen years, France regained a positive trade balance in 1992, when exports exceeded imports by 31 billion francs ($5 billion dollars). Since then, the surplus has considerably increased, reaching 122 billion francs ($20.3 billion) in 1996 and 173 billion francs ($28.8 billion) in 1997.

This performance appears to be solid and lasting. In 1992 and 1993, the upturn had looked vulnerable as it was linked to a significant fall in imports resulting from a slowdown in the economy. But since then the trade surpluses have

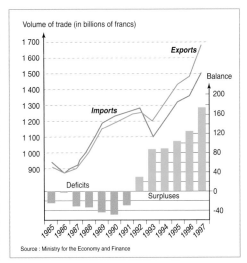

Volume of trade (in billions of francs)

Source : Ministry for the Economy and Finance

Since 1992, France's foreign trade surplus has risen steadily. It reached 173 billion francs in 1997

continued, despite consistent growth in goods purchased from abroad:
the value of imports rose from approximately 1,100 billion francs
($189.3 billion) in 1993 to almost 1,500 billion francs ($250 billion) in
1997. So it is clearly a structural rise in exports, which has put France
firmly in the black as regards external trade in goods.

Office and industrial equipment is
the sector whose overseas sales have contributed
most to France's healthy trade balance, especially
in the fields of aircraft construction, office
machines and professional electronic equipment
and industrial machinery. Food products (in which
there has traditionally been a trade surplus), the
defence industry, luxury goods, cars and other
means of land transport also make a major contribution to the surplus. In the last few years, there
have also been comfortable surpluses in pharmaceuticals and personal hygiene products sold in
pharmacies. France's largest deficits are in energy
products (-80 billion francs [-$13.3 billion]), mine-
rals, tropical food products and products of its traditional industries (textiles and clothing, leather
and hides, shoes, etc.).

If trade in financial and other services (especially
tourism) is added to that of trade in goods,
France has a substantial balance of payments surplus. There was a positive balance of over 230 billion francs
($38.3 billion) on France's current account in 1997, once figures for
trade in services and investment income had been added to the
balance of trade.

In the commercial har-
bour at Lorient (Morbi-
han), 6,000 tonnes of
chickens are loaded onto
a ship bound for Iran

Europe, France's Leading Trading Partner

78% of French trade is with the rich OECD countries and
62% with its EU partners (50% with other euro area countries). Europe
has accounted for an ever increasing share of France's foreign trade
over the last few decades (up almost 20% since the 1960s). So the
European enterprise has created a genuinely dynamic market, from
which France has benefited, since its balance of trade with EU countries
shows a large surplus — in the region of 88 billion francs ($14.6 billion)
in 1997. France's five largest customers are its closest European neighbours: Germany, United Kingdom, Italy, Belgium-Luxembourg and
Spain. These countries are also France's largest suppliers, with the
exception of Spain, overtaken by the USA. Germany has long been
France's leading trading partner, currently accounting for 16.3% of total
French foreign trade, ahead of Italy (9.6%) and the UK (9.2%). In 1996
and 1997, France's chronic trade deficit with Germany was

reversed. Outside the EU, France has three main trading partners: the USA and Japan, with both of which it has a trade deficit, and Switzerland, with which it has a large trade surplus.

Trade with non-OECD countries accounts for only 20% of France's foreign trade, of which over 4% is with East European countries and Russia. Developing countries in Asia, Africa and Latin America account for 14%, less than with Germany alone. From these countries, France chiefly imports energy products, mineral products and raw materials of agricultural origin, together with cheaply produced consumer goods. Exports to these countries are mainly of plant and machinery, consumer durables and agri-foodstuffs. France's balance of trade with these countries varies fairly widely. It is in deficit with China, Russia (except in 1995 and 1997) and South-East Asia, but is positive with Africa, Latin America and the Middle East (with the exception of certain states in these regions, Saudi Arabia and Nigeria, with which it has a significant and chronic deficit due to its oil imports). Trade is rapidly increasing with East European countries and France's balance of trade with these countries became positive in 1996 and remained so in 1997.

The 17 kilometre-long Vasco da Gama Bridge built over the Tagus, north of Lisbon (Portugal) by a French company is a marvel of technology. It was opened in March 1998

Increasing Internationalisation of the French Economy

France's exports account for 21% of its GDP, reflecting a major internationalisation of its trade, which, while the comparable percentage is lower than in Germany (24%), is higher than in Japan (10%) and the USA (9%). The net direct investment flows are another sign of the opening-up of the economy. In 1996, the stock of French direct investment abroad was around 1,000 billion francs ($166.6 billion) and of direct foreign investment in France nearly 750 billion francs ($125 billion).

Between 1990 and 1996, France was the third largest investor abroad, behind the USA and the UK. Worldwide, 16,000 French companies employ 2.6 million people. The country with the largest number of French companies is the USA (1,850 companies and 370,000 employees). Next come Germany (1,100 companies and 224,000 employees), the UK (1,200 companies and 221,000 employees) and Spain (1,000 companies and 218,000 employees). In fact, 45% of all employees of French companies outside France work within the EU. Of developing countries, Brazil has by far the largest number of French companies (in seventh place, behind Italy), but in Latin America the French presence is stagnant, as in Africa, where, although there is a long history of French companies setting up subsidiaries, it has hardly increased at all. By contrast, in the fast-growing Asian economies, France has made a major impact, with French companies increasing their workforce by over 60% between 1990 and 1995. Similarly, in Eastern Europe and the former Soviet Union, the number of employees of French companies was up by 57% over the same period.

At the same time, over 10,000 companies in France, of which half are in the Ile-de-France region, which includes Paris, are foreign-owned. On the industrial front, recent investment has mainly been in growth sectors such as telecommunications, electronics, chemicals and pharmaceuticals and, in the commercial and services area, in financial services, hotels and catering and leisure activities. The country with the highest investment in France is the USA, followed by the UK, the Netherlands, Germany and Belgium. Recruitment by foreign-owned companies plays an important role in reducing high levels of unemployment in France. At present, such firms are creating about 20,000 jobs per year, compared with an average of 10,000 during the 1980s.

Further reading:

H. Tyrman, F. Le Gallo, C. Loisy, *Un demi-siècle d'échanges extérieurs*, INSEE Première, No. 495, November 1996.

A. Bavelier, J.-C. Donnelier, *Les relations économiques internationales*, PUF, Que sais-je?, 1997.

DREE (*Direction des relations économiques extérieures* – external economic relations directorate), *Les échanges commerciaux de la France*, published annually by the *Ministère de l'Économie, des Finances et de l'Industrie* (French Ministry for the Economy, Finance and Industry).

Notes bleues de Bercy, bimonthly journal containing a wealth of articles on and detailed analyses of foreign trade (*Ministère de l'Économie, des Finances et de l'Industrie*).

SOCIETY

11

Lifestyles

Since the 1950s, first economic growth and then social and technological progress have brought about profound changes in France and ushered in the consumer and leisure era. Despite the problems associated with the economic crisis, the French have one of the highest standards of living in the world, with their country among the best placed in the United Nations reports. For example, the UN human development index (HDI) based on economic, social and cultural criteria put France second only to Canada in 1997. However, economic and social development has led to some standardisation of lifestyles and consumer spending, particularly reducing differences between urban and town dwellers. Nevertheless, regional identities remain strong and are an important element in the geographical and cultural mosaic of France, which mirrors the diversity of Europe itself and makes France the world's most popular tourist destination.

Rollerskating is no longer just a sport – it has become the preferred mode of transport for some city-dwellers, as pictured here on the banks of the Seine in Paris

A Richer, Less Unequal Society

Between 1955 and 1995, the average purchasing power of the French quadrupled. Despite the economic crisis, it has gone on rising, albeit more slowly, with household incomes rising by 50% between 1975 and 1995 (up by an average 2% per year). French incomes grew more during those forty years than since the beginning of the industrial revolution which sparked off the country's economic growth. Over the same period, welfare cover was extended to the whole of the population and today anyone with no resources is now entitled to a basic social security benefit, which may take the form of the RMI (minimum integration income), which is a type of income support, of a special "solidarity" allowance paid to the long-term unemployed who have exhausted their entitlement to unemployment benefit, or an attendance allowance for the dependent elderly. All in all, taking the period as a whole, social inequalities have been reduced and France has seen a narrowing of the wage/salary range and disparities in inherited wealth, even though the past two decades of economic crisis have tended once again to widen the gulf between the richest and poorest sectors of society: the poorest 10% of the French receive 2.3% of national income, whilst the richest 10% receive 27%. However, despite this, French society remains one of the least unequal.

In the case of both wage-earning and non wage-earning households (a household averages 2.5 persons), the mean monthly income is between 15,000 francs ($2,500) and 16,000 francs ($2,660) before tax. Taken as a whole, wages/salaries account for half the total income and welfare benefits a third, with the rest coming from self-employment and income from investments and property. The wage/salary range has narrowed over the past thirty years and in 1996 those in the highest income bracket were paid about three times more than those in the lowest: the average income for managerial and professional staff, the best-paid category, was 20,760 francs per month ($3,460), while unskilled workers, the lowest-paid category, received an average of 7,020 francs per month ($1,170). In 1997, average net income, excluding bonuses, of full-time employees was 10,685 francs per month ($1,780) – the gross average was 13,550 francs. In 1950, France was the first country in Europe to introduce a minimum wage for all types of

Standard of living in the European Union in 1995 (GDP per inhabitant)

Austria	124.2
Belgium	117.8
Denmark	129.6
Finland	108.5
France	117.3
Germany	131
Greece	48.5
Ireland	79.7
Italy	82.6
Luxembourg	187.7
The Netherlands	113.5
Portugal	45
Spain	63.3
Sweden	115.5
United Kingdom	83.3

Source : Eurostat
(taking 100 as the EU average).

employment. In 1998, 1.5 million workers (11.2% of employees) were earning the SMIC (*salaire minimum interprofessionnel de croissance*), then 6,797 francs ($1,133) gross a month. The bulk of those on the SMIC are young people, both women and men, with no qualifications, working for small or medium-sized companies. In 1997, the purchasing power of disposable income increased by 2.5%, the largest rise for seven years. However, 4.5 million people – a sixth of the working population – were not in paid employment and were living on benefit: 1.8 million of them on unemployment benefit (just over 1.3 million or so in 1999) and 2.7 million on social security.

The standard of living of the French varies not only with their income but also according to what they own. Over half of average household wealth takes the form of real estate. The remainder is made up of financial assets and the proportion of this constituted by insurance products and shares and bonds has grown fivefold over the past twenty years. Gross average household wealth now exceeds a million francs, but varies considerably according to social category, on a scale of 1 to 8: from slightly under 500,000 francs for the families of wage and salary earners to almost four million for those of professionals.

Housing – Home-owners in the Majority

The French spend an average of 22% of their disposable income on housing, fuel, light and power. This is twice as much as in 1960, for two reasons: more people are buying their own homes, on fifteen to twenty-year loans, and those renting are having to pay more for homes which are roomier and more comfortable than they used to be. Six out of ten French households now own their homes, compared with four out of ten in 1960.

Thanks to the rise in living standards and some specific policies designed to encourage home ownership, a majority of the French have been able to fulfil a strong aspiration and buy their own homes. The schemes introduced in the early sixties were principally geared towards the purchase of flats in large blocks. In 1977, the creation of "PAP" subsidised loans to help people buy their homes boosted the flagging housing market and led to the purchase of houses, particularly small properties in new estates which grew up on the

Time spent watching television has risen by over 30% since 1982 and average viewing time is now two and three-quarter hours a day, almost 20% of waking life

outskirts of towns. 56% of dwellings in France are houses. From the late eighties, the rise in home ownership slowed down, very probably not only because of the low growth in purchasing power during this period, but also due to the high cost of property and mortgages. Conditions have recently improved and the number of homes purchased has risen sharply since 1994, assisted by the October 1995 reform introducing a zero-interest loan (PTZ) for certain categories of buyers.

Housing Conditions

Housing conditions have improved significantly, both in quality and quantity. The average size of the home of a standard French household of 2.5 people is 90m^2, whereas in the sixties, the then average household of three people had approximately 60m^2. Living space per French person is estimated to have doubled since the war. The number of dwellings with "all mod cons" has also risen: whereas in 1955 87% of homes did not have basic sanitary facilities (inside lavatory and bathroom), under 4% are without them today. Thanks to renovation and refurbishment schemes covering whole districts in both urban and rural areas, the quality of older housing is now the same as that of new or more recently built property.

Today, efforts to improve housing conditions are continuing. For instance, local authorities are actively engaged in renovating the public housing estates built in the 1960s and early 1970s (approximately 200 ZUP – priority urban areas – containing around 800,000 dwellings). The passing in 1998 of a law allowing debts to be conditionally written off will eventually help resolve the problems of people who bought their homes on mortgages and cannot afford to keep up the repayments. Lastly, the 1995 emergency plan to house the poorest families who are temporarily unable to pay rent has resulted in a current stock of 20,000 housing units available for temporary accommodation.

New Spending Patterns

The general rise in living standards has brought a sustained increase in consumer spending – up an average of 3% per year since 1970; however the rate of growth has slowed down in recent years (1.5% in 1995 and 1.9% in 1996) and there have been marked variations from one year to another. There have also been significant changes in household spending patterns over this period. French families are allocating a far smaller proportion of their budget to food and clothing, which accounted for only 23% of expenditure in 1997 as against 44% in 1960. Similarly, purchases of household goods have decreased from 11% in 1960 to 7%

today. Spending has sharply increased on housing (22% in 1997 compared with 10.4% in 1960), health (10.3% in 1997 compared with 5% in 1960), transport and communications (16.7% in 1997 as against 11.6% in 1960) and leisure and cultural activities (7.4% in 1997 as against 6% in 1960). Overall, consumer spending patterns in France are typical of a rich country, in which the proportion of spending on essentials is decreasing and that on non-essentials rising.

% of expenditure	1960	1980	1997
Food, drink, tobacco	33.3	21.4	17.8
Clothing and footwear	11.0	7.3	5.2
Housing, heat and light	10.4	17.5	22.2
Furniture and household goods	11.0	9.6	7.3
Medical and health services	5.0	7.7	10.3
Transport and communications	11.6	16,6	16.7
Leisure, education and culture	6.0	7,3	7.4
Other goods and services	11.7	12,6	13.0

Changes in household spending: the percentage spent on food and clothing has fallen from 44% in 1960 to under 25% today

In 1998, 23% of households had a computer. Other would-be netsurfers can explore the Internet in various public places, like the cybercafés (here, in the Rue de Médicis, in Paris)

Multimedia Age

Even though the French allocate less of their disposable income to basic necessities, their spending on these remains substantial: for instance, over 1,000 billion francs were spent on food and clothing in 1997, i.e. twice as much in inflation-adjusted francs as in 1960. Since households are now often fully equipped with the usual white and brown goods, expenditure in these fields tends to be on

replacement items. Nearly 8 out of 10 households have a car, 3 out of 10 have at least two. Indeed, increasingly the only households without these goods are those too poor to buy them (particularly the elderly); over 95% of households have a refrigerator, a television and a washing-machine. Since the 1980s, French consumers have tended to spend their money on such items as video recorders, camcorders, personal computers and multimedia products. This market has grown very quickly: in 1998, 23% of households had a PC, twice as many as in 1992.

Health – a Priority

The proportion of the French household budget allocated to health is growing for several reasons. Firstly, the population is ageing, which means that medical care needs have risen and will continue doing so. Secondly, whilst three quarters of medical expenses are still covered by social security, contributions have steadily increased, as has the direct contribution of households. Finally, people are increasingly turning to the medical profession for help with life's problems and less willing to put up with what was previously regarded as inevitable: pain, physical defects and the effects of ageing.

Mass Consumption, Selective Consumption

These indicators reveal a profound transformation of lifestyles and a society increasingly focusing on consumerism and leisure activities. Spending patterns are becoming relatively standardised, with a rise in the purchase of "ready-to-use" products and services, including frozen food, fast-food restaurants, disposable products, slimming cures, package holidays and organized leisure activities. At the same time, old habits are waning: consumption of wine and bread has fallen sharply and smoking is on the decline, very probably as much a result of public health campaigns as of the changes in lifestyle. However, as if to compensate for these developments, there is a growing demand for high-quality and even luxury products: champagne, fine wines, luxury goods and gourmet cuisine are now within the budget of the middle classes as well as the rich.

The international Car Show in Paris in September 1998 attracted over 1.2 million visitors (a record number)

The Family: New Values

The family and the institution of marriage have been through complex changes as society has become more diverse and the rise in living standards has radically altered living conditions. The drift from the land and the urban development which peaked in the 1970s have been key factors in the weakening of traditional family ties and structures, a process accentuated by the extension to rural communities of urban lifestyles and the increasing number of women in employment. This fragmentation of the traditional family unit is reflected by a marked drop in the number of elderly people living with the younger generation and a rise in the incidence of divorce. Concurrently, the hierarchy within the family has to some extent been blurred with authority no longer so dependent on age or order of birth.

These changes have been accompanied by a fall in the number of marriages and a rise in the divorce rate. Fewer people are getting married and those who do are doing so later and later – the average age at which people get married for the first time is 27 for women and 29 for men – and the number of people staying single is increasing: 7% of those born in 1940, but, it is estimated, probably over 30% of those born in 1970. Practically one marriage in two ends in divorce (about 285,000 marriages are celebrated and over 130,000 divorces pronounced every year); thirty years ago, the ratio was one to ten, with approximately 40,000 divorces for 400,000 marriages.

The French are marrying less (about 285,000 marriages a year) and over 30% of the generation born in 1970 are probably still unmarried.
The photo shows a wedding in the town hall of L'Isle-d'Abeau (Isère)

Changing Laws
for Changing Lifestyles

In reality, the old models are evolving, rather than dying out. The family unit and the couple are still very important in our society, but they have adapted to less rigid conceptions and practices, with a corresponding increase in the flexibility of the legal and social bases of these institutions. In the 1960s, approximately 400,000 couples were unmarried, whereas now there are two million and nearly four in ten births take place outside marriage. There are now large numbers of one-parent families and of families in which children live with one biological parent and one step-parent. Over two million children live in one of these types of family. The law is changing to encompass these new realities and new more flexible legislation on the family unit, marriage and divorce was under discussion in 1998.

Family Solidarity

The family nevertheless remains a major place of refuge in times of difficulty. Young people are leaving home later and later as a result of the increasing length of their studies and subsequent difficulty in finding a job. They now leave home, on average, at the age of 25, while in the sixties the majority did so around 20-21. The existence of a close family able to provide support clearly mitigates the effects of unemployment and financial problems. Inter-generational financial help is estimated at an average of 135 billion francs ($22.5 billion) per year, mainly to young people from their parents and grandparents, and often continues for some time, even when the recipients are well into adulthood. The fact that many homeless people are known to have lost all contact with their relations clearly demonstrates that the lack of a close family hastens the downward spiral of social exclusion.

The French at Work

Thanks to technological progress and more streamlined production, people now work far less, but far more efficiently, than they did in the past. The reduction in the time spent working is clear from the cuts in the statutory working week, which was set at 48 hours in 1919, 40 hours in 1936, 39 hours in 1982 and 35 hours in 1998 (to be fully implemented in 2000). But other factors too have played a part in this change and these are clearer if working life is looked at as a whole: professional careers begin much later and end much earlier and people no longer work either seven days a week or twelve months a year (workers have a legal right to five weeks' paid holiday per year). If all these factors are taken into account, the actual length of working life in France has been halved since 1870, while over the same period France's GDP has risen by a factor of fourteen and hourly productivity by one of twenty. However, conditions vary greatly from one type of work to another and, whilst salaried employees worked

Poster campaign for the 35-hour working week, conducted by the Ministry for Employment and Solidarity in September 1998

Du temps pour soi.
Une chance pour l'emploi.

35h

" JE VIENS DE TROUVER DU TRAVAIL GRÂCE AUX 35 HEURES. ICI ÇA MARCHE, ET CHEZ VOUS ?"

MAXIME SANS - POLISSEUR
AGENCEMENT ET CONSTRUCTION MÉTALLIQUE (91-CHO)

Informations : 08 35 35 2000 (1,09 F/mn) ; www.35h.travail.gouv.fr

an average 1,630 hours per year in 1996, farmers, lorry-drivers and shop-keepers worked far more.

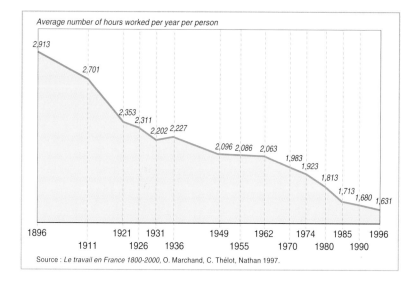

Average number of hours worked per year per person

2,913
2,701
2,353
2,311
2,202 2,227
2,096 2,086 2,063
1,983
1,923
1,813
1,713
1,680 1,631

1896
1911
1921
1926
1931
1936
1949
1955
1962
1970
1974
1980
1985
1990
1996

Source : *Le travail en France 1800-2000*, O. Marchand, C. Thélot, Nathan 1997.

The amount of time spent working has decreased by 45% during the last hundred years, but it is unevenly spread between employees: 13% work fewer than 30 hours a week and 6% over 50

Moving Towards the 35-hour Working Week

The economic crisis, new ways of organising production and wider use of machinery and systems replacing jobs have changed the world of work. The chronic unemployment which set in towards the end of the 1970s with the arrival of the first baby-boom generations on the employment market also played a part in altering people's attitudes to work. A number of developments are taking place in response to the new demands of the labour market. There has been a sharp rise in the number of part-time workers, from 6% of salaried employees in the early seventies to 17% today. Teleworking is enabling more people to work from home. Care for the elderly, new social needs and increasing concern for the environment are also creating new jobs within the community and thus helping reduce unemployment.

The shorter working week introduced in 1998 is clearly one of the possible solutions to France's unemployment problem. However, the measure is controversial, since it could exacerbate the difficulties of some businesses by making them less competitive compared with their counterparts in countries where social legislation is less advanced. Nevertheless, negotiations on the methods for moving to the 35-hour week within companies should result in acceptable compromises in most cases.

In France, working conditions are negotiated between employers and employees in each sector and set by state-backed collective-bargaining agreements. In addition, since 1982, a series of laws and ordinances has strengthened the institutions representing employees and the role of trade unions and established a right to negotiation. Trade union membership, which is still very high in countries like Germany and Scandinavia, is declining in France, despite long-established traditions. It currently stands at approximately 10% (compared to 81% in Sweden) and most of the major trade unions (CGT, CFDT and FO being the most significant) have lost between a quarter and over half of their membership during the last twenty years. Labour relations today are less confrontational than in the past.

Discovering Free Time

Free time is undeniably one of the achievements of this century. In addition to the continuing decrease in the number of hours worked each day, most employees now have two days off a week (the Sunday day of rest was made a legal requirement only in 1906) and five weeks' paid holiday per year (workers gained the right

to two weeks' holiday in 1936, three in 1956, four in 1963 and five in 1981). Sociologists have calculated that in one year an employee spends an average 20% of his or her time at work and commuting, 33% sleeping and the rest, i.e. 47%, on other activities, some, like television, being passive and others, such as DIY, gardening and sport, active, but all of which are regarded as relaxation.

There are 12.5 million vegetable and flower gardens in France: this photograph shows the Hortillonnages (300 hectares of gardens criss-crossed by canals) in Amiens (Somme)

Television – the Most Popular Form of Entertainment

Statistics show that television is the most popular leisure activity. On average, the French spend nearly 1,000 hours per year watching television – 17% of their waking life and two and three-quarter hours a day (30% longer than in 1982). A window on the world for some (it is often invaluable company for people living alone, especially the elderly) and a cultural scourge for others, the small screen is now part of daily life for the French, particularly now that the proliferation of channels, together with transmission by cable and satellite are providing a greater choice of programmes. This trend highlights a real desire for leisure activities which allow people to relax at home. Games consoles are growing in popularity, together with the increasingly sophisticated games, as are home computers equipped with CD-ROMs and, of course, connection to the Internet which is likely to become more widespread in the future with the possibility of access via Minitel.

Access to this new technology has been accompanied by a certain loss of interest in traditional forms of entertainment. The circus is now hardly more than a relic of the past and theatres are often only able to survive through subsidies. Cinema audiences have fallen by two thirds over the past forty years (from 412 million in 1957 to 148 million in 1997). The French film industry is still relatively healthy as a result of active government support and has stood up to competition from America better than its counterparts in other European countries. France produces about 130 films a year and 36% of films shown in France are French and 54% American.

Relaxation: Gardening and DIY Still Among the Most Popular Leisure Activities

Whilst some traditional pastimes are declining in popularity, such as hunting, which was the sport of 2.3 million in 1976 and only 1.5 million in 1996, others have stood the test of time. Two activities in particular are as popular as ever with the French: DIY, for which the market is worth about 90 billion francs a year, and gardening, the favourite hobby of one household in two (there are 12.5 million vegetable and flower gardens in France), on which they spend 35 billion francs per year. Reading also remains a popular pastime: in a recent survey, only a quarter of the French said that they had read no books at all during the past year (compared with 35% in 1986) and 35% said they had read more than five. However, reading appears to be in decline amongst the youngest members of the population, due to the combined effect of television and video games.

A Nation of Sports Enthusiasts

As if to make up for these increasingly sedentary pastimes, growing numbers of French people are turning to sport. Two thirds of French men and half the women say they take part in a sporting activity and nearly a quarter of the French now belong to sports federations, three times more than in 1970. This enthusiasm for sport is mirrored by France's performance in international sporting events. By coming fifth overall in the Atlanta Olympics in 1996, with 37 medals – after the USA, Russia, Germany and China – the French showed their continuing progress in top-level competitive sport.

National and international championships in the most popular sports, such as football, rugby, cycling and tennis, draw huge crowds and record television and radio audiences. The Tour de France cycle race is a genuinely national event and its popularity, which has now spread beyond France's borders, has taken on a European dimension.

France has also organised some prestigious international sporting events, such as the Winter Olympics (Grenoble in 1968 and Albertville in 1992) and the 1998 football World Cup, in which France won the world championship. With a 3-0 win against Brazil, France became world champion for the first time in its history. The victory of the "Blues" (the French team's nickname) was celebrated throughout the country with immense jubilation.

As well as these popular sports, the French can engage in every kind of sporting activity: France's geography and climate provide a wealth of opportunities for water and winter sports. In some fields, such as sailing, judo, fencing and motor-racing, the French are among the best in the world.

The 1998 World Cup final between France and Brazil, on 12 July 1998, at which France won the Football World Cup for the first time

Holidays close to Nature

In both summer and winter, sporting activities are often combined with holidays: by indulging in the joys of skiing, water sports, golf, cycling or walking, holidaymakers combine relaxation with physical exercise. 62% of the French go away on holiday, compared with slightly over 40% in the early sixties (about 36 million people in the summer and 20 million in the winter). Holidays are becoming more varied: long stays devoted solely to rest are being replaced by shorter breaks in which holidaymakers take an active part in sports, crafts or cultural activities. Throughout France, there are an increasing number of festivals and opportunities to discover the countryside, while visits to companies and industrial plants are arousing growing interest. 11 million French tourists go on holiday abroad, with Spain, Portugal, Italy, the British Isles, Morocco, Germany, Austria and Tunisia the favourite destinations.

Far fewer farmers, self-employed craftsmen and small shop-keepers go away on holiday than employees, who have taken the most holidays away from home over the last two decades. An increasing proportion of tourists are retired people, who have benefited from increased pensions and/or holidays organised by their local authorities, works committees or specialised tour-operators. The growth of tourism is also being encouraged by the popularity of the "holiday-cheque" scheme, which allows many low-paid workers to have holidays inside France which they would not otherwise be able to afford: each month, for at least eight months, they pay a set sum into a personal holiday fund to which their employers, and sometimes also their works committees, also contribute.

A walk in the Alps in Haute-Savoie in the summer of 1997, when the fiftieth anniversary of the creation of the Sentiers Grandes Randonnées (a network of hiking trails) was being celebrated

Further reading:

L'état de la France 1998-99, La Découverte, 1998.

« Les chiffres de l'économie et de la société ». *Alternatives économiques*, Special issue No. 34, 4th Quarter, 1998.

« Qui sont les Français ? », *Sciences humaines*, No. 10, September-October 1995.

O. Marchand, C. Thélot, *Le travail en France*, Nathan, 1997.

L. Dirn, *La société française en tendance 1975-1995 : deux décennies de changement*, PUF, 1997.

G. Mermet, *Francoscopie 1998*, Larousse, 1998.

France, portrait social 1997, INSEE, 1998.

12

The Social Welfare System

France has one of the most effective welfare systems in the world. For many years welfare cover was available only to part of the salaried workforce, but since World War II it has gradually been extended to the whole population and now meets such fundamental social requirements as health care, retirement pensions, family policy, unemployment benefit and a minimum income for those who have no other entitlement.

At nearly 2,500 billion francs ($416 billion), over 35% of GDP, the level of France's annual spending on social protection is one of the highest in the European Union, comparable to that of Denmark, Finland, Austria and the Netherlands.

Social security spending is funded and administered separately from the general state budget, whilst a social aid scheme assisting the poorest members of society is financed out of central and local government budgets.

During the thirty or so boom years after the Second World War, France had relatively few problems funding the system created in 1945, despite the regular improvements and reforms required both to keep pace with the needs of the population and ensure the system's survival.

Breakdown of social protection spending in 1997	
Sickness, invality, accidents at work and occupational diseases	34.0 %
Old-age pensions, etc.	43.7 %
Family and maternity	9.5 %
Unemployment and job creation schemes	8.1 %
Housing	4.7 %

However, the economic crisis - which resulted in falls in social security contributions and left some sectors of the population highly vulnerable - growing demands on the welfare system and huge increase in available treatments placed a heavy burden on the public purse. Today, the situation is looking somewhat better: in 1998 France's social security budget had a deficit of 13.3 billion francs ($2.2 billion) and in 1999 it should be balanced.

Health

Health care is provided inside hospitals (which account for approximately 51% of social security spending on health) and by doctors and specialists working outside them. The health sector employs almost 2 million people, of whom about 600,000 work in hospitals, and is one of those in which the most jobs have been created in recent decades. Its dynamism encourages constant improvements in research, diagnostic and treatment techniques, especially in the areas of medicines and imaging devices (echography, scanners and nuclear magnetic resonance imaging). Along with these technical advances, state health care has been reorganised. The provision of health care facilities is now planned and allocated on a regional basis in order to match spending more closely to the requirements of the population. These innovations have left intact the traditional French health-care system in which private practice plays an important role and the patient is free to choose his or her health-care provider.

France's health policy is designed to ensure equal access to health care for the entire population. Although some disparities remain as a result of differences in living standards, education or place of residence, these are much less marked than for many other items of household expenditure.

The public authorities are also endeavouring to develop preventive medicine, by encouraging systematic pre- and post-natal check-ups, increasing the number of workplace consultations and organizing large-scale public-health campaigns on major health risks. These have focused, for example, on smoking and alcoholism, methods of early detection of cancer and preventing AIDS. These efforts have brought some impressive results: France's infant mortality rate is amongst the lowest in the world and its life expectancy amongst the highest, increasing by approximately 100 days every year.

Health spending has doubled since 1980, but life expectancy in France is amongst the highest in the world

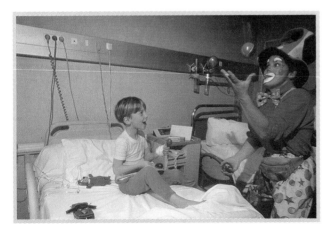

Practically the entire population is now covered against sickness or injury-related expenditure, with 100% cover for long-term, costly serious illnesses and surgical operations, and partial cover for minor illnesses and non-essential expenditure. The costs for which patients remain liable can be covered through private insurance or a mutual.

However, in order to make health care more genuinely accessible to everyone, 1998 saw a wide-ranging reform of the social protection system. This provides for universal medical cover, guarantees complementary protection, and dispenses the poorest patients from having themselves to pay for treatment and wait for reimbursement.

Health-care expenditure now totals nearly 800 billion francs ($133 billion) – this figure includes spending by the state, private individuals, social security, mutuals and other insurance companies offering optional complementary insurance policies. On average, every person in France spends 12,400 francs ($2,066) per year on health care. In other words, nearly 10% of GDP is spent on health, which constitutes an important economic sector.

To cope with ever-increasing health needs, the government has introduced measures to encourage all those involved in the health service to assume more responsibility. Parliament determines the level of expenditure each year and, in the light of its decisions, the authorities negotiate agreements with the Sickness Insurance Funds, and in particular with the *Caisse nationale d'assurance maladie* (the national employed persons sickness insurance fund). The funds in turn sign agreements with doctors' and health professionals' organisations.

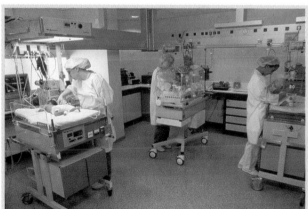

Publicity campaigns are encouraging the patients themselves to limit spending. They are shortly to receive a highly sophisticated smart card, the *Sésame Vitale*, replacing the health record card issued to all French and foreign contributors to the French national insurance scheme, on which doctors record important medical information, such as tests, consultations, prescribed treatments, etc..

A paediatric department
in a Nice clinic

Since 1998, health care has no longer been funded only by national insurance deducted from the salaries of employees, but by a tax, the CSG (generalised social contribution), levied on all gross earned and unearned income.

The Elderly
and the Disabled

The most expensive item in France's social expenditure is the budget for the elderly and dependent elderly, which accounts for just under 13% of GDP (about 1,000 billion francs or $166.6 billion). This includes basic state pensions paid by Social

Security, totalling 380 billion francs ($63.3 billion) and compulsory complementary pensions, totalling approximately 250 billion francs ($41.6 billion). About 10 million retired people receive these pensions.

Retirement pensions in France are funded by national insurance contributions deducted from salaries at source, whose cost is borne jointly by employers and employees. France has a "pay as you go" pension scheme based on contribution and redistribution. It combines the principle of helping those in need (through institutions like the old-age solidarity fund) with incentives to employees to take part in pension schemes.

An old people's home
in Saint-Herblain
(Loire-Atlantique)

As the baby-boom generations born since 1946 gradually reach retirement age, it will become increasingly difficult to finance retirement pensions. Measures have already been taken to try to balance the budget: the 1993 reform increased to forty years the length of time it is necessary to pay national insurance contributions in order to be entitled to a full pension (this was introduced on a gradual basis, adding three months to the period each year from 1994 onwards, with the reform fully implemented from 2003) and altered the basis on which pensions are calculated from the ten best years to the twenty-five best years of earnings.

Old-age pensions are based on a system of contributions, but France also provides for elderly people not entitled to a retirement pension, or whose pension is insufficient for them to live on because they have not paid national insurance contributions or worked for long enough – this is the case, for instance, for many elderly women. A minimum old-age income was introduced in 1956 for all persons over the age of 65 whose resources are inadequate; this has been substantially increased in recent years and now stands at 3,470 francs ($578) a month for a single person and 6,226 francs ($1,037) a month for a couple.

Under the law of 30 June 1975, the disabled must be provided with education, training and integrated both into the work-force and socially. It introduced a disabled adults allowance and structures to help them find jobs in an ordinary or sheltered working environment. Today France has about 2.5 million disabled persons, of whom nearly one and a half million are of working age. Only 170,000 of them are employed in an ordinary working environment, and 80,000 have jobs in sheltered workshops.

Family Policy

A doctor filling in a social security form: he has to indicate the cost of the consultation, wilch will be wholly or party refunded by the patient's social security fund and his/her mutual, if the patient is a member of one

France devotes a higher percentage of its GDP (nearly 4.5%) to family policy than any other country in Europe. Family allowances were first introduced at the beginning of this century for large families in need and certain categories of civil service employees. However, all salaried employees did not receive them until 1932 when it became compulsory for all employers to provide and themselves fund family allowances for their staff. In 1939 the "family code" also extended family allowances to the whole workforce and brought in a grant for the birth of the first child, an allowance for mothers remaining in the home to care for their children and certain fiscal advantages for large families. The chief aim of these measures was to stimulate the birth rate in a country where Malthusian principles were the rule.

Since the 1970s, the focus of family policy has shifted away from encouraging people to produce more children to redistribution of resources to low-income families and lone parents. Family policy has now become more of a social than demographic policy.

Family benefits are largely financed by businesses, whose contributions have, since 1990, been linked to companies' total wage bills. Out of the employers' contributions and government funding (CSG), the *Caisse Nationale d'allocations familiales*, or national family allowance agency, disburses the various family benefits and special allowances such as housing benefit and the RMI (see below).

Most aid to families takes the form of allowances paid to parents, of which the most substantial are the family allowances (28% of the total) paid to over 4 million families. Many other types of benefit are also available to families: the "young child" allowance (paid from the fourth month of pregnancy until the child is three years old), the parental education allowance (paid to compensate for loss or reduction of parental income from paid employment at the birth of a third or subsequent child), family support allowances, the lone parent allowance, grants to pay for child-care, the "new school year" allowance and housing benefit based on the number of children in the family. In all, over 270 billion francs ($45 billion) is paid to over 10 million families.   If indirect benefits such as tax relief, price reductions for families, subsidized mortgage interest rates and whole or part-payment of the costs of certain family requirements (such as crèches, leisure activities and holidays) by local authorities are included, a total of over 300 billion francs ($50 billion) of public money is spent on families.

Breakdown of payments classed as family benefits in 1995

Family benefits in 1995: a total of over 270 billion francs was paid to over 10 million families (one household in two)

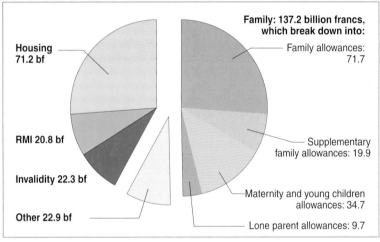

Housing
71.2 bf

RMI 20.8 bf

Invalidity 22.3 bf

Other 22.9 bf

Family: 137.2 billion francs, which break down into:

Family allowances: 71.7

Supplementary family allowances: 19.9

Maternity and young children allowances: 34.7

Lone parent allowances: 9.7

Source : INSEE survey.

Fighting New Forms of Poverty

High unemployment, the difficulties experienced by many young people in finding work and a high rate of separation and debt amongst couples have all contributed to the rise of new forms of poverty. Central government and departmental authorities, which took over some social responsibilities with decentralisation, are having to spend more and more money to combat this growth in marginalisation and job and financial insecurity. Some 170 billion francs ($28 billion) are paid to the poorest households (approximately 6 million persons), mainly in the form of the RMI.

The RMI is a temporary minimum income guaranteed to all individuals over the age of 25 whose income from all other sources is below 2,000 francs a month ($333) for a person living alone. It was introduced in December 1988 and is currently paid to just over a million households (about 2 million people, if you include partners and children). In 1998, the RMI was set at 2,627 francs ($437) per month for a person living alone and just over 5,300 francs

($883) for a couple with two children. It is socially innovative in that it is designed to encourage recipients to enter or return to the world of work. It is mainly financed by central government and allocated by the family allowance agencies. In addition, almost 500,000 unemployed people who have exhausted their entitlement to unemployment benefit receive a state-funded "end of rights" allowance or "specific solidarity" allowance of at least the same amount as the RMI. France's 2.8 million part-time, temporary, or fixed-term contract employees earning less than the minimum wage are also eligible for state benefits of various kinds.

The fight against poverty and social exclusion has become a national priority, mobilizing many players alongside the specialised institutions and the state, which has embarked on a major programme aimed at guaranteeing everyone a set of basic rights (employment, housing, health, education, culture and so on), and at preventing new situations which typically lead to exclusion. Local authorities are taking an increasingly active role in this battle, but a very valuable part is also played by charities like *ATD-Quart-Monde* and *Restos du coeur* which work closely with those in need and are often the deciding factor in reducing poverty.

Volunteers from the Paris "Samu social" (mobile emergency medical service) assisting homeless people

The Battle against Unemployment

Like many other industrialised countries, for twenty years France has had to cope with a continuous rise in the unemployment rate, which in 1998 stood at 11.8% (2.9 million people). However, since 1997, the rise has slowed down and recently unemployment has fallen. Until 1974, the unemployment rate was under 3%, and it was only in 1977 the jobless total topped one million for the first time. The female unemployment rate is higher (14.2%) than the male (10.8%), but it is the young who are suffering the most (23% for those under 25). Overall, the unskilled with no qualifications are most seriously affected, with an unemployment rate of 17%, compared with 7% for those with higher education qualifications.

The battle against unemployment has been waged since the early 1970s focusing first successively and then simultaneously on applying economic and social solutions to the problem. On the economic front, companies are encouraged to maintain or, better still, increase staffing levels. To this end, the state seeks to create a favourable environment: it takes over all or part of the employers' social security contributions for firms pledging to create new jobs and has reduced local business taxes and the tax on reinvested profits. More recently, the government has decided to phase in state financing for family allowances, which were previously paid by businesses. In return for the different incentives, businesses have to recruit additional employees, generally on fixed-term contracts. A total of 1.5 million people have been employed under such schemes. The most common of these are the *contrat initiative-emploi* (employment initiative contract) for people registered unemployed for at least 24 of the previous 36 months, currently held by 400,000 employees; the *contrat emploi-solidarité* (employment support contract) offered for jobs in the community to people registered unemployed for at least 12 of the previous 18 months; and the *contrat d'apprentissage* (apprenticeship contract), which is a type of sandwich course contract. Employment support and apprenticeship contracts are each currently held by over 300,000 people. Since 1997, the government has tackled the problem of youth unemployment by creating new services which benefit the community: 350,000 young people will have been able to take advantage of this scheme by the year 2000.

Efforts on the social front involve taking action on working hours and conditions: lowering the retirement age and encouraging early retirement schemes in sectors in difficulties. Alongside this policy, there are measures to encourage part-time employment and help jobseekers to train and retrain, particularly through paid workplacements. Finally, since economic growth is not sufficient to resolve the unemployment problem, the government has launched a programme of negotiated reductions in working hours.

These measures have, admittedly, slowed the increase in unemployment and reduced the problem of the exclusion of some citizens from society, but just under 3 million people are still out of work and living on benefit. In France, the unemployment insurance scheme is quite separate from the social security schemes and is managed, on a basis of parity

Young people, especially those without qualifications, and women are worst affected by unemployment: one in four under-25s (excluding students) is out of work

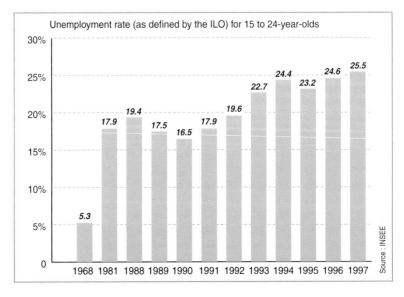

Unemployment rate (as defined by the ILO) for 15 to 24-year-olds

Source : INSEE

between the trade unions and employer's association, by UNEDIC (*Union pour l'emploi dans l'industrie et le commerce*). In 1997, its budget was 116 billion francs ($20 billion), 36% of this coming from employees' contributions and 64% from employers' contributions. Average unemployment benefit was 4,700 francs ($783) per unemployed person per month in 1998, totaling nearly 100 billion francs. The level of benefit decreases over time and the maximum length of time for which benefit may ever be paid is 60 months. The 500,000 jobseekers no longer entitled to unemployment benefit receive the "specific solidarity allowance", which is funded by the state, but also paid through UNEDIC. Jobseekers who are not entitled to unemployment benefit because they have not worked and have thus paid no national insurance contributions are covered by other types of benefit, notably the RMI.

Taken together, the cost of unemployment benefit, approximately 150 billion francs ($25 billion) per year, and job creation schemes comes to a total of around 320 billion francs ($53.3 billion) of public money spent every year combating unemployment. However, on the surface, this effort may seem to have been less effective than that of other countries, such as the United States and the United Kingdom, which have obtained better results at a lower cost. But this is a matter of political choice: industrialised countries which have succeeded in reducing unemployment have done so by cutting back on social protection and increasing the number of people in low-paid work without job security. France has not adopted such recipes.

Nonetheless, it is true that, in the areas of unemployment benefit, health policy, the family and help for the elderly, the French social protection system needs to be rethought to check the continuation of the significant rise in costs which has occurred over recent years and to improve its efficiency. This is the aim of the current reforms to pensions and health insurance and the move to fund the welfare system to a greater extent out of the state budget by increasing the CSG, which is gradually taking the place of the various specific contributions which had been brought in over the years. These changes are not reducing the level of welfare cover, as is sometimes suggested, but tailoring the system to new requirements and they have not prevented its extension to embrace an increasing number of areas and broader sectors of the population.

Breakdown of expenditure on France's employment policy in 1996

Passive spending	**48.0 %**
Unemployment benefit	38.4 %
Early retirement packages	9.6 %
Active spending	**52.0 %**
Vocational training	28.1 %
Job creation schemes	15.1 %
Other	8.8 %

Source : INSEE. *Tableaux de l'Economie française (French economic statistics) 1998-1999.*

Further reading:

Bilan économique et social de la France, Ministère de l'Emploi et de la Solidarité, Ministère de l'Économie, des Finances et de l'Industrie, La Documentation française, 1997.

L'année sociale, Éditions de l'Atelier-Alternatives économiques, Points d'appui series, 1998.

La protection sociale en France, M. de Montalembert Ed., La Documentation française, Les Notices series, 1997.

J.-P. Cendron, *Le monde de la protection sociale*, Nathan, 1997.

J.-B. de Foucauld, J.-F. Chadelat et C. Zaïdman, Commissariat général du Plan, *Le financement de la protection sociale*, La Documentation française, Rapports officiels series, 1995.

T. Lecomte, A. Mizrahi, *Précarité sociale, cumul des risques sociaux et médicaux*, CREDES, 1996.

Ministère du Travail et des Affaires sociales, *40 ans de politique de l'emploi*, La Documentation française, 1996.

Current health
spending in 1996

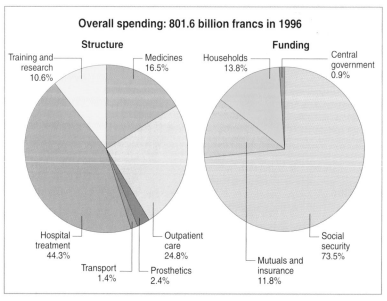

Source : Office of the Minister of State for Health.

13

Education and Training

In the last two centuries, since decrees enacted in 1792 and 1793 assigned the state a primary role in education, France has developed one of the most advanced education and training systems in the world. However, its tasks are increasingly complex, given the rapidity of the social, economic and technological changes and growing expectations of families and society.

There were over 15 million schoolchildren and students in France in 1997-1998, a quarter of the population, and the Ministry of National Education, Research and Technology budget is larger than that of any other ministry. In 1998, it was 334.4 billion francs ($55.7 billion), over 3% up on the previous year, and accounted for 21% of state spending. The education system is also the country's biggest employer, with 1.2 million teaching, administrative and ancillary staff – more than half of all state employees. If spending by local authorities, households and businesses is included, France's total spending on education and training in 1998 amounted to 580 billion francs ($96.6 billion), 7.4% of French GDP.

	1975	1997
Total spending (billion francs)	330	592
Average spending per pupil (francs)	21,400	35,700
Percentage of GDP spent on education	6.5 %	7.3 %

Growth in spending on education in France (at 1997 prices). Average spending per pupil has risen by 65 % over a twenty- year period: education has definitely become a French national priority

Issues in Education

As in most industrial countries, the French education system is constantly being tailored to the far-reaching socio-economic and cultural developments. The past 30 years have seen changes at every level of the system, from nursery school through to university, and given rise to widespread debate on the fundamental role of education and particularly on the necessity to strike a balance between preparing young people for working life and equipping them all with the general knowledge they need to enable them to make free choices and exercise to the full their rights and duties as citizens. This has led to clashes between different conceptions of secular education, teacher training, the teacher-pupil relationship and new teaching methods, etc..

The decisions taken over the years have enabled the system to carry on working, but from the debate some fundamental principles have emerged, including, in particular, the need to enable as many pupils as possible to move from the *collège* (approximately 11-15 years) to the *lycée* (from approximately 15 years) and then take the *baccalauréat* examination and go on to university, while continuing as far as possible to offer a wide range of subjects treated in adequate depth - a very difficult balance to achieve. The trend towards giving greater autonomy to the schools themselves has also been confirmed, although genuine decentralisation has been limited by France's adherence to some Republican principles, some of which have, in fact, been formally called into question, such as central state control of examinations, diplomas and university degrees and secondary school teacher recruitment.

Continuity and Change in the System

The education system in France is largely the responsibility of the state and thus of the Ministry of National Education.  Sometimes the Education Minister is assisted by another minister or junior minister responsible for a specific sector such as higher education or vocational training. Other ministries may also have responsibilities, for instance the Ministry of Agriculture for agricultural *lycées*.

Schools have always had great symbolic importance in France. One of their tasks has from the beginning been to develop and maintain national unity by providing all pupils with the same education, irrespective of their social and geographical origins, thereby, for example, integrating the children of foreign parents into French society. Four basic principles govern the public education service: equal access, non-discrimination, neutrality and secularity. Schools, whether at the primary, secondary or university level, may be freely established if these principles are respected and if

Public examinations are open to all pupils. Here, candidates are sitting a *baccalauréat* paper in the examinations hall in Arcueil (Val-de-Marne)

certain rules of health, safety and respect for public order are met. State education is free, except for registration fees at university, which are far lower than in most large industrialised nations. Only the state may define and establish diploma levels and degrees; public examinations are open to all pupils.

For many years, the education system was highly centralised, hierarchical and uniform in its organisation and operation. The situation began to change in the 1960s, when two trends emerged. On the one hand, syllabuses and teaching methods began to be brought up to date and decisions concerning the internal organisation of schools to be discussed at meetings of their *Conseils d'établissement*, which are composed of representatives of teachers, administrative and ancillary staff, parents, pupils and local authority officials, thereby involving them in decision-making. And, on the other, the state has had to take steps to cope with a substantial rise in pupil and student numbers, both for demographic reasons, and, more fundamentally, because of the growing length of courses and a deliberate government policy of increasingly extending access to *lycées* and universities designed to ensure that France has the skills it needs for its future development.

Nursery Schools: an Underestimated Success Story

French nursery schools, which have existed since 1887, are neither day nurseries (day care centres) nor kindergartens, but educational establishments for children aged from two to six. The majority of the teachers are women.

School attendance is not compulsory at this age but there is a strong demand for it. The situation in France is unusual in that 99% of three-year-olds attend nursery schools, most of which are state-run. Detailed studies have shown that attending school in early childhood has a favourable influence on children's subsequent education. For the 2.1 million children who attend them, nursery school teaches them to get on with others and develops their personality and language skills. It can also allow identification of any sensory, motor or learning difficulties so that they

Early learning means a more successful school career, so children are starting nursery school earlier and earlier. Here, pupils are being introduced to books and pictures at a nursery school in Tremblay-en-France (Seine-Saint-Denis)

can be treated early. It is extremely effective in helping children from disadvantaged backgrounds to integrate. Finally, older children can begin to develop reading skills.

The building and maintenance of nursery schools are the responsibility of the *communes*, which also supply ancillary staff. The teachers are employed by the Ministry of National Education.

New Challenges for Primary Schools

With rare exceptions, children start primary school at the age of six. State primary schools are locally-based: since 1833 the *commune*, or a group of *communes*, has been responsible for primary-school building, equipment and maintenance. Since the laws adopted in 1881-1882 at Jules Ferry's instigation, primary education has been compulsory and in state schools has been both secular and free of charge.

Teachers are state employees, generally recruited by competitive examination. Nowadays, both primary and secondary-school teachers are trained at university-level schools of education, the *Instituts universitaires de formation des maîtres* (IUFM). The primary-school teachers trained in the former specific primary-school teacher-training colleges, the *Écoles normales d'instituteurs*, are gradually being integrated into the new school teacher profession. Running costs and teachers' salaries in private schools under state contract are borne respectively by the *communes* and central government.

Children normally spend five years at primary school. The first three years - CP (*cours préparatoire*) and CE1/CE2 (*cours élémentaire* 1 and 2) - are coordinated with the last year of nursery school to provide a grounding in the basic skills. The next stage - CM1/CM2 (*cours moyen* 1 and 2) - takes the children up to the end of primary school, strengthening their grasp of the basics and, since the start of the 1998-1999 school year, including a compulsory introduction to a foreign language.

Playground games
at a primary school
in Vironchaux (Somme)

The primary school population is currently 6.4 million (including 800,000 in private schools) with 300,000 teaching staff. The number of pupils has fallen by nearly 900,000 over a period of 30 years, and this trend has become more marked since the start of the 1990s as a result of the fall in the birth rate since 1981-1982. This has led to a reduction in average class size, but it has also resulted in the closure of classes and sometimes schools (in the least populated areas), which threatens to exacerbate the drift away from rural areas, despite the introduction of school buses.

In some urban and suburban communities, primary schools have to cope with problems of cultural and linguistic diversity resulting from immigration. Children of foreign parents, who account for about 10% of primary-school pupils, are unequally distributed geographically: 97% of them attend state schools.

	1985		1997	
	in francs	%	in francs	%
Pre-primary (pre-elementary)	51,600	33.5	76,400	39.1
Primary (elementary)	102,300	66.5	119,200	60.9
Total	153,900	100	195,600	100

Rising cost of pre-primary and primary education per pupil (at 1997 prices). It now costs almost 200,000 francs to educate a pupil up to the standard required for the first year of *collège* (sixth form)

Collèges: a Vital Link

Over three million pupils currently attend almost 7,000 *collèges* [1] catering for the first four years of secondary education (approximately 11-14 years). *Collège* schooling is divided into stages, known as "cycles"1. The first year (sixth), the "adaptation stage", is followed by the "central stage" (fifth and fourth forms) and an "orientation stage" (third form). Since 1975 all children have entered a *collège*, whatever their level of achievement. Consequently, the number of *collège* pupils has increased by nearly a million in the last 30 years. Despite France's system of insisting on pupils who do not reach the required educational standard in the national curriculum repeating the year, the vast majority of pupils complete this first stage of secondary education before the school leaving age. Those who reach sixteen before finishing *collège* may legally leave school. 94% of all *collège* pupils go on to a general or technical *lycée* to prepare the *baccalauréat* or to a vocational *lycée* to prepare for a CAP (*certificat d'aptitude professionnel*, which sanctions training in a specific vocational skill) or BEP (*brevet d'enseignement professionnel*, which sanctions the completion of adequate training within a range of technical skills required in a particular trade, industrial, commercial, administrative or social field).

Collèges are currently attended by over three million pupils. Collège Victor Hugo in Noisy-le-Grand (Seine-Saint-Denis), with the Arène Picasso (designed by Nunez) in the background

Approximately 80% of pupils attend state *collèges*. As part of the decentralisation policy, the building, equipment, maintenance and operation of *collèges* are financed by the *départements*, whilst central government is responsible for recruiting, training and paying teachers, as well as their appointment and promotion in schools all over France. The state also supplies

[1] In the French system, the *collège* and *lycée* forms are numbered from 6 to 1 followed by *terminale*, with the youngest children, approximately 11 years of age, in form 6.

school books and equipment (IT, audiovisual, etc.). It grants additional funds to schools in so-called "priority education areas" (ZEPs) where a disadvantaged social and cultural environment makes educating the pupils especially difficult.

In 20 years the number of pupils in private *collèges* has increased by an average of 2.5%. In the case of private *collèges* which have association contracts with the state (only 10,000 pupils attend private institutions which do not have such contracts), the state pays all teachers' salaries. The schools' running expenses are shared between the state and the *département*.

Whereas in primary school one teacher covers every subject, each *collège* teacher generally teaches only one. In the first two years of the *collège*, pupils learn one modern foreign language and in the third year (fourth form) they choose a second. Nowadays, each school has to produce a development plan, intended to define its identity, for which it draws heavily on recommendations made at the national level, tailoring them to regional or even local situations and, where appropriate, to its pupils' specific needs.

The 1977 Haby reform establishing a "single *collège*" and then the abolition, in 1989, of a selection procedure at the end of the fifth form (12-13-year-olds) revolutionised the composition of *collège* classes, which are now mixed-ability. Before that, pupils experiencing difficulties had been steered towards special classes (pre-vocational, pre-apprenticeship, etc.). There are, of course, still support systems, reorientation classes (facilitating changes of courses at school) and special education sections, but considerable thought is being given by the Education Ministry and other partners to finding better ways of addressing the vital problem of bringing up to standard pupils who are having problems. Indeed, 85% of pupils who are a year behind when they start *collège* still manage to move on to the *lycée*, but only 8% of them go on to pass the *baccalauréat*.

*For **lycée** pupils, the objective of an 80% pass rate in the baccalauréat is in sight. Lycée Martin Luther King in Bussy-Saint-Georges (Seine-et-Marne)*

Lycées: Aiming at an 80% Baccalauréat Pass-rate

78% of *lycée* pupils (aged approximately 16 to 18) attend the 2,600 state lycées, which are of two types, general and vocational.

The curriculum in general *lycées* leads their one and a half million-plus students to either a general or a technical *baccalauréat*, often known as the bac, in three years (second, first, and *terminale* forms). The general *baccalauréat*, frequently modified over the years, is still a national examination seen as the first step to a university qualification; it has been restructured into three broad subject areas, known as "*séries*" – literature (L), science (S), and economics (ES). The technological *baccalauréat* is also divided into several *séries*: science and tertiary technologies (STT), science and industrial technologies (STI), science and laboratory technologies (STL) and medical and social sciences (SMS).

Vocational *lycées* prepare about 700,000 pupils for jobs in industry and the services sector. The three-year CAP courses have become far less popular, while the numbers of those preparing the two-year BEP are rising fast. A vocational *baccalauréat* was introduced at the end of 1985 and is now taken by over 100,000 pupils every year. The types and content of training courses offered by the vocational *lycées* are decided on at national level in conjunction with business and industry, but determining businesses' quantitative and qualitative requirements is more difficult in these vocational spheres than in purely academic ones. To ease this problem, the Education Ministry is trying to increase the number of sandwich courses and the use of continuous assessment.

The greatest increase in the school population has occurred in the *lycées* not only because of the arrival in them of the large numbers of young people born in the late seventies and early eighties but also, and chiefly, because of the government policy target of 80% of pupils reaching *baccalauréat* level. This contrasts with the 1950s, when fewer than 10% of young people attained this level and the 1980s when fewer than 30% did so. In 1997, almost 70% passed the exam and in 1998 the overall pass rate for all types of *bac* was 79%.

This skills training centre at Clermont (Oise) teaches the CAP (*Certificat d'Aptitude Professionnelle*) vocational certificate course in welding

The *lycée* network is determined at regional level within the framework of a regional education plan. The regions are responsible for the building, equipment and running of *lycées*, whilst central government pays the salaries of teaching and ancillary staff. It also provides teaching equipment and has invested heavily in IT equipment, with the current aim of giving all *lycées* access to the Internet. The regions have also made substantial financial contributions in the last ten years to the renovation and improvement of *lycée* buildings and the building of new schools.

Higher Education: Preparing the Third Millennium

In France, the term "higher education" covers all courses open only to students with the *baccalauréat*. In 1998 France's overall spending on higher education amounted to 95 billion francs ($15.8 billion), two and a half times more than twenty-five years ago, reflecting the need to cater for a spectacular increase in the number of students. There were 123,000 students in higher education in 1946, 850,000 in 1970, 1.2 million in 1980 and 2.1 million in 1998. Universities employ nearly 130,000 teaching and research staff.

For historical and technical reasons, some two-year post-*baccalauréat* courses are taught in the *lycées* and administered as a part of the secondary school system. This is the case essentially for the course leading to the BST (*brevets de techniciens supérieurs* - higher technical qualifications) prepared by over 200,000 students - three times as many as ten years ago - and for the 80,000 or so students who, instead of going straight to university, for which the entrance requirement is the *baccalauréat*, opt to

spend two years preparing the competitive entrance examination for the *grandes écoles*.

The first *grandes écoles* date from the 18th century, when the universities were going through a period of crisis. They were set up by the authorities in order to prepare candidates for competitive examinations for high-level government posts and by the professions to provide companies with the skills

INSA mechanical engineering school at Saint-Etienne-du-Rouvray (Seine-Maritime). Many new higher education establishments have opened since 1990 to meet a constantly rising demand

they needed for their development. Currently attached to various ministries, these institutions have over 200,000 students and cover all areas of learning and knowledge, from the pure sciences to the arts, and including the social sciences and engineering as well as literature, law and administration.

Some of these schools, including the most prestigious of them, were originally intended to train the top servants of the Republic, the "*grands corps de l'État*" – the *Écoles normales supérieures* for teachers, the *Polytechnique* and *Saint-Cyr* for the armed forces, the *École des Chartes* for public archivists, curators and librarians, and the *École nationale d'administration* (ENA), founded in 1945, for top civil servants. While retaining these objectives, most of these schools have broadened their courses and their students no longer automatically go into the civil service. The business and management schools among them, such as HEC (*Hautes études commerciales*), ESSEC (*Ecole supérieure de sciences économiques et commerciales*) and the *École supérieure de commerce*, and the engineering schools (ENSI) have recently been attracting ever growing numbers of applicants due to companies' increasing need for highly qualified staff.

The vast majority of students – about 1.5 million, of whom 10% come from overseas, mainly Africa – go to the universities, which are open to anyone with the *baccalauréat* or an equivalent qualification. By contrast, places at the *Instituts universitaires de technologie* (IUT) which prepare a two-year technology degree, are awarded following an application selection procedure; nearly 110,000 students are currently studying in IUTs.

The breakdown of students by subject is as follows: arts and social services 35%, law and economics 24%, science 20%, medicine, pharmacy and dentistry 14%, with the remainder either studying in IUTs or specialising in sport and physical education. As at primary and secondary level, studies are organised in "*cycles*", of which higher education has three. The first theoretically lasts two years and leads to a *diplôme d'études universitaires générales* or *diplôme d'études universitaires scientifiques et techniques* (DEUG - comparable to a Diploma in Higher Education); the second "*cycle*", also two years, leads first, after one year, to the *licence* (comparable to a bachelor's degree) and then, after a further year, to the *maîtrise* (comparable to a higher degree or master's). The third, one-year "*cycle*", open only to selected postgraduate students, leads either to a *diplôme d'études supérieures spécialisées* (DESS - in a specialised subject) or a *diplôme d'études approfondies* (DEA), a preparatory research qualification opening the way to a doctorat (PhD).

About 60% of students go on to the second *cycle*, after obtaining a DEUG, some taking longer than others - 28% in two years and 32% in three or more years.

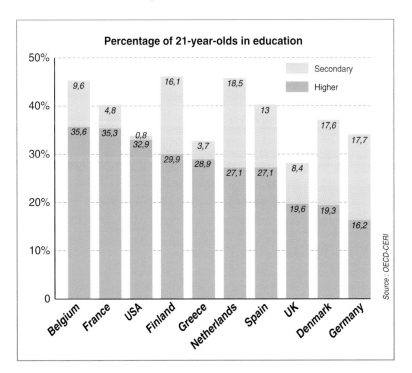

Percentage of 21-year-olds in education

Source : OECD-CERI

About 40% of 21-year-olds in France are in education, 35% of them at university

The organisation of French universities changed remarkably little between 1896, when they were reestablished by the Third Republic, and the Edgar Faure Law of 1968 which introduced a number of reforms following the student unrest of May 1968, and the 1984 Savary Law establishing administrative, pedagogical and financial independence and academic freedom for the universities. Two new bodies have replaced the traditional "faculty": the Training and Research Units (*unités de formation et de recherche* - UFRs) which are headed by a director whose task is to coordinate teaching; and the university itself, which brings together the UFRs, the related services of libraries, student careers guidance and information and professional development, as well as the schools and institutes which also form part of the university.

The *président* (principal or vice-chancellor) of each university, elected for five years, is assisted by administrative and financial services and manages a budget funded principally by the state, but also from other sources of its own (gifts, support from businesses, subsidies from local or regional government bodies, registration fees). The universities are autonomous, despite the fact that the bulk of their resources come from the state, their staff members are state employees and university directors of administration (*secrétaires-généraux*) are appointed by the Ministry of Education. Councils, elected by university staff and students, participate in university administration; one of these includes leading figures from outside the university.

Successive reforms in the 1980s and 1990s have sought to tailor university courses to the increasingly varied needs of the economy and society as a whole and make them more suitable for a larger, more heterogeneous student population. The most recent, in April 1997, instituted a semester system for universities, allowing students, if necessary, to change courses more quickly, greatly extended the number of modular courses and introduced a work experience module as an integral part of courses, and student tutorials. Further moves in this direction are being studied, with the aim of increasing decentralisation and giving a greater vocational focus to courses.

Universities and equivalent institutions vary greatly in size and are distributed very unevenly within the country. The city of Paris alone has nearly a sixth of France's students and the Paris region (i.e. Paris together with Versailles and Créteil) a quarter of them. Small universities usually offer many different subjects and contain a high proportion of "first-*cycle*" students. The major provincial metropolises each have several, often more specialised universities, with large numbers of second and third-*cycle* students: this is the case of Lille, Toulouse, Lyon, Aix-en-Provence, Bordeaux, Grenoble, Montpellier and Nancy.

The constant rise in the number of students and the financial drain on the local authorities which have to cater for this influx have led to university branches being set up in a great many medium-sized towns. To cope with these new requirements, the University 2000 Plan launched in spring 1990 provided for an additional investment of 32 billion francs ($5.3 billion), half from central government and half from local authorities, and in November 1997 Prime Minister Lionel Jospin announced a University 3000 Plan to meet the new demands of the next millennium. The new university branches act as a powerful lever for regional development and promoting new activities in the provinces. They encourage an "access for all" policy in higher educa-tion not only through a system of grants to the least well-off students, but also on a more general level, through greater provision of university can-teens and accommodation and general student support services.

To enable French universities to increase their international ties, especially within Europe, individual institutions are being given more autonomy in the management of their affairs. The same concern lay behind the Ministry of Education's policy of encouraging the creation of a small num-ber of European university centres. The idea is for universities located within the same town to form links among themselves and with major research teams, thereby creating dynamic, highly reputed centres, large enough to participate in European university exchange programmes and working in partnership with businesses. Such centres have, for example, been formed by the universities of Grenoble, Toulouse, Lille, and Rennes-Nantes.

Adapting Vocational Training

"Vocational training" takes a variety of forms. It includes studies leading to vocational qualifications, but also and perhaps more frequently, on-the-job training for first-time job-holders along with peri-ods of retraining, mid-career development and adaptation.

Vocational training comes under the joint aegis of the Min-istry of National Education, Research and Technology and the Ministry for Employment and Solidarity. The decentralisation legislation of the early 1980s gave the regions authority in this sphere except for programmes for priority groups – young people with no qualifications, job seekers, migrant workers and women wishing to return to work – which are state-run.

Training programmes are financed either from public sources, principally the state budget, or out of the mandatory 1.1% of the gross wage bill all employers with ten or more employees are required to contribute for the purpose. Employers can themselves use this sum to finance training for their employees or pay it into the *Fonds d'assurance formation* (state-managed training insurance fund), or to an approved training organisation or the *Trésor public* (public revenue department). The total annual cost of training, funded by all these bod-ies, comes to nearly 140 billion francs ($23.3 billion) and one in three members of the workforce receives some training each year.

Both private and public training bodies organise courses for private-sector workers, civil servants (in both these cases the employee is usually granted training leave) and the priority groups referred to above. Nearly 4,000 private institutions cover over 87% of the training course market, with public agencies competing with them under market conditions. Training institutions are of many types, with clearly distinct areas of operation. The association for the vocational training of adults (AFPA), which has over

100 centres, trains people for over 300 trades, giving priority to job seekers and employees working under contract or taking personal training leave. The GRETAs (*Groupements d'établissements de l'Education nationale*) offer training periods negotiated with companies, courses for priority groups (in particular, a fifth of all young people in their first jobs), introductory, advanced and career development courses. Private, non-profit-making bodies train a third of young people in their first jobs and nearly a third of the unemployed. Half of salaried workers receiving additional training do so in centres run by government departments or private, profit-making bodies.

Between 1983 and 1996, spending on professional development rose by 75%

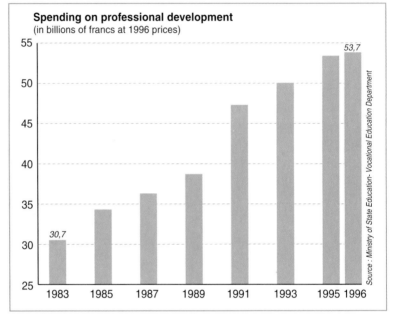

Spending on professional development
(in billions of francs at 1996 prices)

Source : Ministry of State Education- Vocational Education Department

Further reading:

Direction de l'évaluation et de la prospective, *L'état de l'école* (periodical report), Ministère de l'Éducation nationale.

" Le système éducatif ", *Cahiers français*, No 285, La Documentation française, March 1998.

M. Allaire, M.-T. Frank, *Politiques de l'éducation en France : de la maternelle au baccalauréat*, La Documentation française, Retour aux textes series, 1995.

B. Bouyx, *L'enseignement technologique et professionnel*, La Documentation française - CNDP, Systèmes éducatifs series, 1997.

R. Fauroux, G. Chacornac, *Pour l'école*, Commission de réflexion sur l'école, Calmann-Lévy-La Documentation française, 1996.

J. Fialaire, *L'école en Europe*, La Documentation française-IIAP, Vivre en Europe series, 1996.

R. Hérin, R. Rouault, V. Veschambre, *Atlas de la France scolaire : de la maternelle au lycée*, La Documentation française, Dynamiques du territoire series, 1994.

R. Périé, J. Simon, *Organisation et gestion de l'Éducation nationale*, Berger-Levrault, 1998.

C. Rault, *La formation professionnelle initiale*, in *Notes et Études documentaires*, No 4987, La Documentation française, 1994.

THE ECONOMY

14

Economic Policy

France is the world's fourth largest economic power and its fourth largest exporter. In 1997, its GDP (gross domestic product) was 8,183 billion francs ($1,363 billion) and its population has one of the highest standards of living in the world. This can partly be explained by the country's rapid economic growth since the Second World War. Benefiting from the development of the European Community, in which it is playing an essential role, and a buoyant foreign trade situation, the French economy has achieved an impressive metamorphosis over the past fifty years. Its agriculture has been modernised to such an extent that it can now often compete with the USA in a number of foreign markets; its industry has been restructured and encouraged to move into high-tech areas, whilst, supported by an impressive transport infrastructure, the tertiary sector, particularly banks, retailing and tourism, has become a spearhead of the national economy. (See next chapter for more detailed information about specific sectors.)

Changing Needs

The recession of the 1930s and the Second World War left the French economy completely drained. In 1945, infrastructures had been destroyed, plant and machinery were hopelessly outdated, the country was in a state of financial ruin and foreign trade was non-existent. But, like the other industrialised countries, from 1945 to 1974 France enjoyed a long phase of economic growth known as the *Trente Glorieuses* ("Thirty Glorious Years"), which enabled it to get the economy back on its feet and emerge from its former commercial isolation.

From 1945 to 1958, France set about rebuilding the country and modernising its industry. The state played an essential role in this process, through its national plans and the extension of the public sector. It took control of the major banks, the coal industry, gas and electricity distribution and some sectors of industry by nationalising companies like Renault. It also received American aid, under the Marshall Plan. The authorities initially made transport, energy production and heavy industry their top priorities. From 1948, production reached pre-war levels and the demand for labour was such that there was full employment. France became a consumer society and a high rate of population growth maintained domestic demand. In terms of trade, however, France remained relatively isolated, dealing chiefly with its former colonies. In 1958, exports represented only 9% of GDP and the former colonies accounted for a quarter of France's imports and almost a third of its exports.

From 1958 to 1973, the rate of growth accelerated, with an average annual growth rate of 5.5%, compared with 4.8% in Western Germany and 3.9% in the United States. Only Japan did better. In inflation-adjusted francs, GDP doubled during this period and industrial production increased by 5.7% per annum. Private firms followed the state in making investments and there was a first wave of mergers. Companies benefited from the low cost of energy and raw materials and devaluations of the national currency allowed them to remain competitive in foreign markets despite a higher level of inflation than in many competitor countries. Meanwhile, trade opened up considerably for France following decolonisation and, above all, entry into the European Coal and Steel Community (ECSC) in 1951 and the European Economic Community (EEC) in 1957. By 1973 the franc area countries (i.e. France's former colonies) accounted for only 3.5% of French imports and 5.1% of exports. In contrast, 76% of France's foreign trade was conducted with other industrialised countries, and 64% of flows were taking place within the EEC. The process of modernisation continued in agriculture and industry. The Government improved transport infrastructures, focusing particularly on motorways, and subsidised ambitious pro-

Percentage change in GDP at 1980 market prices, 1972-1997

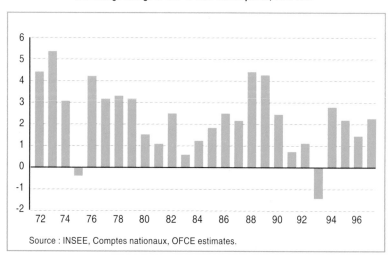

Source : INSEE, Comptes nationaux, OFCE estimates.

grammes of aircraft construction and nuclear energy production. The economic imbalance between Paris and the regions lessened as industry was decentralised and a nationwide town and country planning policy implemented.

The "Thirty Glorious Years" came to an end as monetary instability set in after the dollar's convertibility to gold was abandoned in 1971 and especially following the first oil crisis in 1973. The effects of a second sharp rise in oil prices in 1979 were exacerbated by the rising cost of the US dollar. France's energy bill rose spectacularly from 14 billion francs ($2.3 billion) in 1972 to 187 billion francs ($31 billion) in 1984. It was not until 1985 that the price of a barrel of oil and the rate of the dollar began to come down, thereby relieving this external pressure. These years saw the French growth rate slow down and, to make matters worse, there were sharp fluctuations from one year to the next. In order to become more competitive, companies increased productivity and cut jobs. Until the end of the 'eighties, France also had to cope with high inflation, which pushed up prices just as the country had to fight off competition on two fronts: from the United States and Japan in high-tech industries and from developing countries for everyday consumer goods. Certain sectors, like textiles, footwear, toys, iron and steel and electrical appliances, were badly hit by this competition and the impact was increased by the fact that these industries often constituted the main (and sometimes the only) economic activity of a region or a town. Their disappearance has had genuinely tragic social consequences, witness the chronically high levels of unemployment in the textile-manufacturing valleys of the Vosges and the former centres of the iron and steel industry of Valenciennes and Longwy.

Economic Reform

During the last few years, France has witnessed a distinct improvement in most economic indicators. As a result, it was able to meet the criteria set by the Treaty of Maastricht and was one of the eleven countries to join the Single Currency in 1999.

For a start, the growth rate improved. After a period of moderate growth between 1990 and 1996, it rose to 2.3% in 1997 and was close to 3% in 1998. This recovery reflects the healthy state of foreign markets, particularly in the industrial countries, which account for over 80% of France's foreign trade. It also underlines the growth of the domestic market since 1997, as a result both of increased demand on the part of households and of a rise in investments by businesses wishing to compensate for lack of investment over several years. Order books are filling up and businesses are rebuilding their stocks.

For a long time inflation was higher in France than in most of the countries with which it was trading, but it has now been reined in. Whereas prices were rising by as much as 14% per year in the early 'eighties, the rise was kept to below 3% in 1991 and the latest statistics show the downward trend continuing: 1.5% for 1996, 1.3% for 1997 and about 1% in 1998. This is the result of long-standing consensus and a policy of price stability waged continuously for more than a decade by successive governments from both left and right.

France's remarkable foreign trade figures are another favourable indicator for the national economy. There was a structural deficit in foreign trade until the beginning of the 1990s, but then the balance tipped in favour of an increasingly spectacular surplus — 31 billion francs ($5.1 billion) in 1992, 122 billion francs ($20 billion) in 1996 and 175 billion francs ($29 billion) in 1997. The figure has been positive for manufactured goods since 1992 and France has trade surpluses with most of its EU trading partners, which account for over 60% of its foreign trade.

However, unemployment remains a serious economic and social problem, as indeed in most European countries. The number of unemployed people has been rising alarmingly for over twenty years now: it was 430,000 in 1974, 1,400,000 in 1980, 2,483,000 in 1990 and almost 3,000,000 in 1998. The greatest job losses have been in the construction and manufacturing industries. Conversely, the number of jobs in the tertiary sector has increased, despite considerable gains in productivity. Combating unemployment has become the chief priority of all French governments, irrespective of their colour. For several months now, there has been a slight fall in unemployment due to a combination of economic recovery and job creation schemes, particularly reduced

Inflation defeated – retail price inflation, 1962-1997

Year-to-year % change*   * Rise in prices over the preceding 12 months

Source : INSEE

national insurance payments for low-paid employees. Nevertheless, it must be said that France has been less successful in combating unemployment than its principal partners.

Budget deficits are another major problem. As in neighbouring countries, sizeable deficits are a constant feature. The situation worsened sharply in the early 'nineties, but has been improving since 1994. At that time, spending requirements for financing the administrations accounted for 5.8% of the GDP: they subsequently fell to 4.2% in 1996, 3.1% in 1997 and 3% in 1998. This improvement is the result of curbs on spending by central government, local authorities and the social security system. Whereas in 1995 there was a budget deficit of 323 billion francs ($53.8 billion), in 1997 France succeeded in reducing its deficit to 268 billion francs ($44.6 billion). The French government, like those of the other European countries, has begun a programme to improve public finances known as the "convergence programme"; at the same time, it is taking selective action in sectors which are sensitive to economic cycles, so as to reduce unemployment and government debt. High levels of public spending mean that compulsory payments to the state are also high, whether they are extracted in the form of taxes or national insurance contributions and such spending inevitably increases the national debt, which currently amounts to 58% of the GDP. This may be lower than in most European countries, but interest payments now account for over 14% of budget spending.

An Advantageous European Environment

European integration has had a profound influence on the French economy. It has forced businesses to become more competitive not only in order to resist new challengers, but also to take advantage of the opportunities offered by such a huge market. In 1993 the principle of free movement of people, goods, services and capital came into effect with the establishment of the Single Market and opened up an economic area of 376 million consumers to French companies, benefiting all sectors of the national economy.

Construction of the Puymorens tunnel between France and Spain (here, western Pyrenees entrance to the tunnel) was partly financed by the EU

The Common Agricultural Policy (CAP) has been a vital factor in bringing French agriculture up to date. Based on the principles of free movement of goods, financial solidarity and preferential treatment for EC products, it has helped improve farmers' incomes, stimulated investment and accompanying rises in levels of production. The European Agricultural Guidance and Guarantee Fund (EAGGF), responsible for managing the CAP, channels substantial amounts of aid into rural development, modernisation of farms and land improvements. It also grants continuing support to agriculture in mountain regions and other disadvantaged areas. France is the foremost agricultural producer in Europe and receives over 55 billion francs ($9 billion) in the form of various categories of aid from the EAGGF every year.

In industry, free movement of goods and capital has given French companies a significant boost and has resulted in higher investment rates, a high level of financial concentration and an increase in the number of subsidiaries of French companies established abroad. Almost 40% of the latter are located in the European Union, with Germany, the United Kingdom and Spain being the most popular host countries. In addition, the EU has brought in a number of measures which are advantageous to French businesses. It has provided incentives to restructure ageing companies by offering various types of aid and by setting limits on imports. For example, under the Multifibre Arrangements (MFA), it succeeded in getting large-scale third-world textile exporters to agree to limit their exports to European countries. It also devotes considerable effort to promoting high-tech industries by encouraging cooperation between laboratories, universities and businesses in the member countries, and has financed numerous research programmes to help European research catch up with that in Japan and the USA. It also encourages SMEs (small and medium-sized enterprises) to develop a more international outlook within the EU, by providing them with structures for sharing information and working together on joint projects.

The tertiary sector has also benefited from Europeanisation. Through aids and loans, the European Community has had a hand in modernising transport networks, co-funding major civil engineering projects such as the Puymorens tunnel between France and Spain. Judicial and technical harmonisation and the advent of free competition have also helped bring the various modes of transport up to date. Freedom of movement has encouraged the growth of tourism in France, where four fifths of visitors are Europeans. It has also revitalised the banking and insurance sectors by spurring French companies to modernise and merge to stand up to foreign competition and attack other neighbouring markets.

European cooperation has also helped stabilise currencies and reduce fluctuations in exchange rates, which are damaging to the climate of healthy competition the Single Market needs to function properly. Under the EMS (European Monetary System) introduced in 1979, narrow margins were set for fluctuations in exchange rates between currencies and cooperation between the central banks of participating countries organised. The Treaty on European Union, which came into effect on 1 January 1993, committed France and its fellow member countries to a process leading to EMU (Economic and Monetary Union). This led to a degree of economic convergence between the member countries and in particular to a reduction of their budget deficits. The introduction of the euro on 1 January 1999 eliminates the hazards of fluctuating exchange rates and the costs of converting from one currency to another – considerably benefiting both individuals and businesses. Today, for France and its partners, EMU is a fundamental component of European integration.

Flourishing Businesses

The state plays an important role in the French economy. It is the number one employer, producer and customer in the country. It is also the leading transporter and owns the largest amounts of land and real estate.

The state defines the general outlines of economic policy through a planning system introduced in 1947. Although the Plan recommends rather than imposes the directions the economy should take, it has successfully guided investors towards priority sectors, as well as encouraging the construction of large-scale infrastructures and stimulating regional development. For a long time, the state also played a key role in production in that it controlled many businesses, but the see-sawing between left and right which has prevailed in French politics over the past twenty years has resulted in significant changes. First, state control was strengthened in 1982 by a wave of nationalisations designed to bring the country's means of production up to date and restructure companies. A quarter of industry and 90% of bank deposits came under state control. Then a right-wing majority was elected and, whilst it was in office (from 1986-1988), twelve or so companies were privatised. After a further period of left-wing government, the right came back to power in March 1993 and launched a further programme of privatisations, returning 21 large industrial concerns, banks and insurance companies to the private sector. This programme was pursued in 1995 with the privatisation of several industrial concerns like Péchiney, Usinor-Sacilor and Elf-Aquitaine and several banks and insurance companies like the BNP and the UAP. Since the left regained power in 1997, the state has reduced its share in several companies and is preparing to do so in others, as the forthcoming privatisation of Crédit Lyonnais demonstrates.

Industry has seen a significant trend towards concentration, which has led to the emergence of some major groups, although this is less marked than in many competitor countries. France has only nine companies among the world's 100 largest, far behind the USA (31) and Japan (21), and also behind Germany (12). The largest French company, Elf-Aquitaine, is only the 28th largest company worldwide. The leading French companies continue to be characterised by a complex framework of cross-holdings involving the country's major banks. They tend to rely less than their foreign competitors on the stock market to increase their capital, although in the last two decades the general public have shown great interest in stocks and shares, particularly following the many privatisations.

Whilst large companies have been reducing the size of their workforces, the SMEs, which are more flexible and can more easily adapt to rapid changes of strategy, have become the new spearheads of the national economy. Almost half France's industrial workforce now work in companies with fewer than 500 employees and these companies account for 42% of sales. Some of them, specialising in sectors which are booming, now occupy prime positions in the international market. This is, for example, the case for Zodiac (inflatable dinghies and emergency escape chutes for aeroplanes), Béneteau and Jeanneau (boating and sailing equipment) and Salomon and Rossignol (ski equipment). SMEs are particularly active in the agri-foodstuffs, construction and clothing sectors, but are as yet not sufficiently present in foreign markets, so the state is encouraging the development of both public and private initiatives to help them increase their exports.

Budget in 1998

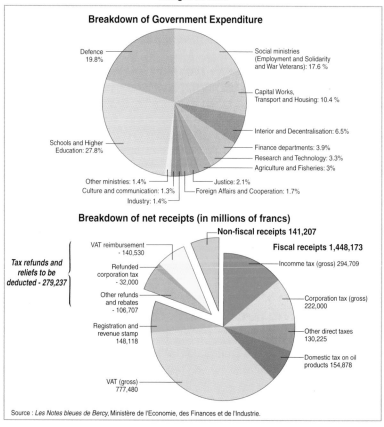

Breakdown of Government Expenditure

Defence 19.8%

Social ministries (Employment and Solidarity and War Veterans): 17.6 %

Capital Works, Transport and Housing: 10.4 %

Interior and Decentralisation: 6.5%

Schools and Higher Education: 27.8%

Finance departments: 3.9%

Research and Technology: 3.3%

Agriculture and Fisheries: 3%

Other ministries: 1.4%
Culture and communication: 1.3%
Industry: 1.4%

Justice: 2.1%
Foreign Affairs and Cooperation: 1.7%

Breakdown of net receipts (in millions of francs)

Non-fiscal receipts 141,207

Fiscal receipts 1,448,173

VAT reimbursement - 140,530

Incomme tax (gross) 294,709

Tax refunds and reliefs to be deducted - 279,237

Refunded corporation tax - 32,000

Corporation tax (gross) 222,000

Other refunds and rebates - 106,707

Other direct taxes 130,225

Registration and revenue stamp 148,118

Domestic tax on oil products 154,878

VAT (gross) 777,480

Source : *Les Notes bleues de Bercy*, Ministère de l'Economie, des Finances et de l'Industrie.

Modernisation has made French businesses more competitive. In addition, the presence of a skilled work force with wage costs 25% lower than in Germany (France's number one trading partner) is encouraging a large number of foreign firms to set up in France, especially in Alsace and Lorraine. Although wage costs are higher in France than in Italy, Spain and the United Kingdom, this handicap is wholly or partially compensated for by higher productivity. The situation is more delicate with regard to developing countries, where production costs are sometimes thirty or fifty times lower than in France, providing industrial firms with an incentive to relocate factories, particularly to South-East Asian countries. To try and limit the number doing so, the authorities are striving to cut labour costs by reducing some of the non-wage costs for employers and promoting the use of new technologies capable of bringing down production costs.

After the period of intense modernisation at the end of the 'seventies and in 1987-1988, investment slowed somewhat during the early 'nineties. Since 1997 it has again picked up. Businesses are taking advantage of the economic recovery, which is easier for them today now that they have more room for manoeuvre when it comes to borrowing and investment. Strengthening their capacity for innovation, investing in new technologies and moving into markets with a high growth potential are now seen by French businesses as the keys to economic success.

Further reading:

Annuaire statistique de la France, 1997 edition, INSEE, 1997.

Les tableaux de l'économie française 1999-2000, INSEE, 1999.

L'économie française. Rapport sur les comptes de la Nation 1999-2000, Le Livre de poche, 1999.

Le budget de l'État 1998, Les Éditions de Bercy, Ministère de l'Économie et des Finances, 1998.

Études économiques de l'OCDE, France, OCDE, 1997.

J.-F. Eck, *La France dans la nouvelle économie mondiale*, PUF, 1994.

S. Marti, V. Ragot, *L'euro en poche*, La Documentation française, 1998.

J.-P. Vesperini, *L'économie française sous la Ve République*, Économica, 1993.

Periodicals:

Cahiers français, La Documentation française; *Capital* (monthly); *L'Expansion* (fortnightly); *Le Nouvel Économiste* (weekly); *Le Revenu français* (weekly); *Valeurs actuelles* (weekly); *La Vie française* (weekly); *Problèmes économiques*, La Documentation française (weekly).

15

Key Economic Sectors

Agriculture

France is the EU's leading agricultural economy, ahead of Germany, accounting for 22% of the fifteen member states' total production. It is also the world's second largest exporter of agri-foodstuffs, behind the USA, and in 1997 had an agricultural trade surplus of over 50 billion francs ($8.3 billion). Although French agriculture now employs only 6% of the total workforce and accounts for only 2% of the national GDP, it is nonetheless one of France's most dynamic sectors. During the last three decades, it has undergone a remarkable modernisation leading to a spectacular increase in productivity and yields. This radical change has affected not only rural landscapes and production methods, but also people and their attitudes. The traditional farmers with their small family farms have been replaced by modern farmers running farms as businesses using modern technology and management methods.

An Ever-More Efficient Agriculture

33.4 million hectares of land – 55% of the country's surface area – is given over to farming. 61% of this is arable land, 35% grassland and 4% under crops, used especially for vineyards and orchards.

Agricultural modernisation has been accompanied by a steady trend towards concentration, with the number of farms falling from 1,588,000 to 735,000 between 1960 and 1997, but their average size doubling to 39 hectares. The combining of smaller holdings has chiefly benefited the really large farms of over 100 hectares. While these account for only 10% of the total number of farms, they now cover 40% of farmland. There are an especially large number of them in the Paris basin, especially on the rich soil of Beauce, Brie and Picardy, whilst the south-west and Mediterranean coastal areas still have many small farms. Keen to encourage the development of competitive operations, the state facilitates farm reorganisation through regional land agencies (SAFER - *Sociétés d'aménagement foncier et d'établissement rural*) which are entitled to buy land and earmark it for agricultural use. These agencies, which have

a first option to purchase, buy land, sometimes make improvements and then re-sell to new farmers or farmers wishing to expand. The state also encourages elderly farmers to retire and helps young farmers get started. It also encourages cooperation between farmers, especially through GAEC (*groupements agricoles d'exploitation en commun* - agricultural partnership schemes). Farmers running their own farms, who long

Large-scale cereal farming – plaine de la Beauce (Eure-et-Loir)

dominated the agricultural scene, are now outnumbered by tenant farmers, who work 63% of French farmland. At the same time, the system of payment of rent in kind has practically disappeared from the French countryside.

This concentration of units has affected the agricultural landscape. 40% of agricultural land has been reparcelled, facilitating the creation of vast geometrical fields suitable for mechanised farming. This has particularly been the case in northern and eastern France. In western regions such as Brittany, it has led to the destruction of most of the hedges which used to be a feature of mixed wood and pasture land. However, because of the presence of many specialised farms and continued existence of large numbers of owner-run farms, the South has seen less restructuring. Irrigation and land drainage schemes are increasingly being developed, especially in the south-west and the Paris basin.

Today's larger holdings are also better equipped. France now has 1,310,000 tractors and many farmers own several. The use of other types of agricultural machinery has also increased, e.g. combine harvesters, grape harvesters, potato and sugar-beet lifters. New farm equipment is constantly coming on the market, such as the modern vine-pruning machines, and this mechanisation explains the rapid fall in the numbers of farm workers, from 2,700,000 in 1970 to 1,080,000 today.

The development of agricultural production also reflects the growing recourse to chemicals. The amount of chemical fertiliser used has increased sixfold since 1950 and extensive use of plant-health products has eliminated most of the diseases, weeds and parasites which used to affect harvests. French production is now amongst the highest in the world, especially now that genetic research has led to the development of plant varieties with increasingly high yields. Livestock farming has made similarly remarkable strides. Vaccinations, milk monitoring and selective breeding through artificial insemination have contributed to increased milk yields and meat production and improvements in product quality.

Crops

Just over half of France's agricultural earnings come from crops, of which the most important remains cereals, both in terms of total output and of exports. Producing 36 million tonnes of wheat, France is the fourth largest wheat producer in the world and the leading one in the EU. Wheat is grown mainly on the rich soil of the Paris basin, Berry and the Toulouse area. With 17 million tonnes in 1997, maize production now outstrips that of barley which has not risen over the last decade (10 million tonnes). Maize, which used to be grown only in the south-west, has spread to the Paris basin thanks to irrigation using sprinkler systems and the development of new hybrid varieties. Cultivation of other grains, such as oats and rye, is rapidly declining.

However, production of oilseeds and protein-giving plants, boosted by high demand from industry, has been rising over the last fifteen years. Oilseed rape, mainly grown north of the Loire, and sunflowers, grown in the south-west and Paris basin, make up the bulk of this output. More recently, more land has been planted with soya in the Midi and the Rhône valley.

Sugar beet, often grown in association with cereals, is an extremely important crop in France. In 1997 France produced 34.2 million tonnes and is the world's leading producer, ahead of Germany. In addition, cane sugar is produced in Martinique, Guadeloupe and Réunion. Fewer potatoes, another industrial crop, are now being grown, even though agri-foodstuffs companies are now using them in a wider variety of ways.

A smaller proportion of agricultural land is devoted to specialised crops, but these often generate a high income per hectare. This is particularly true of vineyards. In 1997, French wine production totalled 56 million hectolitres, surpassing that of Italy (54 million). France is also the leading producer of quality wines, which are produced in clearly defined areas in which growers are entitled to use an *Appellation d'origine contrôlée* (AOC) label which attests to the geographical origin of the wine. This applies especially to Champagne, the Bordeaux area, Burgundy and the Loire and Rhône valleys. Elsewhere, as in Armagnac and the Cognac area, grapes are used to make France's renowned brandies. In the Languedoc, which mainly produces table wines, production has been substantially restructured to improve the quality of wines by changing to new types of vine and reducing the yields.

France is the third largest producer of fruit and vegetables in the European Union, behind Italy and Spain. Production is mainly concentrated in the Mediterranean regions such as Roussillon and Comtat Venaissin, the Garonne and Loire valleys and the market-gardening belts around the major conurbations. Flowers are grown mainly in the coastal areas and low-lying valleys of Provence.

Livestock

France is also the EU's leading meat producer. It has the largest national herd of cattle (20.6 million head), mainly concentrated in the Atlantic coastal regions, such as Normandy,

Brittany, Pays de la Loire and Poitou-Charentes, where grass grows quickly in the damp maritime climate. Cattle are also farmed in medium-mountains areas with a humid climate such as the Jura and northern Pre-Alps. All these regions concentrate mainly on dairy production. Although this is still regulated by European quotas intended to avoid surpluses, France is one of the world's leading cheese and butter producers. The same regions also produce a substantial proportion of French beef, but livestock fattening is concentrated in fertile areas with lush meadows, like Charolais and the Limousin edge of the Massif Central.

France is the EU's leading beef producer: the Les Essarts GAEC (agricultural partnership scheme) in Plan (Isère)

Pig numbers in France, currently exceeding 15 million, are the second highest in the EU (behind Germany), 50% up on 1970. As in other EU countries, consumption of pork, which is cheaper than other meats, is rising rapidly (34.2 kilos per inhabitant) and now even surpasses that of beef (26 kilos per inhabitant). Traditional pig farms have been replaced by industrial piggeries, concentrated mainly in the north and Brittany. Poultry farming has seen a similar expansion and there are now many large battery farms in the west and south-west. However, in response to consumer demand, some farms are specialising in quality production guaranteed by special labels, for example, *foie gras* in Alsace and the south-west, and chickens in Bresse.

Sheep-farming has picked up to a certain extent over the past two decades, benefiting from increased demand for meat and for sheep's milk cheeses like Roquefort. However, the size of the national flock remains modest, at 10 million head. It is concentrated mainly in southern regions like the Causses, Southern Alps, Basque Country and Corsica. In the west, lamb raised on the salt meadows of Brittany and Normandy is much prized.

Agri-foodstuffs Industry

The agri-foodstuffs industry is agriculture's chief customer. One of the French economy's strong points, it has a turnover of over 750 billion francs ($125 billion), over half of which is generated by the processing of animal products (meat and dairy sectors combined); the soft and alcoholic beverages, fruit and vegetables and animal feed products sectors also report healthy sales figures. With almost 400,000 employees, the flourishing agri-foodstuffs sector is France's third largest industrial employer and includes 4,200 companies, of which many are SMEs (small and medium-sized enterprises) or farming co-operatives.

Three of the sectors big names are Générale des Grandes Sources, Miko and Fromageries Bel.

In addition, this sector is highly geared to the export market and achieved a record trade surplus of 50 billion francs ($8.3 billion) in 1997. Wines and spirits topped the list of exported products with a trade surplus of 31 billion francs in 1997 ($5.1 billion), followed by cereals with one of 25 billion francs, ($4 billion) and dairy products with one of 13 billion francs ($2 billion).

Working towards New Goals

French agriculture owes its success in part to the EU's Common Agricultural Policy (CAP), which provides substantial support for production and is helping to bring rural areas up to date by financing various improvements such as land drainage and the building of country roads. Rapidly increasing yields have led in France, as in most other European countries, to large surpluses, despite twenty years of regulatory measures. This is why, since its most recent reform in 1992, the CAP has moved towards lowering guaranteed prices to bring them more into line with world prices and thus facilitate exports. It is also increasing aid to small farmers and encouraging the development of extensive farming, which shows greater respect for the environment. To curb the depopulation of some rural areas, the CAP is also encouraging farmers to diversify, in particular by giving grants for re-planting woodland and promoting farm holidays. True, the French farmer of the year 2000 is still primarily a producer, but he or she is being called upon to play an increasingly active role in maintaining the ecological balance of the countryside.

Energy

Although France has few resources, it now manages to satisfy 50% of its total energy needs, compared with only 24% in 1973. This means that France's energy independence is comparable to Germany's and very much greater than that of Italy or Japan. The improvement in France's energy situation in recent years stems primarily from the rapid development of its nuclear power generation industry, now second only to that of the United States, but is also due to a slow-down in the growth of consumption. After doubling every decade during the boom years, the growth in energy consumption has been slowed down by the austerity measures adopted from 1973 onwards and by the decline of industries like steel which have a high energy consumption. National energy consumption stood at 237 million TOE (tonne oil equivalent) in 1997, compared with 183 million in 1973. Although France is still heavily dependent on outside producers (for 50% of its needs), the energy bill has gone down. In 1997 it was 85 billion francs ($14.1 billion dollars) compared with 187 billion francs in 1984, when it was at a record high.

Primary energy consumption in 1979 and 1998

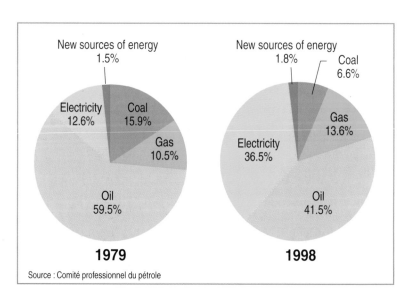

New sources of energy 1.5%

Electricity 12.6%
Coal 15.9%
Gas 10.5%
Oil 59.5%

1979

New sources of energy 1.8%
Coal 6.6%
Gas 13.6%
Electricity 36.5%
Oil 41.5%

1998

Source : Comité professionnel du pétrole

Heavy Dependence on Hydrocarbons

France is still heavily dependent on hydrocarbons. Its Les Landes and Brie oilfields produce only 2.1 million tonnes of petroleum, whereas it imports 83 million tonnes of crude oil and 25 million tonnes of refined petroleum products. Middle Eastern countries still supply 38.7% of France's crude oil imports, Saudi Arabia 22%. However, the policy of diversifying suppliers has put North Sea countries in second place (35%).

Natural gas production is concentrated in the southwest. Gas reserves at Lacq, which previously provided over 50% of the natural gas used in France, are now running out and produce only 3 billion m^3. To compensate for the decline in production, France has increased its purchases of gas from other countries and signed many long-term contracts to guarantee supplies. It imports gas from the CIS (33%), Algeria (22%), Norway (30%) and the Netherlands (15%).

World's Second Largest Nuclear Industry

Electricity production in France has increased almost tenfold during the past 43 years, reaching 490 TWh (terawatt hours) in 1998 compared with 50 in 1955, and now satisfies over 40% of the country's total energy requirements. Electricité de France (EDF) has become one of the world's leading electricity companies. It exports over 72 billion kWh (kilowatt hours) every year. This is the result of the policy of developing nuclear power generation plants conducted since 1974. Nuclear power now accounts for 75% of France's total electricity production. EDF has 57 nuclear reactors generating a total output of 60,000 MW (megawatts). The nuclear power stations are located on the Loire and Rhône rivers. The Creys-Malville Superphénix fast breeder reactor fuelled by plutonium has now been shut down.

Conventional power stations now provide only 11% of France's electricity.

Electricity generated by nuclear power satisfies 40% of France's energy requirements: Dampierre-en-Burly nuclear power station (Loiret)

Hydroelectric power stations in the Alps, Pyrenees and Massif Central now supply 13% of France's electricity, compared with 55.7% in 1960.

Inexorable Decline of Coal

Coal now accounts for only 6.6% of total energy consumption, as against 22.7% in 1970. After peaking at 60 Mt (million tonnes) in 1958, production has steadily declined, falling to 7 Mt, plus 900,000 tonnes of lignite, in 1997. The mines of the Nord-Pas-de-Calais region have been closed since 1990 and all the others, both in Lorraine and around the edges of the Massif Central, will have done so by 2005. Because of the low productivity of France's coalfields, the bulk of the coal used by power stations and blast-furnaces is now imported. The United States, Australia and South Africa are the chief suppliers.

Still Marginal Role of New Energy Sources

New energy sources provide only 3.6% of the energy consumed in France, despite the research efforts carried out in this field. However, geothermal energy is used to heat over 200,000 homes in the Paris area and the south-west, and solar energy to heat houses in the southern regions. The role of wind-power and biomass also remains modest. However, the past few years have seen the emergence of new fuels such as ethanol and diester, extracted from oilseed rape and used by buses in several large towns.

Industry

France is Europe's second largest industrial power and the world's fourth largest behind the USA, Japan and Germany. The manufacturing sector, including construction and civil engineering, accounts for 29% of jobs, 40% of investments and almost 80% of French exports. But although industrial output has quadrupled since 1950, nearly 1.5 million jobs have been lost during the past twenty years. This shrinkage reflects not only steadily rising productivity, but also the major restructuring of industry in the wake of the oil crises and globalisation of the economy. In this respect, French industry has seen a rapid concentration of its firms and a sharp rise in direct investments abroad. French companies now control 15,788 subsidiaries outside France, employing 2,548,000 people. These investments allow the companies concerned to grow to the critical size needed to break into new markets; the same is true of take-overs of foreign companies such as the acquisition by Michelin of Uniroyal and by Alcatel-Alstom of the American ITT group. On the other hand, 2,860 companies controlled by foreign capital, of which the majority come from the USA, Germany, Switzerland and the UK, are responsible for 28% of France's output, 24% of the jobs and 30% of its manufacturing sector. France is the third largest destination of inward investment in the world, behind the USA and UK, above all in the fields of information technology, pharmaceuticals, machine-tools and precision instruments.

The manufacturing industry as a whole has for some years had a comfortable trade surplus. This is due not only to French skills in traditional industrial sectors like the automotive, railway locomotive and rolling stock industries, haute couture and agri-foodstuffs, but also to France's success in high-tech industries like nuclear power, telecommunications and aerospace.

Traditional Industries

The importance of heavy industry, long regarded as symbolising a country's economic might, is gradually diminishing in France, as in other developed countries. Stagnating demand and growing competition from other countries have led to significant reductions in production capacity and transformed the geographical distribution of plants.

The steel industry, which has an annual output of 17 million tonnes, is the twelfth largest in the world and fourth largest in the European Union, behind Germany, Italy and the UK. Production has decreased by over a third since 1974 and the workforce by 70%. This downward trend reflects the combined effects of the economic crisis, competition from other products such as aluminium and plastics, and the emergence of serious new rivals like the East European countries, Brazil and South Korea. Thanks to measures to reduce capacity and for restructuring adopted in the European Union framework, firms have modernised their plants, concentrated production in the most profitable sites and restored their financial health. The steel industry, marked by the rapid growth in the production of oxygen-steel, is dominated by the Usinor-Sacilor group, the fourth largest in the world. Over 45% of French steel production is now carried out in the Nord-Pas-de-Calais region, and especially in the major Dunkirk steel centre, which has taken over from the former inland plants. Similarly, in Lorraine, production is concentrated in the Moselle valley, for example

Removal of foundry plates from moulds in the Péchiney aluminium plant in Dunkirk (Nord)

at Gandrange, south of Thionville. There are also plants outside the steel-making centres such as that of Fos-sur-mer, near Marseilles, and Ugine in the Alps.

The aluminium industry, originally based in the Alps and Pyrenees near hydroelectric power stations, is now centred in areas near ports, which are more convenient for receiving shipments of imported bauxite. The most important French aluminium manufacturer and the third largest in the world is Pechiney, which also has several factories abroad, including in Australia, the USA and Greece. Privatised at the end of 1995, it has a state-of-the-art plant at Dunkirk, near the Gravelines nuclear power station. It has upgraded its production by manufacturing finished products and in 1988 took control of the major American packaging group, American Can.

Amongst the first-generation industries, the textiles and clothing sectors still employ 254,000 people and have a total turnover of over 170 billion francs ($28 billion). Although they export a third of their output, these industries recorded a trade deficit of 26 billion francs ($4.3 billion) in 1997 and, above all, have shed over 250,000 workers since 1974. They are suffering from the slow growth in domestic demand and above all from ever fiercer international competition from Italy, Germany and especially from Eastern Europe, the Mediterranean basin countries and south-east Asia, which offer far lower production costs than France and have been attracting an increasing number of French firms to relocate there.

Upstream, the textile industry as such, including in particular spinning, weaving, printing and rug and carpet manufacture, is still traditionally capital-intensive. It is dominated by large companies such as Chargeurs-Textiles, the leading world group in the wool trade, and DMC, a company based in Mulhouse specialising in cotton. These firms work with imported raw materials such as cotton and wool, but especially with man-made fibres. Operating alongside these major groups are small and medium-sized family businesses. To keep up with their competitors, textile companies have begun a process of financial and technical concentration and invested heavily in modernising their equipment to improve productivity. In many cases, textile industries are still in their original locations – Roubaix-Tourcoing and Armentières for spinning and weaving wool and cotton, Mulhouse for cotton and printed fabric, the Lyon region for silk and synthetic fibres and Troyes for hosiery.

Downstream, the clothing industry, however, remains a labour-intensive sector in the hands of a large number of SMEs, some more specialised than others, concentrated in the large conurbations of the Nord-Pas-de-Calais, Rhône-Alpes and Ile-de-France regions. In a bid to become more competitive, companies are not only making increasing use of high-tech production methods such as marking out fabrics by computer and cutting by laser or pressurised water-jet, but are also increasingly relocating abroad. They are also benefiting from the agreements concluded between developed countries and the main third world textile exporters under the multifibre arrangements (MFA). These arrangements, which are scheduled gradually to be phased out in the framework of the World Trade Organisation, allow the temporary imposition of limits to the quantities of cheap textile imports. Other firms, particularly in the Sentier district in Paris, specialise in customer-led production, capable of responding quickly to the rapid changes in fashion.

Haute couture: a fitting at the house of Christian Dior

Like the textiles industry, **leather goods manufacturers** have to compete with low-wage countries, especially in the case of bottom-of-the-range products. Shoe production in France has fallen by a third since 1970 and glove-making has lost nine tenths of its workforce over the past 25 years. Areas which specialised in these industries, like Romans and Fougères, have been hard hit by this decline.

The Normandy bridge, built by the French Bouygues and Campenon-Bernard groups and a Danish company, spans the Seine estuary; its main span is 856 metres long and at its highest point is 52 metres above the Seine

The construction and civil engineering industries employ 1.4 million people directly and provide almost as many spin-off jobs. Excellent barometer of changes in the economic situation, this sector has shed a large number of jobs in recent years, but is now picking up slightly. It has a turnover of almost 800 billion francs ($133.3 billion). **Civil engineering** is carried out almost exclusively by large companies, and the sector has become much more concentrated during the last two decades. The largest firms are Bouygues, the SGE (Société Générale d'Entreprise), Dumez-GTM, Eiffage, Spie-Batignolles and Sogea, which all make use of increasingly sophisticated technology, including prestressed

reinforced concrete, cable-stayed bridges and off-shore platforms. Inside France, they undertake construction work ranging from motorways to the Stade de France, the Normandy bridge and the Puymorens tunnel. They are also very active abroad, where they often have to compete with foreign groups, including those of the newly industrialised countries. La Lyonnaise des Eaux and La Générale des Eaux (now renamed Vivendi) water companies have won many contracts abroad for the installation of water supply and treatment systems in large metropolises like Buenos Aires and Beijing.

By contrast, the **building trade** is very fragmented, with its 30,000 SMEs. To improve productivity, these firms are industrialising their construction processes, especially for roof structures, doors and window frames and joinery. The building trade is directly affected by the level of government support for home building, in the form of various grants and of loans with interest-rate subsidies, totalling some 120 billion francs per year. However, the number of starts has sharply declined during the past twenty years or so, from 556,000 in 1973 to just under 300,000 in 1997. Admittedly, the demographic pressure has eased.

Capital Goods

Renault Scénic automated assembly line: welding of the bodywork

The **capital goods** sectors, including the automotive industry, are an essential part of France's industrial fabric. They generate a turnover of over 1,200 billion francs ($200 billion) and employ 1.5 million people. Whilst several branches of this sector, such as shipbuilding, machine-tools and motorcycle and bicycle manufacturing, have significantly declined in the face of foreign competition, others are positively thriving.

A notable success is the automotive industry, which recorded a trade surplus of almost 31 billion francs ($5 billion) in 1997. France is the world's third largest exporter of private cars; it produces 3.4 million cars and over 500,000 commercial vehicles. This makes it the fourth largest vehicle manufacturer in the world. Over 350,000 people are directly employed in car manufacturing, with 2.6 million spin-off jobs, which makes the sector an extremely important one for the national economy. Virtually all the vehicles are produced by Renault and the private group PSA, which controls Peugeot and Citroën. As regards car parts, a few large groups have emerged from a concentration of manufacturers, such as Michelin, the world's leading tyre manufacturer since it bought Uniroyal, Valéo, which specialises in electrical fittings, and Epéda-Bertrand Faure, which makes seats.

French motor manufacturers export more than 60% of their output, but have lost 40% of the domestic market to their competitors, especially Germany and Italy. In addition, an agreement between the European Union and Japan has lifted restrictions on imports of Japanese cars as of 1999. To become more competitive, French manufacturers have invested massively in robotisation, which has resulted in large numbers of redundancies. They have also increased the number of technical cooperation agreements with other firms, moved to just-in-time production and developed their presence in foreign markets, particularly Spain, Portugal and Brazil.

France's **shipbuilding industry** has shrunk considerably, having fallen victim to the over-capacity of the world fleet and competition from Asian shipyards. A world leader in the 1970s, French shipbuilding is today a marginal player. Some shipyards, such as Chantiers de l'Atlantique at Saint-Nazaire and the Ateliers and Chantiers du Havre have specialised in building cruise liners and LPG tankers. France is also one of the leaders in the boating and sailing equipment industry, thanks to the Bénéteau and Jeanneau boatyards in Vendée.

France's **chemicals and chemical products industry** is the world's fourth largest, with an annual turnover of over 430 billion francs ($71 billion) and a labour force of 250,000. The chemicals industry in the strict sense of the term is concerned with the processing of raw materials found in France, such as potash (from Alsace), sulphur (Lacq) and salt (Lorraine and the Camargue) and of imported products, hence the concentration of some activities around ports. The petrochemicals sector, dominated by the Compagnie française des pétroles (CFP-Total) and Elf-Aquitaine, has taken over from the former organic chemistry industry. The sector is dominated by Orkem, a former subsidiary of Charbonnages de France, Atochem, which belongs to the Elf group, Rhône-Poulenc and Air liquide, the world leader in industrial gases with subsidiaries in over 50 countries. Nevertheless, engaged principally in the manufacture of fertilisers, plastics and synthetic fibres, the chemicals industry is experiencing a period of low growth.

France is one of the world leaders in the boating and sailing equipment industry: boatyard in Lorient (Morbihan)

By contrast, the **chemical products and pharmaceuticals** sectors are booming, with trade surpluses exceeding 50 billion francs ($8.3 billion). Because of the high level of investment and costly research required, they are dominated by large groups such as Procter and Gamble, Unilever and Colgate-Palmolive for soap and detergent products and the French firm L'Oréal for perfumes and beauty products - a sector in which famous perfume manufacturers such as Saint-Laùrent and Chanel also perform well. Pharmaceuticals laboratories tend to belong to the major groups like Rhône-Poulenc, which has taken control of the American firm Rorer and is now the world's seventh-largest pharmaceutical firm. Synthélabo, which is part of the L'Oréal group, has taken over the Delagrange and Delalande laboratories. Sanofi, a subsidiary of Elf-Aquitaine, is another major player in this sector.

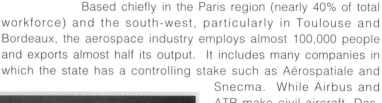

High-Tech Industries

Dependent not only on constant technical innovation, but also on high levels of research and a highly skilled workforce, the high-tech industries currently provide 20% of industrial jobs and exports. France is one of the most successful countries in the aerospace and defence industries. To meet the increasingly stiff international competition and reduce research and production costs, French companies have developed links with their counterparts in other countries. For example, the Airbus Programme is the result of cooperation between France, Germany, the United Kingdom and Spain and Aérospatiale is working with the Italian firm Alenia on the ATR (avion de transport régional - regional transport aircraft).

Successful launch of the Ariane 5 rocket from the Kourou centre in French Guiana, October 1997

Based chiefly in the Paris region (nearly 40% of total workforce) and the south-west, particularly in Toulouse and Bordeaux, the aerospace industry employs almost 100,000 people and exports almost half its output. It includes many companies in which the state has a controlling stake such as Aérospatiale and

Snecma. While Airbus and ATR make civil aircraft, Dassault-Industrie specialises in military aircraft such as the Mirage and the Rafale, and executive planes like the Falcon. Snecma, in partnership with the American firm General Electric, produces jet engines and other aero-engines.

Industrial space activities have also burgeoned in the framework of a European programme involving fifteen countries including Norway and Switzerland, which are not in the European Union. This is largely due to the success of the Arianespace programme, which has a very full order-book for the next few years for Ariane 5, which can place a 6-tonne payload into orbit, 2 tonnes more than was the case for Ariane 4. It owes its success to the reliability of its launch vehicles, which are winning it many foreign clients, despite the competition from the USA, Russia and more recently China. The rockets are launched from the Kourou centre in French Guiana. France is also active in the field of telecommunications and observation satellites, such as SPOT and Hélios, built by Matra Espace, Alcatel Espace and Aérospatiale Espace.

The electronics and electrical equipment sectors both produce a very wide range of products. They are also dominated by large companies and depend to a large extent on business from the public sector. Alcatel-Alstom, which has acquired a large number of companies over the past ten years, is still the world leader in telecommunications. In addition to being a major railway equipment (TGV) manufacturer, Alstom specialises in equipment for power stations and is the world's number one producer of combined-cycle turbine generators. Thomson's product range is vast, ranging from military electronics, with Thomson-CSF, to domestic appliances and other consumer equipment, with Thomson Multimédia. Schneider is a major company in the electromechanical sector and Legrand is the world leader in electrical equipment.

While France is in a strong position in telecommunications and telematics, largely due to France Telecom, the picture is less rosy when it comes to information technology. Admittedly, the software and services industry is very active with Cap Gemini-Sogeti, but France depends largely on foreign suppliers of micro-processors, and is subject to competition from the US and Japan, with their larger domestic markets. SGS-Thomson is Europe's third largest microchip manufacturer, but accounts for only 3% of world production. Although there is a trade surplus in electrical equipment and telecommunications this does not make up for the deficits in the computer and consumer electronics sectors.

For some years now, the weapons industry has been seeing a marked slowdown in the wake of the end of the Cold War and cuts in the defence budget. France is the fifth largest arms exporter world-wide and its trade surplus has been averaging over 30 billion francs ($5 billion). This is a strategic, high-tech industry which is heavily dependent on the government, which decides on procurement programmes through the intermediary of the Délégation générale à l'armement (weapons procurement agency) and controls exports. It is dominated by large companies: GIAT-Industries for land-based equipment, Dassault and Aérospatiale for aircraft and Aérospatiale, Thomson-CSF and Matra for missiles. To counteract excessive production capacity and the high cost of some projects, French companies are merging - for instance, Aérospatiale and Matra Hautes Technologies merged in 1998 - and increasing the number of joint ventures with their counterparts in other European countries, for example Eurocopter for the production of a fighter helicopter. The bulk of the industry is concentrated in Ile-de-France, Brittany, the south-west and the Provence-Alpes-Côte d'Azur region.

The French **biotechnology industry** is one in which the stakes are high and in which France is well-placed, be it in the area of fermentation, flavourings or the genetic engineering used especially in agriculture to develop new seeds. Biotechnology is a very varied field with spin-offs in many economic sectors: pharmaceuticals, with antibiotics, the agri-foodstuffs industry, with the use of enzymes in the dairy industry, horticulture, with the in vitro cultivation already extensively used by the rose-grower Delbard, and

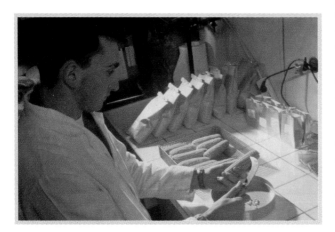

the energy and environmental industries, with the production of diester and ethanol. Indeed, the green-technology industry now has a turnover of 30 billion francs ($5 billion). Water treatment is the leading activity, followed by air purification and waste processing. Many specialist organisations are involved in research in this area, including national bodies such as Inserm, INRA and the Pasteur Institute, and major industrial groups: firms in the agri-foodstuffs industry like BSN, chemicals firms like Rhône-Poulenc and Lafarge-Coppée, oil companies like Elf-Sanofi and pharmaceuticals companies such as Roussel-UCLAF.

At INRA, the French national institute for agronomic research (Gif-sur-Yvette, Essonne), a scientist selects seed for transgenic hybridisation to improve varieties of maize

A New Industrial Map

The geographical distribution of French industry remains very uneven. There is still a clear divide between the France north-east of a line between Le Havre and Marseille and south-western France, where the industrialisation, more recent, remains unobtrusive. But the divide, which was very sharp in the 1950s, is nevertheless quite quickly becoming blurred. Indeed, the industrial decentralisation policy conducted in the 'sixties and 'seventies helped bring industry to the western regions, with car plants in Caen,

Rennes and Le Mans, and electronics and electrical goods manufacturing in northern Brittany. The regions around the edge of the Paris basin, and especially Centre and Burgundy, also benefited considerably from these measures. All in all, over a million jobs were created in the provinces and a third of jobs in industry are now located south-west of a line between Le Havre and Marseille, with the Paris area now accounting for only 20% (compared with 25% in 1950). Without going so far as saying that the situation has been totally reversed, industrial activity now clearly seems to be shared more equally between the various parts of France, with this trend accelerated by the different developments of the sectors.

The old industrial heartlands, which relied on first- or second-generation industries, like the Nord and Lorraine, are in crisis. Jobs in manufacturing are fast disappearing, resulting in growing areas of industrial wasteland. These areas are now being deserted. The other industrial centres, such as the Paris area and Rhône-Alpes, have not been hit quite so hard by the economic crisis. This is because their industrial base is more varied and they are home to some high-tech industries and a host of flourishing SMEs. The same applies to Alsace, which benefits from its proximity to the German market. Today, the momentum for French industry is coming from France's southern regions. New industrial centres have been developed at Sophia-Antipolis, France's leading science and technology park, Montpellier and Toulouse. These towns, which have not had to bear the cost of industrial restructuring, also have the advantage of being extremely attractive because of their environment and particularly their climate.

Services

The tertiary sector now accounts for 70% of GDP and 65% of jobs. Whether in non-market services, provided by local and central government, the health service, etc. or market services such as the hotel trade, restaurants, retailing and banks, this sector is the chief source of employment at a time when the fight against unemployment is intensifying. However, for several years now, substantial gains in productivity, often resulting from computerisation, have been reducing the number of situations vacant.

Banking and Insurance

Banks play a major role in the French economy. Banking generates almost 4% of GDP, a proportion comparable to that of transport, energy or agriculture, sylviculture and fishing. Judged by the number of employees (400,000) and market capitalisation, the main banking groups are amongst the largest French companies. Just how large the banking system has become can also be gauged by the total number of credit institutions (1,400) and the number of bank branches offering the full range of services (about 25,500, not including the 17,000 post offices).

The banking sector has witnessed some major upheavals since the early 'sixties. The traditional distinction between deposit banks and merchant banks has become blurred since the former have invested in industry and the latter have been allowed to develop a network of retail branches. The main banks, like the BNP, Société Générale, Crédit Agricole and Crédit Lyonnais, have huge networks covering the whole of France and sometimes extending even beyond its borders: there are over 1,000 French banking establishments in 139 foreign countries. The former merchant banks, Paribas and Indosuez, the latter now being in the Crédit Agricole group, still deal mainly with corporate investments and have control of a good number of French and foreign companies through a complex framework of cross-holdings. To these should be added

regional banks like the Banques Populaires, establishments linked to a specific region, the network of Caisses d'Epargne (savings banks) and specialised institutions like the Crédit National and the Crédit Foncier de France. Banking activities have become increasingly international, thanks to the globalisation of trade, France's determination to make Paris a major financial centre, and freedom of move-

Telebanking at the
BNP (Banque nationale
de Paris)

ment of capital within the European Union, which came into effect on 1 July 1990. To become more competitive, French banks have computerised very many of their services and encouraged customers to use debit cards rather than cheques, which are costlier to process. They have also increased their own stockholders/shareholder's equity to provide a financial safety-net and have invested more heavily in industry. Finally, several banks have created subsidiaries specialising in life assurance in order to diversify their activities and broaden their client base. The restructuring of French banking speeded up from 1985 onwards: the modernisation of the banking system resulting from the Law of 24 January 1984, together with the general trend toward liberalising and deregulating banking and financial services, increased competition. Banks have had to adapt to these new conditions and will have to adapt further with the completion of European integration, the move to the single currency (euro) and globalisation of the economy.

Within the framework of European Economic and Monetary Union, France now has an independent central bank. Since the Banque de France's establishment in 1800 by Napoleon Bonaparte, its decision-making structures have been modified four times by major reforms. The Law of 24 July 1936 transformed the bank's organisation in order to strengthen the government's authority over the monetary institute. This reform was the prelude to the nationalisation of the central bank, which came after the Liberation, in December 1945. Next, in 1973, the bank was modernised in response to technological changes in the financial and credit field. In 1993 the Banque de France became independent. While previously it had operated as the state bank, its new independent status formally prohibits it from authorising overdrafts or granting any other type of credit to the *Trésor public* (public revenue department) or any other public body or enterprise. However, it continues to maintain the current accounts of the *Trésor public*, contribute to the management of government debt and hold the current accounts of government bills. It also draws up the nation's balance of payments.

The Paris financial market is a capital market accessible to all buyers and sellers and offering all financial services, with transactions ranging from the day-to-day to the most long-term securities and forward transactions. The stock and bond markets are among the world's largest. The Paris market does a brisk trade in derivatives, both over the counter and on the organised markets: the financial futures market MATIF (*Marché à terme international de France*) and the traded options market MONEP (*Marché des options négociables à Paris*). The Paris market has been comprehensively modernised in recent years and today there are no technical, fiscal or statutory obstacles to the international movement of securities or capital. It offers all international investors a wide range of markets and products and guarantees absolute security and transparency. With a capitalisation of 4,098 billion francs ($673 billion) in 1998, the French stock market ranks fifth in the world, behind those of New York, Tokyo, London and Frankfurt. Listings on the Paris stock exchange reflect the sectorial and geographical diversity of the French economy. The 40 principal market capitalisations are listed on the CAC 40 index and the Paris Bourse has also developed new and broader indexes including average values. Since 1983, SMEs with strong growth potential have had access to the second market. In 1996, the New Market was set up, also designed to encourage SMEs to expand. The bond market is the largest section of the French financial market and the third largest of its kind in the world.

The French **insurance** sector is the fourth largest in the world with a turnover of over 1,050 billion francs ($175 billion). It is made up of nearly 600 French companies employing 146,000 people. The sector is dominated by large firms such as AXA, AGF and Groupama. There are also large numbers of mutuals like the GMF (*Garantie mutuelle des fonctionnaires*) for civil servants and the MAIF (*Mutuelle assurances des instituteurs de France*) for primary-school teachers. Apart from Paris, the leading centre for insurance, the towns of Niort and Le Mans, where some important mutual societies have their headquarters, have specialised in this field. Insurance companies, which own large amounts of property, are diversifying in order to improve their profitability. They are buying shares in industrial firms, stepping up their foreign investments to increase their influence and also broadening their product range, notably by offering funded pension funds. The liberalisation of services in the EU framework has also caused major strategic and structural upheaval in the insurance sector. Mergers and take-overs are on the increase, both within France, as in the case of the take-over of UAP by AXA, and at European level.

Hypermarkets and Small Shops

Over the past thirty years, the retail sector, which employs over 2.5 million people, has undergone a radical transformation of both the distribution network and selling methods, with the rapid rise of one-stop shopping. Although this type of retailing first appeared in the nineteenth century, with department stores like Bon

Marché and La Samaritaine in the heart of Paris, it got a further boost after the Second World War, with the arrival of the Prisunic and Monoprix chains, and then mushroomed from the 'sixties as self-service supermarkets and hypermarkets caught on. With its 1,120 hypermarkets (one for every 52,000 inhabitants) and 7,600 supermarkets, France has one of the highest levels anywhere of this type of retailing. Con-

Leclerc shopping-centre
in Ibos
(Hautes-Pyrénées):
as well as a hypermarket,
it has an arts centre,
cinema,
theatre and gallery

sumers now buy over 60% of their food products and 30% of their non-food products from one-stop retail outlets. Hypermarket specialists like Carrefour, Auchan and Promodès dominate the sector, along with the Leclerc supermarkets. These groups rely on powerful central purchasing organisations which dictate prices to manufacturers and compete fiercely with each other, mounting increasing numbers of advertising campaigns. They are expanding abroad: for example, Carrefour and Auchan have outlets in Spain, Asia and Latin America and Promodès in Germany. Originally selling mainly food products, the hypermarkets quickly branched out into other areas, such as ticket agencies for shows and travel agencies. Specialist retailers, such as Darty for household appliances and hi-fi equipment and Castorama and Leroy Merlin for DIY, have also emerged. Hypermarkets need vast amounts of space, so they are located either on the outskirts of large conurbations or in shopping centres which include specialist shops and many other services such as chemists' shops, cinemas and post offices.

On the other hand, small outlets are fast losing trade and protective legislation restricting the numbers of new supermarkets has not sufficed to halt their decline. Very vulnerable in rural areas, they survive better in towns, especially in the case of specialist shops or shops which open late and are particularly useful for last-minute shopping.

Other forms of retailing, such as mail order, have also developed. This is a highly concentrated market, dominated by a few large groups: La Redoute, La CAMIF and Les Trois Suisses. These companies are making increasing use of the telephone, Minitel and Internet and rely on the rapid processing of orders. Here too, markets are becoming increasingly international, as demonstrated by the German companies Neckermann and Quelle which have successfully penetrated the French market, while La Redoute is expanding its activities in Italy. More recently, France has seen a rise in the number of factory shops and discount warehouses which cut profit margins to the bone in order to attract customers.

Tourism

Enjoying a trade surplus of over 60 billion francs ($10 billion) in 1997 and with 67 million foreign tourists, France attracts more tourists than any other country in the world. Residents of other European countries, especially the Germans and British, are the most frequent visitors, accounting for 87% of arrivals. Furthermore, over 35 million French people also holiday in France. In the nineteenth century, France was a favourite haunt of aristocrats and the bourgeoisie, but over the last three decades, it has seen the advent of mass tourism.

Paris attracts over 10 million foreign tourists every year; the queue for the Louvre

Visitors come in such huge numbers because France has so much to offer them, with a wide variety of landscapes and a remarkable cultural heritage, demonstrated by its 12,000 listed monuments and 1,200 museums. Well situated geographically, remarkably well served by public transport and with an excellent road network, it also has extensive overnight accommodation facilities with over 17 million beds. Its 45,000 hotels have more than a million bedrooms and there are 8,200 campsites, 830 holiday villages, over 42,000 *gîtes* (rural self-catering accommodation) and 2,820,000 second homes. The French hotel trade is thriving, as evidenced by the strength of chains like the Accor group, which has 1,010 hotels in France and over 1,300 abroad. Tourism has now become a powerful economic engine of growth. It provides over 1.5 million direct or spin-off jobs and total spending by tourists exceeds 750 billion francs ($125 billion). Tourism has also triggered development in some coastal regions, like the Languedoc and Les Landes, slowed down the depopulation of mountain areas and boosted the construction and civil engineering sectors, as well as specialised industries such as sailing and boating equipment and clothing and cultural activities.

Nearly half the holiday-makers choose to go to the seaside. Established resorts like Deauville, Arcachon and Biarritz have now been joined by newer ones, particularly on the Languedoc and Aquitaine coasts. The Provence-Alpes-Côte d'Azur region continues to attract the highest numbers and, together with Languedoc-Roussillon and Corsica, dominates seaside tourism on the Mediterranean coast. On France's Atlantic coast, Brittany receives more visitors than Aquitaine or Vendée, which started to cater for mass tourism later. Mountain tourism, which began at Chamonix, rapidly developed after the war, benefiting from the wider range of activities offered and the Grenoble (1968) and Albertville (1992) Winter Olympics. 18% of the world's ski-lifts are in France. The most popular mountains are the Northern Alps, France's highest mountains, which have the best snow and remarkably well equipped resorts like Chamonix, Courchevel, Les Arcs and Tignes. The Southern Alps, with resorts like Serre-Chevalier, Vars and Isola 2000, confirm the supremacy of the Alps. Not so high and less easily accessible from the major population centres, the other mountains see fewer visitors. In the Pyrenees, the most popular tourist destinations are the spas, like Cauterets and Luchon, and ski-resorts such as La Mongie and Superbagnères. The Massif Central depends primarily on the attractions of its volcanoes and its many spas, whilst the Jura and the Vosges are popular with Swiss and German visitors who do not have far to come. Green tourism increased substantially during the 'sixties and 'seventies, with the rise of the ecologist movements and because of its affordability. It allows farmers to diversify by renovating cottages and letting them out as *gîtes*, providing bed and breakfast accommodation and creating farm campsites. Especially successful in the Rhône-Alpes region and the Massif Central, this helps to give a seasonal boost to many sparsely-inhabited villages.

Package tours mainly visit the Paris area and the Loire Valley. The French capital receives over 10 million foreign visitors every year, attracted by its outstanding architectural heritage, its intellectual and cultural role and successful development of facilities for business tourism, which has a turnover of over 20 billion francs ($3.3 billion) per year. In fact, more conferences are held in Paris than anywhere else in Europe. The Loire Valley owes its popularity to its many châteaux, of which Chambord, Chenonceaux and Azay-le-Rideau are the finest examples.

Transport

The various modes of transport play a vital role in the country's economic development and the accessibility of every part of it. France has one of the densest and most efficient communications networks in the world, with 146 kilometres of roads and 6.2 kilometres of railways per 100 km^2. Both the domestic and international networks have Paris as their centre, thereby reinforcing the capital's all-important role. While France used to build its networks with a view to national integration, today it thinks European. Indeed, the development of the single market is being accompanied by a progressive harmonisation and liberalisation of transport services in the EU framework.

An Efficient Road Network

With over 965,000 kilometres of roads, the French network is the longest in Europe. A large number of motorways have been built since 1965 and the motorway network now spans over 9,000 km. There are an increasing number of international links, with the construction of the Paris-Lille-Brussels, Macon-Geneva and Perpignan-Barcelona motorways and the Mont-Blanc (1965), Fréjus (1980) and Puymorens (1994) road tunnels. The motorway construction programme slowed down somewhat during the 'eighties, but received a new boost with the major development plan launched in 1990, which will extend the network to over 12,000 km by 2010.

Because almost every area of France is accessible by road and vehicle ownership is widespread (25 million cars and 3.4 million commercial vehicles), and because of the advances made in road building and maintenance technology, roads now carry 60% of domestic freight, as opposed to 40% in 1970. Nearly 90% of passenger journeys are made by road, mainly by private car, although use of public transport is rising sharply, especially for tourism.

Road transport is in the hands of over 39,000 firms with a total of 350,000 employees. It is a highly fragmented sector. Specialist groups like Calberson, a subsidiary of the SNCF, operate alongside large numbers of self-employed hauliers to whom haulage contracts are often subcontracted. This fragmented structure could well hamper the French haulage companies at a time when the European economic area is opening up in this sector - indeed, for this reason, the French government has asked the European authorities to delay opening up France to cabotage.

Railways: TGV to the rescue

Although the railways have long been given favourable treatment by the government, only 20% of freight (50.5 billion tonne-kms) is now carried by train. They not only face competition from road hauliers, but are suffering from the decline in heavy goods transport, particularly of coal, iron ore and hydrocarbons. Freight traffic is concentrated in the north-east quarter of the country and on the Paris-Lyon-Mediterranean route. Passenger trains are more successfully resisting competition, both due to the density of commuter services between

Paris and its suburbs and the opening of the TGV (high-speed) routes to the south-east and the Atlantic coast. Speed, punctuality and safety are valuable assets for these services, which also give passengers direct access to city centres. However, despite these assets, only 9% of domestic passenger travel is by train. There are now 34,450 km of track, compared to 52,000 km in the early 'thirties. The electrified network is only 14,200 km, but carries 80% of the total volume of traffic.

At the Gare du Nord (Paris), Eurostar, which takes passengers from Paris to London in three hours, and Thalys, which links Paris and Brussels in an hour and twenty-five minutes

The SNCF, a state-owned company, is heavily in debt and has a substantial financial deficit, despite state aid designed to compensate for its public-service obligations. It has to invest over 22 billion francs ($3.6 billion) a year to continue its modernisation. A public industrial and commercial company, RFF (*Réseau Ferré de France* - French rail network) has been founded to manage the rail transport infrastructure. In addition to completing the high-speed network, modernisation includes renewing rolling stock, increasing the range of services (e.g. motorail, family compartments and tickets including hotel accommodation) and pursuing an active marketing policy. Concurrently, the drive to improve productivity has led to a rapid reduction in the workforce, from 500,000 in 1939 to 180,000 in 1998. The future of the railways now depends on developing the high-speed rail network and piggyback transport. Use of the latter, already frequent for long distances, is likely to be expanded, particularly between Lille and Marseille, via Lyon, because of the saturation of the motorway network, and also along international routes to the UK and Italy, as recent plans for a rail tunnel between Lyon and Turin illustrate.

Eurostar: London to Paris in three hours

Paris-London direct, from the Gare du Nord to Waterloo International in three hours - that was the experience on 14 November 1994 of the 794 passengers on the first commercial Eurostar service linking the two capital cities. Today there is a train almost every hour. The return fare is about 690 francs ($115). For 2,750 francs ($458), you can travel first class, which includes breakfast or dinner brought directly to your seat. Travelling by Eurostar is rather like a plane journey, with futuristic terminals, check-in 20 minutes before departure, boarding cards and facilities for separate transport of luggage. Even the journey times are similar: it takes three hours to get from central Paris to central London, whether you travel by Eurostar or plane. Only the view is different: passengers on Eurostar race across Picardy at 300 km/h, before travelling through the 54-kilometre Channel Tunnel and enjoying the scenery of Kent at a more leisurely 160 km/h.

Thalys – Paris to Brussels in an hour and twenty-five minutes

Since 14 December 1997, the journey between Paris and Brussels has been 45 minutes shorter. This is the first TGV to travel from one European capital to another at a speed of 300 km/h all the way. From 7.00 a.m. to 10.00 p.m., there is a train every hour and every half-hour at peak times. Return fares cost between 316 francs ($52) and 996 francs ($166). Thalys also serves many Belgian, German and Dutch towns as far away as Cologne and Amsterdam.

Inland Navigation - Modest Volume of Traffic

The inland waterway transport undertakings, which have to compete with railways and pipelines, carry 5.7 billion tonne-kms, less than 2.5% of domestic freight. They have been affected by the collapse of the heavy goods transport sector, which has caused freight tariffs to fall and led the French authorities and the EU to finance the destruction of part of the fleet to reduce overcapacity. French operators have to compete with German and Dutch companies, which are more concentrated. A further problem for this sector is that many of the canals in the 8,500 km long network are in a poor state of repair. Although some major waterways have been improved, like the Rhine, the Rhône below Lyon, the Seine below Montereau and the Moselle, and several wide-gauge canals such as the Dunkirk-Valenciennes link, the links between them are older, smaller-gauge canals. Only 1,860 km meet the European norm for 1,500 tonne vessels. The traffic is concentrated in the northern half of the country, with the main river ports being Paris, Strasbourg, Thionville and Rouen.

Shipping

The French-registered merchant fleet (210 ships, total gross tonnage of 6.6 million) is only part of the total number of ships belonging to French shipping firms. Like their counterparts in other industrialised countries, shipping firms use flags of convenience on some of their ships to reduce their labour and non-wage costs. Other vessels sail under the Kerguelen flag, which was created in 1986 and allows up to three quarters of a ship's crew to be foreign, whereas those sailing under the French flag must have all French crews, which is more expensive. The Compagnie Générale Maritime, privatised in 1996, dominates French shipping and also operates the sea link between Corsica and mainland France, through a subsidiary, Société Nationale Corse Méditerranée. Of the other shipping firms, the largest are SCAC/Delmas-Vieljeux/SDV, the Dreyfus Group, which specialises in grain transport, and the Compagnie française de Navigation, a subsidiary of the CFP, which transports hydrocarbons.

Although France is the world's fourth largest exporter, its merchant fleet ranks only 27th. Goods traffic is shared mainly between seven of France's seventy ports — Marseille-Fos (90.7 million tonnes), then Le Havre (56 million tonnes), Dunkirk, Calais, Nantes-Saint-Nazaire, Rouen and Bordeaux. Efforts to improve productivity have led to a rapid decline in the number of dock workers and the emergence of new handling techniques, with, in particular, greater use of containers and trailers. Passenger transport is rising fast, due to the growth of tourism. Traffic is particularly busy on the Cross-Channel routes, despite the opening of the Channel Tunnel. Calais (with 1.8 million passengers) is ahead of Cherbourg (1.5 million), Boulogne and Dunkirk, whilst on the routes between mainland France and Corsica, Bastia handles more passengers than Marseille and Nice.

Air Transport Crossroads

France's size and geographical position have made it a veritable hub for air transport in Europe. Benefiting from a rapid democratisation of air travel, mainly because of charter flights, the advent of large passenger aircraft and increasing competition, the sector is growing fast. Air France, the state company, has taken control of Air Inter. The group is also developing commercial cooperation with foreign companies. Serving 164 airports in 92 countries, it carried 33 million passengers on international flights in 1997. It also carried 15 million passengers on domestic flights, despite fierce competition from companies like AOM and Air Liberté.

Aéroports de Paris is Europe's second (after London) and the world's seventh largest airports authority. In 1997 it handled

60.4 million passengers and 644,500 aircraft movements, far more than the other major French airports of Nice-Côte d'Azur, Marseille-Provence, Lyon, Toulouse and Bordeaux.

Postal and Telecommunications Services

The French postal system (La Poste), which in 1997 delivered over 24 billion letters, packages, newspapers and periodicals, is noted for its reliability and rapidity. Through the establishment of about ten subsidiaries, the La Poste group has developed three important activities: financial services and express letters and parcels services. It has almost 310,000 employees. In 1990, France's postal and telephone services were separated and two public law companies set up, with France Telecom taking responsibility for telecommunications. Thanks to considerable state investment during the 'seventies and 'eighties, France now has a network of over 33 million telephone lines and prices have been steadily falling, especially for long-distance calls, as a result of increased competition between France Telecom and private operators like Cégétel and Bouygues. The meteoric rise of the mobile phone sector (over 8 million subscribers since the start-up in 1996) has also resulted in fierce competition.

The mobile phone sector has seen spectacular growth since 1996; there is fierce competition between France Telecom, Cégétel and Bouygues, the three leading operators

From Minitel to Internet: Swift Conversion

The development of French telematics, with 7.4 million Minitel computer terminals, 30,000 on-line services and 85 million hours online per year, has slowed down the growth of the Internet. France is now trying to catch up and to this end the government has entrusted France Telecom with the task of piloting several projects in the field of the new IT and communications technologies.

These have had a promising start and growth has been rapid. The number of Internet surfers had risen to around two million at the end of 1998, most using service providers such as France Telecom's Wanadoo, Club-Internet, AOL or Micronet. The number of French websites has expanded in record time: there are now some 44,000 and government departments, newspapers, television and radio stations, businesses and voluntary organisations are all accessible on the Web.

Further reading:

Les chiffres-clés de l'industrie française 1997-1998, Ministère de l'Industrie, Direction générale des stratégies industrielles, Service des statistiques industrielles, SESSI, 1998.

G. Colletis, J.-L. Levet, *Quelles politiques pour l'industrie française ?* Commissariat général du Plan, La Documentation française, 1997.

B. Coriat, D. Taddéï, *Made in France*, LGF, 1993.

La France, industries et services depuis 1945, Sirey, 1994.

P. Le Roy, *Les agricultures françaises face aux marchés mondiaux*, A. Colin, 1993.

L'agriculture, la forêt et les industries agroalimentaires, Graph Agri France 1999, Ministère de l'Agriculture et de la Pêche, 1999.

L'agriculture et l'agroalimentaire dans les régions, Graph Agri 1999, Ministère de l'Agriculture et de la Pêche, 1999.

D. Zerah, *Le système financier français : dix ans de mutation*, La Documentation française, Les Études series, 1993.

"Le commerce international", *Cahiers français*, N° 253, La Documentation française.

D. Plihon, *Les banques. Nouveaux enjeux, nouvelles stratégies*, La Documentation française, Les Études series, 1998.

16

Town and Country Planning and Regional Development

After centuries during which centralisation, at both the political and economic levels, had been a key feature of France, the end of the Second World War found the country with huge disparities between the regions; for instance, there was an excessive concentration of power and resources in Paris - at that time home to over 15% of the population -, a divide between the rich, industrial, north-east and the poorer south-west, which had remained largely rural, and a general contrast between urban and rural areas (where the level of development was noticeably lower). Since the mid-sixties, governments have been implementing an active town and country planning and regional development policy to level out these imbalances and encourage a more even distribution both of the population and of economic activity.

New Objectives

Following the Second World War, recognition of this serious regional imbalance led the government in 1949 to set up a regional development agency, the *Direction de l'aménagement du territoire*. Thereafter, the authorities began to have a clearer understanding of these disparities that became more complex as economic changes affected the country. In 1955, the Government defined a number of regions for planning purposes and instituted structures and specialised funding instruments. DATAR (*Délégation à l'aménagement du territoire et à l'action régionale* - town and country planning and regional development agency), established in 1963, became the state's chief instrument in this sphere. It pilots development, assisted by various local bodies with expertise in areas such as tourist facilities, industrial and urban development and since 1997 the relevant minister has been able to draw on its services. There is also the Interministerial Committee on Regional Development (CIAT), which decides on objectives and takes decisions, and a Regional Development Fund (FIAT - *fonds d'interven-*

tion pour l'aménagement du territoire), which provides finance for development initiatives, alongside other partners such as local authorities and state-owned and private companies. Initially, central government determined regional development objectives within the framework of the Plan and ensured overall control of the operations.

DATAR conducts several different types of operation. It coordinates large-scale projects to encourage economic development in particular regions – as was the case in the 'sixties and early 'seventies when tourist facilities were improved on the Languedoc and Aquitaine coasts and major winter sports resorts built in the Alps. It was also involved in the development of the docks and industrial estates at Dunkirk and Fos, designed to promote heavy industry in those coastal areas by improving access for imported raw materials and energy products.

From 1964 onwards, DATAR also attempted to reduce the supremacy of Paris by encouraging the development in eight regional centres not only of industry, but also of high-level services such as universities and teaching hospitals. To restabilise the structure of the conurbations, it also contributed to the building of new towns in the areas surrounding Paris (Marne-la-Vallée and Saint-Quentin-en-Yvelines), Lille (Villeneuve d'Ascq) and Lyon (L'Isle d'Abeau). In addition to these direct interventions, measures were taken to restructure the country's economy. Accordingly, decentralisation of industry and services was promoted by giving grants to companies locating in specific regions and the number of industrial jobs rose sharply in the areas around the Paris basin, such as the Centre and Picardy, and Brittany. By contrast, businesses wishing to set up in other regions, notably the Ile-de-France, must obtain the authorities' approval and face fiscal disincentives.

The state has also set an example by decentralising some of its own services: bank notes are now manufactured near Clermont-Ferrand, whilst the meteorological office has moved to Toulouse. The net result of these various initiatives has been the creation of over 600,000 jobs in industry in the regions surrounding the Paris basin and a substantial increase in amenities in the regional metropolises, much better served by public transport. Elsewhere, there have been some radical changes: the regions in the west and south, which previously had little industry, are seeing more rapid development than the old industrial regions of the north and east. The picture is marred only by the continuing drift from the countryside.

Over the last few decades, over 40% of *communes* in rural areas have seen their population decline. This is particularly true of the sparsely populated area forming a diagonal band stretching from the Central Pyrenees to the Ardennes, and of the Southern Alps, Corsica and the hinterland of Brittany. To combat the population drain, the government, helped by EC subsidies, has been granting substantial aid to farmers and encouraging additional economic activity, particularly silviculture and tourism. Nature reserves have been created in some of these regions with a view to preserving the ecological balance and attracting tourists.

Slower rates of growth from 1974 onwards and the economic crisis hitting many of the old industrial sectors, such as textiles and steel, led the Government to revise its regional development objectives, especially as the funds available to achieve them were decreasing. The emphasis shifted from large-scale development schemes to initiatives intended primarily to facilitate the restructuring of the former industrial heartlands through environment improvement projects, retraining the workforce and bringing in new economic activities. The state has been encouraging French and foreign car-manufacturers to locate factories in the Nord region and Lorraine and, to limit the magnetic pull of regional capitals, it gave priority first to schemes in medium-sized towns and then to rural areas. The authorities have also had to confront two worsening problems – rural depopulation and the difficulties of some problem urban areas.

Impact of Decentralisation

Decentralisation legislation adopted in 1982 and 1983 led to the central government's gradual disengagement from regional development, with many of its development resources transferred to the local authorities. The regions, which have become fully-fledged local authorities, were given responsibility in many areas, particularly with respect to regional development. They prepare "concerted regional development programmes" (PACT - *programmes d'aménagement concerté du territoire*), liaising with central government and ensuring consistency of these with the national plan. The subsequent "planning contracts"

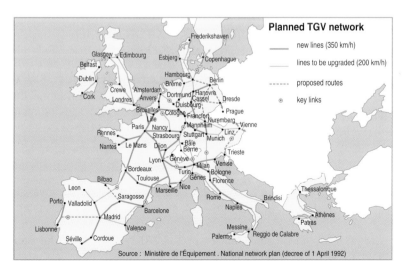

Planned TGV network

—— new lines (350 km/h)

—— lines to be upgraded (200 km/h)

------ proposed routes

⊛ key links

Source : Ministère de l'Équipement . National network plan (decree of 1 April 1992)

A pioneer in the field of high-speed railways, France is well placed to benefit from its integration into the European rail network

are co-financed by a number of bodies: central government, the regional authorities, the national regional development fund (FNADT - *Fonds national pour l'aménagement du territoire*) and, in some cases, aid allocated by the European Union. The 1994-1998 period saw the conclusion of "planning contracts" worth over 250 billion francs ($42 billion), with the funding breakdown as follows: 85 billion francs ($14 billion) from central government, 85 billion francs from the regions, almost 40 billion francs ($6.6 billion dollars) from other local authorities and 55 billion francs ($9 billion) from the European Union. Nearly one third of this funding was spent on roads, 18% on economic development and 10% on urban regeneration. The *Université 2000* project, the environment and the arts have also required substantial investment.

The other local authorities have also seen their powers and areas of responsibility increased by decentralisation. France's 36,500 *communes* have considerable autonomy in the area of town planning. They draw up and approve land use plans (*Plan d'occupation des sols*) which determine the permitted uses for each part of the *commune* (farming, residential, open spaces, etc.), while the mayor is responsible for granting planning permission. Departments are in charge of some areas of agricultural planning, such as *remembrement* (reparcelling of holdings) and for their network of secondary roads.

In addition the European Union has increased the level of funding allocated to regional development. The various EC structural funds were of substantial assistance to France from 1994 to 1999. These funds aid regions whose development is lagging behind such as Corsica and the overseas departments, regions suffering industrial decline, such as Nord-Pas-de-Calais and Lorraine, and vulnerable rural areas. They are also available to create employment and help provide training schemes to enable workers who have been made redundant return to work. The European Regional Development Fund (ERDF) is the main instrument for these schemes, along with the European Social Fund and the European Agricultural Guidance and Guarantee Fund (EAGGF).

New Approach: Reordering Priorities in Favour of Job Creation and the Environment

New guidelines have now been defined for town and country planning and regional development. The Outline Act of 4 February 1995, amended by the bill adopted by the Council of Ministers in 1998 and presented to Parliament in 1999, stresses the need for sustainable development and adopts a new approach to planning with the aim of achieving a better balance between the roles of central government and local authorities. A budget of 1.8 billion francs ($0.3 billion) has been allocated to this task.

In the years leading up to 2020, the priority for development policy will be to reduce the disparities between rural and urban areas. The first aim is not only to pursue the effort to stem the depopulation of over 400 rural *cantons*, but also to support still populated, but vulnerable rural areas in order to prevent the disintegration of the fabric of rural life. Accordingly, it has been decided to halt the decline of local public services and encourage a broadening of employment possibilities. A fund for managing natural habitats in rural areas will also be established.

The new guidelines also include the renovation of urban areas (inner cities, industrial estates undergoing restructuring and overseas territories, etc.) which is vital to improve social harmony. Initiated in the 'seventies, the urban regeneration policy was expanded in the 'eighties and especially since 1990. The primary aim is to improve the urban environment by renovating housing, creating parks and open spaces and providing more community facilities. The number of schemes encouraging local job creation initiatives is also being stepped up.

Sustainable development is an integral part of town and country planning (see Ch. 2), which aims to restore a balance between the development of urban and country areas by strengthening the local communities shaped by geography, history and economic factors. The geographical framework for this development has been modified and now has three levels: regions, conurbations and *pays* (localities or groups of *communes*). Sharing geographical, cultural, economic or social characteristics, these now seventy groups of communes can work together on joint intercommunal development plans. Conurbations are also being encouraged to organise cooperation on an intercommunal basis.

In the face of rural depopulation, France's regional development policy is designed to support vulnerable rural communities

Finally, as the 20th century draws to a close, France is thinking in European terms, and no longer only national ones. Today French regions are far less likely to be competing among themselves than with their European counterparts such as Flanders, Bad Würtemburg, Bavaria and Lombardy, with which they are in fact not just competing, but also developing cooperation agreements. The same holds true for cities: Paris is no longer in competition with Lyon, Lille or Marseille, but must instead vie with London, Brussels, Frankfurt and will soon also have to do so with Berlin. Consequently, the French capital is striving to increase its influence and attract the major foreign decision-makers and the headquarters of multinational companies by offering them tax incentives and developing office space, hotels and conference facilities. To counterbalance Paris' increasing importance, there are also plans to stimulate development around a dozen regional cities (Lyon, Marseille,

Lille, Strasbourg, Bordeaux, Rennes, Nancy, Metz, Nantes, Toulouse, Grenoble and Clermont-Ferrand) which have the potential to become European and international centres, because of their tertiary infrastructures (e.g. higher education and research establishments), communications networks and other amenities.

The new approach also involves identifying the new spheres on which, if there is to be development, attention must be focused, such as education, research and new information technologies which allow professional mobility.

New terminal at
Roissy-Charles de Gaulle
airport, Paris

Further reading:

F. Auriac et V. Rey (Eds), *Atlas de France*, volume 8, *L'espace rural*, Reclus-La Documentation française, 1998.

J. Bourdin, J. Boyon, A. Zeller, Commissariat général du Plan, *Économie et territoires*, La Documentation française, 1997.

J.-P. Delevoye, Commissariat général du Plan, *Cohésion sociale et territoires*, La Documentation française, 1997.

R. Brunet, "L'aménagement du territoire en France", in *La Documentation Photographique*, N° 7041, La Documentation française, 1997.

J.-P. de Gaudemar (Ed.), DATAR, *Environnement et aménagement du territoire*, La Documentation française, 1996.

M. Kotas, DATAR, *Politique de pays*, La Documentation française, Rapport de mission series, 1997.

SCIENCE, TECHNOLOGY, CULTURE AND MEDIA

17

Science and Technology

France has a long tradition of scientific achievement and French science is today highly competitive at the international level. In all branches of science, France's scientists are contributing to the development of fundamental scientific knowledge and related technologies.

The Tradition of Fundamental Research Continues

The French school of **mathematics**, which has continued and taken considerably further the work begun by the Bourbaki group in the interwar years, is still amongst the most important in the world. It has been awarded seven Fields medals, including two in 1994, and is considered authoritative in the areas of fractal geometry, equations with partial derivatives, and chaos theory (i.e. the mathematical study of complex systems which are very sensitive to initial conditions or to changes in them, for example stock market fluctuations, growth of cancerous tumours, meteorology and concert hall acoustics). French mathematicians including Benoît Mandelbrot, Alain Connes, Jean-Pierre Serre, René Thom, Alexander Grothendieck, Pierre-Louis Lions and Jean-Christophe Yoccoz have won international recognition for their work.

These achievements in mathematical research have naturally earned France a prominent place in the related sector of software and application packages, in particular complex software for powerful machines tailored to meet specific needs such as signal processing, imaging, high-power scientific computation, etc.. In a field with ever greater possibilities for the future, some excellent French teams at Paris-Sud, and particularly Marseille and Grenoble, are outstanding in their development of interaction between man and computer using direct spoken instructions.

Today's French **physicists** are carrying on the tradition of prestigious forerunners from Henri Becquerel and Pierre and Marie Curie to Alfred Kastler and Louis Néel. They continue to excel in a wide variety of fields including quantum optics, nuclear physics, solid-state physics and magnetism, hydrodynamics and materials for microelectronics, as the Nobel prizes for physics awarded to Pierre-Gilles de Gennes in 1991, Georges Charpak in 1992 and Claude Cohen-Tannoudji in 1997 acknowledge. De Gennes has successfully investigated many areas of physics and current molecular physical chemistry. Particularly focused on possible applications, his work has led to progress in the following areas: liquid crystals, superconducting materials and the composition of polymers and adhesives. Charpak invented an ultra-

sensitive radiation and particle detector which has led to many new discoveries in sub-atomic physics. Cohen-Tannoudji has worked on low temperature, low level atomic interactions involving atomic nuclei and radiation emissions which could make the atomic chronometers of the future. French physicists are also contributing to the development of research instruments of international importance. The world's largest particle accelerator, the

Georges Charpak (on right), 1992 Nobel prizewinner for Physics, congratulates Claude Cohen-Tannoudji on winning the same prize in 1997

LEP 2, was installed at CERN (the European Organization for Nuclear Research) in 1996 and France is among the most active participants in European research on the physics of elementary particles. The GANIL (*grand accélérateur national d'ions lourds*), a very advanced heavy-ion accelerator located near Caen, enables the international scientific community to carry out research in atomic and nuclear physics.

Chemistry is another area in which French scientists have had a long tradition of excellence with the great names of the past including Lavoisier, Gay-Lussac and Frédéric and Irène Joliot-Curie. One area where France is currently at the forefront is supramolecular chemistry which makes, virtually to order, complex molecular associations with completely new properties, such as the famous cryptands discovered by Jean-Marie Lehn (winner of the 1987 Nobel Prize for chemistry) which can selectively absorb ions in solution. France also leads the field in solid-state chemistry, where the work of Professor Raveau led to synthesis of the first high-temperature superconductor solids; organic chemistry synthesising new materials at normal temperatures; and the synthesis of medicines for cancer therapy and the production of vaccines following work done at the Institute on the chemistry of natural substances. In the field **of life sciences**, especially biology, French teams such as those at the Pasteur Institute and

INSERM (National Institute for Health and Medical Research), including Luc Montagnier, Pierre Chambon and others, have pioneered important research in molecular genetics, immunology (on in vitro genetic recombination and AIDS) and the hormones associated with reproduction and embryonic development. It is now recognised that the HIV virus associated with AIDS was first isolated at the Pasteur Institute in Paris.

The Pasteur-Mérieux group is actively pursuing research into a vaccine to prevent HIV infection, an area in which French scientists and a few American biotechnology firms are the only groups still working. Professor Etienne-Emile Baulieu's work is also of great importance: his development of the contraceptive pill RU 486 in 1982 led to the INSERM team's recent discovery of the ability of the female hormone progesterone to mend damaged nerve cells – a finding which could have important implications for treatment of motor and sensory problems and those with paralysis.

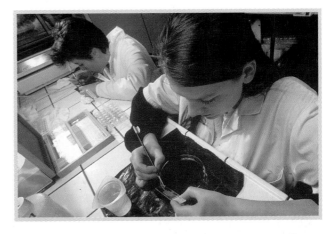

An INSERM team (U161) studies sections of guinea-pigs' brains in order to analyse the cerebral mechanisms of pain

Mapping the human genome is perhaps the most exciting challenge facing biologists in the next few years, and here too French and American scientists lead the field. Scientists are attempting completely to decode all the genes of each of the 23 human chromosomes – a job which can be compared to reading a text of three and a half billion characters in an unknown language – and to identify their functions in the hope of one day preventing or curing most genetic diseases. As recently as ten years ago, this would have seemed impossibly far-fetched, but international cooperation has made it a reality and French teams have been responsible for a number of breakthroughs. Discovery has followed discovery: in September 1992, at Généthon in Evry (one of the world's best-equipped laboratories for the study of the genome) Daniel Cohen drew up the first complete physical map of Chromosome 21; the following month, Jean Weissenbach published details of 1,400 genetic markers in almost the whole of the human genome (22 chromosomes out of 23). At INSERM in February 1993 Patrick Aubourg's team isolated the gene for adrenoleukodystrophy (Schilder's disease), a congenital disease which destroys the brain. A month later, after successful experiments on rats, other French teams (including Axel Kahn, Michel Perricaud, Marc Peschanski and Jacques Mallet) announced a way to treat

Alzheimer's disease by gene therapy and succeeded in curing Duchenne muscular dystrophy in mice by gene transfer. France also has the *Centre national de séquençage* (national centre for sequencing) which specialises in studying DNA in order to identify specific genes. In 1994 the first complete map of the genome was produced as a result of international cooperation in which French research played an active part. The boom in genetic research led to the establishment of French biotechnology firm Genset, the largest in France, employing 500 scientists and technicians and working closely with the giants of the pharmaceutical industry.

The *Institut national de la recherche agronomique* (INRA - national institute for agronomic research) is obtaining

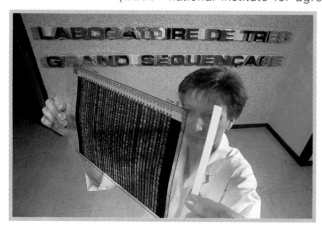

remarkable results in the areas of plant and animal biology. For example, in viticulture, horticulture and cereal cultivation, rapid propagation by in vitro tissue culture techniques has created, by the introduction of specific genes, varieties with a resistance to particular diseases. INRA has also made a new hybrid variety of oilseed rape and developed software for organising forest planting.

At Evry (Essonne), a private gene-sequencing laboratory, on the Généthon site

Exciting discoveries are also being made in the **earth sciences and the study of the universe**. In the first area French teams have made important contributions to the development of seismology and the theory of plate tectonics. French scientists are also participating in major international projects such as the Franco-American ocean valley exploration programme Famous and IPOD (International Project for Ocean Drilling), exploring the ocean depths. France is also at the forefront in space research where it has many successes to its credit, several achieved through joint projects with European or international teams: the launch vehicle Diamant, the rocket Ariane, the SPOT programme (satellite positioning and tracking) for monitoring the earth's resources, the Franco-American TOPEX/Poseidon ocean monitoring programme launched by Ariane in 1992, and many telecommunications, meteorology, astrophysics and cosmology projects. **Social scientists** are constantly gaining new perspectives on mankind as a result of research carried out within French universities and other major higher education institutions such as the *Ecoles normales supérieures, Ecole pratique des hautes études, Ecole des hautes études en sciences sociales* and CNRS (national centre for scientific research).

French **historical research** is recognized as among both the most illustrious and prolific in the world, particularly as a result of the work of the *Annales* school founded by Lucien Febvre and Marc Bloch, but also through that of internationally reputed historians like Fernand Braudel, Georges Dumézil and Georges Duby (now deceased) and Jacques Le Goff, Pierre Chaunu, Jean Favier and Emmanuel Leroy-Ladurie. Meanwhile, the many archaeological units working in France and other Mediterranean countries, Asia and Latin America have totally revamped a discipline in which France was already prominent in the 19th century, when a French expedition unlocked the key to the ancient civilisation of Egypt and, a few decades later, the *Ecole d'Athènes* was set up by French archaeologists. At the same time, other branches of learning are gaining in importance: sociology, anthropology (largely thanks to the work of Claude Lévi-Strauss) and demography, in which the *Institut national d'études démographiques* (INED) has kept up the tradition of Alfred Sauvy and acquired an international reputation.

Economics is still to a large extent dominated by English-speaking countries, but French economics has gained worldwide recognition through the work of Maurice Allais (winner of the 1988 Nobel prize for economics) and Edmond Malinvaud on the response of market economies to risk situations and the combined effects of planning and decentralisation.

Finally, **legal scholarship** in France is heir to a venerable tradition. To cope with the growing complexity of the world of law and the interdependence of its various specialities, the trend in this area is now towards an increasingly collective approach. Jurists are responsive to current concerns and are anxious to bring fundamental areas like constitutional law, civil liberties and comparative law up to date and are turning their attention to newer issues such as bioethics, European Community law and IT-related law.

New Technologies: Alliance of Science and Industry

As the world's fourth-largest industrial power and exporter of goods, and second largest exporter of services, food and agricultural products, France has acquired the modern technologies required for its economic and social growth, whilst encouraging the research and development effort it needs for the future.

In order to be competitive, French high-tech industries have to take on board advances in electronics, microelectronics,

Claudie-Andrée
Deshayes,
France's first
woman astronaut

information technology, biotechnology, nuclear engineering and composite materials. These technologies have applications in both new and traditional industries which they are helping to modernise.

Strategic Technologies

The Colibri, the latest model developed by the Franco-German company Eurocopter, at the Marignane airbase (Bouches-du-Rhône), January 1998

In addition to the defence industry, which brings together many generic technologies (materials, precision engineering, electronics, information technology, etc.), the aerospace, and energy sectors are helping maintain France's independence and its leading place in high-tech industry.

In aerospace, France (in association with its partners on the Ariane and Airbus programmes) has clearly emerged as the only major rival to the United States. Thanks to its overall design, the performance of its liquid hydrogen engine and its reliability, more than 50% of the world's space launches are carried out by Ariane. It is also largely thanks to Ariane that the European space programme has recorded many successes in the observation and communications sciences. The dynamism and skills of the French teams involved in European aerospace joint ventures are epitomised in the major technological advances of the Airbus A340: number one in its category as regards the economy, low level of pollution and quietness of the engine and the use of composite materials in parts of the plane's structure which are critical for its safety. If we look at the numbers of aircraft ordered by carriers in 1997 and 1998, Airbus is almost on a level with its great American rival, Boeing, the world leader in aircraft construction. The Franco-German company Eurocopter is the world's leading helicopter manufacturer.

Energy is another area in which French technology excels. France is a major player in every area of the nuclear power sector - supply of fuel, electricity production and reprocessing of nuclear waste. It has the world's largest nuclear waste reprocessing plant in the Hague in Normandy and its expertise is clearly recognised by countries as demanding as Germany, Sweden and Japan. This industry has demonstrated by its reliability and security that protection of the environment does not have to be sacrificed in order to keep energy costs down. France also has proven expertise in conventional energy production and exports its technology and skills by building hydroelectric and conventional power stations, particularly those equipped with the new combined-cycle gas turbines which have been especially successful in many other countries. French research in petroleum exploration and petrochemical processes and related engineering skills have helped establish the French oil industry in many regions of the world.

Land Transport, Civil Engineering and Materials Engineering

As for the technology used in the transport sector, France holds more than 12% of the world's patents and 22% of European ones. Many factors account for the success of France's shipbuilding, railway equipment and car industries; notable achievements include: thermal and electrical propulsion (synchronous and asynchronous), reliable technology and materials for braking and the reduction of noise inside vehicles to increase passenger comfort, performance of safety, command and control and signalling software and the light weight of its increased shock-resistant systems. These factors have encouraged many countries to choose French-built transport equipment (underground trains, trams and automated driverless trains like the VAL) and French companies to build their conventional and high-speed rail systems — South Korea and Florida both have the TGV.

France is also one of the world leaders in civil engineering. The Grand Arch of La Défense in Paris, Channel tunnel and Normandy bridge, as was the case in its time for the Garabit viaduct (Cantal), all use the latest technologies in construction, civil engineering and associated scientific disciplines. The

world's biggest cable-stayed bridge, which is 17 kilometres long and spans the river Tagus north of Lisbon, was built by the French and opened in March 1998. France's skill in building infrastructures and urban equipment is also famous world-wide, especially in the field of water conveyance treatment. In fact, French companies are in the lead in all these areas: the world's two largest water-supply and treatment companies are French (CGE [now Vivendi] and Lyonnaise des Eaux), as are Europe's three leading construction and civil engineering firms (Bouygues, GTM and SGE).

Météor, the new Paris metro line with state-of-the-art driverless trains, was officially opened in October 1998

Electronics and Information Technology

Electronics occupies a special place in the development of science, for progress here leads not only to advances in the electronics industry itself, but also contributes to progress in many other fields such as image and signal processing, telecommunications, robotics and - more prosaically - electronic money, with the smart cards (bank and telephone) invented by Frenchman Roland Moreno the best-known example. In many sectors of activity, from cellular phones to data compression and virtual imaging, France has increased its capabilities, not only through the efforts of big multinationals (the number one telecommunications firm in the world, Alcatel, is French), but also through those of a large number of innovative SMEs (small and medium-sized enterprises), which in some cases have even managed to get a foothold in the American market.

French telecommunications and telematics companies have benefited from an active policy of Government support. While the famous Minitel system has had little success in export terms, it did give France a head start in telematics and may yet enjoy a new lease of life, as the latest version of the Minitel can function as an Internet terminal. Alcatel has also developed ADSL technology, which allows Internet access via standard telephone networks. Meanwhile, the *Centre national d'études des télécommunications* (CNET) has developed a technology for high-speed data transfer (ATM - asynchronous transfer mode), which should speed up the development of electronic superhighways. France, which already uses more digital technology than most other countries, has entered the information society.

Food, Health and the Environment

French cuisine has traditionally enjoyed a reputation for excellence, but this has now been consolidated, as regards quality and safety, at the highest scientific level by advances in bio- and food-processing technology and the constant quest for absolutely safe food through developments in predictive bacteriology. French technical and scientific cooperation in the form of large-scale, multi-disciplinary research projects designed to find ways to protect crops in southern hemisphere countries, aid drought-stricken regions, make the best use of all available water resources and develop agricultural methods better tailored to humid tropical zones is valued highly by the countries concerned. This approach constructively complements the universally recognised work of French scientists in the fields of immunology and vaccines (e.g. vaccines against rabies, polio and meningitis, or combined vaccines against five diseases at once).

In the environmental sphere, the wide range of technologies developed by government and private research include remote sensing (used to predict what problems need to be addressed, so that the requisite projects can be scheduled), soil conservation, reforestation, water purification, waste processing and measures to combat pollution. France currently holds over 12% of patents worldwide and almost 20% of European ones for environmental technologies. So, combining tradition with a pioneering approach, France's scientific community today is simultaneously cooperating with other countries and making a vital contribution to the competitiveness of the French economy.

Xavier Vignon and J.-P. Renard, the INRA scientists who successfully cloned a calf, Marguerite, born in March 1998

Further information:

The principal French research establishments are:

**Ministère de l'Enseignement supérieur et de la Recherche
(Ministry of Higher Education and Research)**
1, rue Descartes. 75231 Paris Cedex 05
Direction de la Technologie (Technology department)
Fax: 33 1.46.34.48.58 - http://education.gouv.fr
Direction de la Recherche (Research department)
Fax: 33 1.46.34.49.49
http://www.recherche.gouv.fr
**Centre national de la recherche scientifique (CNRS - National Centre for
Scientific Research)**
3, rue Michel-Ange. 75794 Paris Cedex 16
Fax: 33 1.44.96.50.00 - http://www.cnrs.fr
Centre national d'études spatiales (CNES - National Space Research Centre)
2, place Maurice Quentin. 75039 Paris Cedex 01
Fax: 33 1.44.76.76.76 - http://www.cnes.fr
**Institut national de la santé et de la recherche médicale (INSERM -
National Institute for Health and Medical Research)**
101, rue de Tolbiac. 75654 Paris Cedex 13
Fax: 33 1.45.85.68.56 - http://www.inserm.fr
**Institut national de la recherche agronomique (INRA - National Institute for
Agronomic Research)**
147, rue de l'Université. 75338 Paris Cedex 07
Fax: 33 1.47.05.99.66 - http://www.inra.fr
**Institut français de recherche pour l'exploitation de la mer (IFREMER -
French Research Establishment for Marine Resources)**
155, rue Jean-Jacques Rousseau. 92138 Issy-Les-Moulineaux Cedex
Fax: 33 1.46.48.22.96 - http://www.ifremer.fr
Commissariat à l'énergie atomique (CEA - Atomic Energy Commission)
31-33, rue de la Fédération. 75752 Paris Cedex 15
Fax: 33 1.40.56.29.70 - http://www.cea.fr
**Institut national de recherche en informatique et automatique (INRIA -
National Institute for Research into Computers and Automatic Systems)**
Domaine de Voluceau. Rocquencourt. BP 105.
78153 Le Chesnay
Fax: 33 1.39.63.59.60 - http://www.inria.fr
Institut français du pétrole (IFP - French Petroleum Institute)
1 and 4, avenue de Bois-Préau. BP 92852. 92506 Rueil-Malmaison Cedex.
Fax: 33 1.47.52.70.00 - http://www.ifp.fr
**Institut de recherche pour le développement (IRD, formerly ORSTOM -
French Research Institute for Development)**
213, rue La Fayette. 75480 Paris Cedex 10
Fax: 33 1.48.03.08.29 - http://www.ird.fr
**Centre de coopération internationale en recherche agronomique pour le
développement (CIRAD - Centre for International Cooperation in Agro-
nomic Research for Development)**
42, rue Scheffer. 75116 Paris.
Fax: 33 1.53.70.21.33 - http://www.cirad.fr

18

Culture

For many people, France is synonymous with culture – hence the many foreign tourists who flock to the Louvre and the Pompidou Centre and queue up for performances at the Opéra Bastille and the *Comédie-Française*. The lively cultural scene is sometimes held to be the result of a distinctive French tradition of constant state intervention in cultural policy - an issue which frequently arouses heated debate.

State intervention in the arts in France goes back a long way. As early as the 16th century, the royal decree of Villers-Cotterêts (1539) stipulated that French must be used in legal decisions and notarised acts, and changes to the language have been monitored by the French Academy since it was founded in 1635. In the 17th century, the state declared itself to be the protector of the arts, especially during the reign of Louis XIV, and as such began encouraging artists and writers by providing them with stipends and commissions: the construction of the Palace of Versailles and the creation of the *Comédie-Française* (1680) are examples of this ambitious royal patronage.

In 1793 the state opened a museum in the Louvre Palace, thereby becoming a curator as well as a patron of the arts. Other landmarks along this road were the establishment of a department of historic monuments (1832) under the direction of Prosper Mérimée and the work of the architect and restorer Viollet-le-Duc.

It was not until the mid-20th century that a third objective was clearly defined in addition to the first two of lavishing encourage-

Greek sculpture room at the Louvre

ment on artists and preserving the cultural heritage: that of making culture more widely accessible. The pioneering work of Jean Zay, Minister for Public Education and Fine Arts in the Popular Front government was taken a step further after the Liberation, with a policy designed to afford the widest possible access to artistic treasures previously seen only by an élite. One example was the public subsidy for the work of Jean Vilar, director of the *Théâtre national populaire* (TNP). Under the Fifth Republic, André Malraux, appointed Minister for Cultural Affairs by General de Gaulle in 1959, stated before the National Assembly that his aim was to do for culture what the Third Republic, with its republican ideals, had done for education: make it truly democratic.

On the eve of the 21st century, this threefold approach to cultural policy is as pertinent as ever. In fact, each of these goals can now look to increased support. But the state no longer acts alone in this area.

The Players

The State

Over the years the funds allocated to the Ministry of Culture have risen steadily, in 1998 approaching the symbolic threshold of 1% of the total state budget or 15.1 billion francs ($2.5 billion). If expenditure on the arts undertaken by other ministries (such as the Ministry of National Education and the Ministry of Youth and Sport), or passed on to third-party bodies (CNRS, *Centres d'action culturelle*, a third of whose funding is state-subsidised) plus appropriations channeled through social projects, town and country planning and the development of tourism are added to this figure, it may be considered that the state spends in the region of 40 billion francs a year on culture.

With this increase in funding, the Ministry of Culture has undergone internal reorganization. By 1998 it had a staff of nearly 15,000 to look after national heritage and architecture, museums, archives, music, dance, theatre and other performing arts, the visual arts, books and reading. It has also developed training programmes for arts specialists and administrators at the *Ecole nationale du patrimoine* (National Heritage School) which opened in 1993.

Local Authorities

The decentralisation legislation of 1982-1983 widened the cultural responsibilities of local authorities and gave them the wherewithal to act. Departmental and regional budgets for culture grew five-fold during the 1980s and those of the municipalities more than doubled. Overall, local authorities now provide more arts funding than does central government (50.3% and 49.7% respectively). The pooling of local and central government resources undoubtedly has a multiplier effect and culture is now benefiting to the tune of 80 billion francs per year.

Towns and cities play a key role: they provide 40% of public arts funding, with an annual contribution of over 30 billion francs ($5 billion). The Paris municipality alone spends 2 billion francs ($0.3 billion) on culture, but many provincial towns also spend large sums on conserving their heritage and organising specific cultural events. In addition, a number of towns are home to cultural institutions of national or even international importance, like the modern art museums of Lyon, Saint-Étienne and Grenoble, the national photography school in Arles, the national higher school of dance in Marseille, the national comic-strip centre in Angoulême, the *Archives du monde du travail* (archives of the world of work) in Roubaix, and the Matisse Museum in Nice. After centuries in which Paris dominated the scene, culture is now starting to flower in all parts of the country.

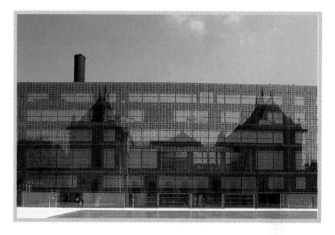

Lille Fine Arts Museum (Nord-Pas-de-Calais), designed and restored by the architects Ibos nd Vitart

Voluntary Organisations and Businesses

The contribution of non-profit-making associations and the private sector to culture should also be stressed. Cultural associations now employ nearly 20,000 people and are usually subsidised by the state and local authorities. They help attract audiences to a wide variety of events and assist in the training of amateurs with the potential to become real professionals. Associations are generally the prime movers behind the many festivals which now take place all over France. Some associations are linked to a particular monument or museum and take an active part in restoration, often alongside foreign organisations and sponsors, as in the long, painstaking process of reconstruction under way at the Palace of Versailles.

Cartier Foundation in Paris, which sponsors many young artists

Private patronage of the arts has a long history, but US-style sponsorship

by businesses is a more recent phenomenon. The Law of 23 July 1987 provided a legal framework for these operations, which represent a total contribution to the arts of over a billion francs a year. For many large companies, setting up foundations and sponsoring prestigious cultural projects are now key strategies in their public relations policy. The Cartier Foundation for fine arts, the Vuitton Opera Foundation, the GAN (*Groupe des assurances nationales*) Foundation for the cinema and many others make an important contribution to cultural events and help to nurture emerging talents. Costly heritage conservation projects have also been wholly or jointly funded by businesses: EDF contributed to the restoration of the dome of the Invalides in Paris; Kodak assisted in restoring the Lascaux prehistoric cave-paintings; and in 1998 the Japanese company NTV pledged funding for renovation of the room containing the Mona Lisa at the Louvre.

Culture, an Economic Sector in its Own Right

Each year, the French spend almost 150 billion francs ($25 billion) on audiovisual products and equipment, books, newspapers, magazines and theatre and cinema tickets. When expenditure by businesses, central government and local authorities is added to this consumption by households, the total market for culture turns out to be worth nearly 200 billion francs ($33 billion). The industries and services which meet this demand now constitute an economic sector in its own right – one which employs over 300,000 people and is steadily expanding.

Of the economic activities relating to culture and the arts, the press, publishing and graphics lead the field (with a turnover of over 100 billion francs [$16.6 billion]), followed by the audiovisual industries — television, the record industry and the cinema (with a collective turnover of about 70 billion francs [$11.6 billion]). The art market is also a sizeable earner: sales at auction, buoyed by increased demand for contemporary works, are in the region of five billion francs ($0.8 billion) per year. The number of art galleries outside Paris doubled during the 1980s. In Paris itself, besides traditional locations like the Faubourg Saint-Honoré and Saint-Germain-des-Prés, two new neighbourhoods have become centres of the art trade: the Beaubourg area around the Pompidou Centre and, more recently, Bastille.

Memory and Heritage

The notion of heritage has gradually broadened to encompass many previously neglected vestiges of the past, but it now also has an aesthetic dimension, particularly as concerns landscapes. However, the traditional focus of heritage conservation – public monuments, religious edifices and archaeological sites – remains central, benefiting from additional financial support and increasingly sophisticated technology.

Conservation, Restoration, Archaeology

Major thematic programmes, particularly those devoted to cathedrals or parks and gardens, show that traditional heritage sites are not being neglected. In all, the number of monuments officially classified as historic has risen at the rate of several hundred a year since 1980. There are now nearly 40,000 "classified" or "listed" buildings.

Restoration is at the heart of the work of the Ministry of Culture's heritage department, which draws on techniques developed by both French and foreign laboratories. All the materials which have historically been seen as fragile or under threat from the ravages of time — stone, stained-glass, painted panels or walls, fabrics — come under the research workers' scrutiny. Some impressive achievements show the progress made in this area: the use of laser technology to clean the cathedral of Amiens; restoration of the stained-glass windows of the cathedrals of Chartres and Troyes; renovation of the organs of Notre-Dame and the church of Saint Eustache in Paris. Advanced technology has also been

In the National Museums' restoration department, experts use a miscroscope to examine *The Resurrection of Lazarus*, a late sixteenth-century work by Gérard Saint-Jean

used to analyse the various types of pollution suffered by the 69 statues in the Napoleon courtyard of the Louvre before their restoration and to restore the dome of the Invalides using a special gold leaf gilding process designed to be weatherproof.

As regards archaeology, over 200,000 sites have now been catalogued throughout the country. Their excavation takes us back to the very beginnings of the national heritage. Important discoveries have added to our knowledge of the neolithic period and iron age: three miraculously preserved pirogues were dug out of the banks of the Seine upstream from Paris, pile houses characteristic of the period have been reconstituted at the Lake Chalain site in the Jura, whilst at La Combe d'Arc (Ardèche) a magnificent bestiary comparable to that at Lascaux was discovered in late 1994. Mediaeval archaeology has benefited from urban renewal schemes in a number of cities: in Paris, construction work on the Grand Louvre led to unprecedented excavations which revealed important vestiges of the medieval period, notably the remains of a keep built by King Philip Augustus at the end of the 12th century.

New Objects of Interest

Imperceptibly, the very notion of heritage has expanded over the past few decades, so that it now encompasses a whole range of previously neglected elements: folk arts and traditions, urban architecture from the late 19th and 20th centuries, industrial architecture, and all the other sites associated with human activity which deserve to be rescued from oblivion, including the recent addition of rural landscapes which are typical of a particular area. The impetus came initially from ethnologists who were anxious to preserve records of ways of life in rural societies. It is one of them, Georges-Henri Rivière, with the assistance of Claude Lévi-Strauss, whom we have to thank for the *Musée des Arts et Traditions Populaires* in the *Jardin d'acclimatation* in Paris. This example inspired others all over France to preserve the memory of regional and local traditions: that is the purpose of the *Musée Camarguais* between Provence and Languedoc, the *Musée Dauphinois* in the Alps, or the many "eco museums" recently opened in most regions. An Ethnological Heritage Mission has been established to preserve the memory of these age-old traditions.

Le Palais du Luxembourg opens its doors to the public on the increasingly popular *Journées du Patrimoine* (annual heritage days), 20 September 1998

Town centres have enjoyed special protection since the adoption of the 1962 Malraux Law stipulating rehabilitation procedures to be used in urban redevelopment schemes. But age and the presence of historic monuments are no longer the sole criteria for preservation; industrial and urban landscapes typical of the past two centuries are now also protected. In the coal mining areas of eastern and northern France, national and local authorities have endeavoured to preserve the sites which symbolise the history of mining and the labour struggles associated with it, such as the Simon pit head in Forbach (Moselle), or the Denain mine which served as a model for Zola's novel *Germinal*. Finally, many urban buildings or sites of architectural or historical interest have likewise become part of the heritage: railway stations, restaurants, theatres and even former brothels can be classified as historic monuments if they are typical of a period or society.

New Media

France, the country of Niepce, Daguerre, Nadar, Doisneau and Cartier-Bresson, can hardly neglect the art of photography, to which it continues to contribute so much. Since 1981 more than five million negatives by the greatest photographers have been stored at the Saint Cyr fort near Versailles.

One of the tasks of the Photographic Heritage Mission is to acquire and manage collections of works of particular significance to the history of photography, such as the Harcourt collection or the series of photographs taken all over the world at the instigation of Albert Kahn at the beginning of this century. It has also benefited from the generosity of several famous photographers: Jacques-Henri Lartigue, who donated photos taken over a period of more than 80 years, extending from the Third Republic of Emile Loubet (1899-1906) to the France of François Mitterrand; Amélie Galup, who took 2,800 plates of rural society at work and play, during the years from 1895 to 1920; and Willy Ronis, who observed life in the working-class neighbourhoods of Paris in the 1950s. The Georges Pompidou Centre has adopted a policy of systematically purchasing the work of contemporary photographers in order to hand down a record of our time to posterity.

Another important task is protecting the cinematic heritage. Henri Langlois, who founded the French *cinémathèque* (film archive library) was a forerunner of cinema conservators today. Copies of films are now systematically given to the CNC (*Centre national de la cinématographie* or national centre for cinematography), but the photochemical medium of film presents especial difficulties for conservation and, where necessary, restoration. In 1990 an emergency 15-year plan was drawn up to save 250,000 films made before 1954 from corrosion. Among the works which have thus escaped destruction are masterpieces of the cinema like Abel Gance's *Napoleon* and Jean Vigo's *Atalante*.

France has a long tradition of systematically preserving archives and printed documents which in the 20th century has been extended to photography and the cinema: this is the *dépôt légal* rule (registration of copyright), which requires that a copy of each document be filed with the *Bibliothèque Nationale* (National Library). This system, which was reorganised by 1992 legislation, is another example of the way the notion of heritage has been broadened; the *dépôt légal* rule now also applies to audiovisual material broadcast by the principal radio and television channels and to computer software. The necessity of keeping a photographic record for future generations has also been borne in mind: since it was founded in 1992, the National Photographic Observatory records changes to the environment at sites which are characteristic of French geography.

A Passion for History

These strenuous efforts to preserve France's heritage are perhaps related to a new French infatuation with history, whether national, regional or even family history, with the development of genealogical research. In recent years there have been numerous commemorations of great national events: the thousandth anniversary of the Capetians coming to power (1987), bicentenary of the French Revolution (1989), centenary of General de Gaulle's birth (1990) and the fiftieth anniversaries of the Normandy and Provence landings and the Liberation of France (1994-1995). These celebrations were a great success with the public, as demonstrated by the proliferation of local initiatives. The record shows that between 1986 and 1992 more than a thousand events — exhibitions, conferences, concerts, celebrations and reenactments — were organised locally. Some commentators have spoken of an "age of commemoration" and "a rush to the past" to describe the French people's new interest in their collective memory.

The Arts Today

This concern to protect France's heritage does not mean that French culture today is entirely preoccupied with celebrating the achievements of the past. The last decades of the 20th century have been marked by a new upsurge of creative activity.

The Place des Terreaux in Lyon (Rhône) enhanced by artists Buren and Drevet

Architecture and the Visual Arts

Since the late 19th century, French artists have played a decisive role in the development of modern painting: thus the work of the Impressionists, Cézanne and the Fauvists inspired the Cubist movement. The millions of art lovers flocking each year to the Louvre, the Musée d'Orsay, the National Museum of Modern Art at the Georges Pompidou Centre and the Picasso Museum bear witness to France's role as a centre for the arts. The Picasso Museum also reminds us of the extraordinary pull Paris has had over the years for artists from all over the world. Van Gogh, Miro, Van Dongen, Modigliani, Soutine, Chagall, Brancusi and Giacometti and many more besides all came to work in the studios of Montparnasse and Montmartre.

Since the 1950s, a plethora of new trends and schools of painting, ranging from abstract expressionism to pop art, have sprung up, once again revolutionising modern art and probably shifting the focus of the avant-garde from Paris to New York. But French artists have kept pace creatively: the work of Daniel Buren, Pierre Soulages, César and Ipoustéguy has won international recognition and the new generation is continuing to influence the major trends in contemporary art.

State encouragement for this creative activity is expressed first of all in art teaching and in the facilities made available to young artists: the award of grants and prestigious scholarships (for example, to the *Académie de France* at the Villa Medici in Rome); it is also expressed in various kinds of assistance for publication or for a first show administered by the Ministry of Culture's FIACRE programme — fund for encouraging creativity. In recent years state sponsorship of the arts has also taken the form of commissions to artists for works to be displayed in public (a type of patronage which had gone out of fashion), and of a programme of major public buildings.

The Paris Conservatoire, La Villette, designed by architect Christian de Portzamparc

Some of the works commissioned from contemporary artists have had an enormous impact. Daniel Buren's columns in the Palais Royal courtyard caused months of heated debate reminiscent of the passions stirred up a century earlier when Rodin's statue of Balzac was erected in the capital. In Paris alone, these new public works include Arman's assemblages of clocks and suitcases in front of the Saint Lazare railway station (1985), César's homage to Picasso (1985), Jean Dubuffet's *Tour aux figures* on the island of Saint Germain (1988) or the curtain painted by Jean-Pierre Chambas at the Athénée theatre (1989).

Finally, the new public buildings which have sprung up in Paris since the beginning of the 1980s are a tribute to the creativity of architects from all over the world. The Georges Pompidou National Centre of Art and Culture was designed in the 1970s by the British architect Richard Rogers and the Italian Renzo Piano. The old Gare d'Orsay, a fine example of railway architecture from the end of the last century, was remodelled by three French architects and an Italian and has now become the Musée d'Orsay, dedicated to 19th-century art. To celebrate its bicentenary, the most famous Parisian museum of all had a face-lift: the Grand Louvre was entirely refurbished by the American architect Mario Pei. The new-look Louvre, with its glass pyramid, spans a magnificent perspective which extends through the Tuileries Gardens, along the Champs-Elysées to the Grand Arch of La Défense — the work of a Danish architect, Von Spreckelsen. In the north of Paris, the park at La Villette, designed by Bernard Tschumi, forms a city-garden which takes in a whole series of buildings: the Zénith, where big variety shows are staged, Adrien Fainsilber's astonishing Géode (a cinema where spectators are surrounded on all sides by the action) and the multi-purpose musical venue *Cité de la Musique* designed especially for sound by its creator, Christian de Portzamparc. Finally, the banks of the Seine up-river from Notre-Dame also catch the eye, with Jean Nouvel's *Institut du monde arabe* (Institute of the Arab World) on one side and the new headquarters of the Ministry of Finance at Bercy, designed by Paul Chemetov, on the other. Farther back from the river on the Right Bank is the Opéra-Bastille, the work of architect Carlos Ott, while on the Left Bank at Tolbiac four towers in the shape of open books rise up. They make up the new Bibliothèque Nationale de France, designed by Dominique Perrault and opened to the public in 1996.

Music

Music is very popular in France and the French enjoy a very wide variety of musical styles. The authorities encourage all forms of music from the purest classical traditions to the most popular of tastes (such as rock, variety, rai and rap). The Government subsidises the *Centre de musique baroque* in Versailles along with the *Centre national du patrimoine*

de la chanson et des variétés, dedicated to popular songs and variety shows, the *Orchestre national de jazz* and the *Centre d'information du rock*.

Highbrow contemporary music has won new audiences with the performance of works by composers such as Olivier Messiaen, Pierre Boulez, Yannis Xenakis and Henri Dutilleux from IRCAM (*Institut de recherche et de coordination acoustique/musique*). On its tours in France and abroad the *Ensemble intercontemporain* acquaints audiences around the world with this 20th-century repertoire.

The composer and conductor Pierre Boulez conducts the Ensemble Court-circuit at Aix-en-Provence, June 1998

Opera has been generously supported by the French government in recent years. The Opéra-Bastille, which opened its doors in 1988, has the most modern technical equipment at its disposal and can seat an audience of 2,700 in its main hall. The Opéra-Comique specialises in the French repertoire; the Châtelet theatre, once a shrine to operetta, now alternates performances of recitals, concerts and opera; while the Palais Garnier – the older Paris opera house – now focuses more on dance. Away from the capital, the *Théâtre français de la musique* in Compiègne is developing a reputation as an outstanding centre for French opera. The opera houses of Lyon, Toulouse, Rouen and Nantes, amongst others, consistently offer high-quality productions.

Dance

As in the case of music, it is becoming increasingly difficult to establish a rigid distinction between classical and modern dance. The ballet company of the Paris Opera continues to uphold its long tradition of excellence and, under the aegis of Claude Bessy, its ballet school has become one of the best in the world. The many companies founded during the past twenty years are contributing to a radical renewal in contemporary choreography. Since Maurice Béjart revolutionised the

"Shazam", choreographed by Philippe Decouflé and performed by the DCA company

world of dance, others have also made their mark, from Régine Chopinot to Jean-Claude Gallota and Dominique Bagouet to Angelin Preljocaj. Dance in France has also been enriched by the experimental work of foreign choreographers and dancers such as William Forsythe, Merce Cunningham and Pina Bausch, all of whom are regularly and enthusiastically welcomed in Paris and other French cities.

Cinema

Juliette Binoche, winner of 1997 Oscar for Best Actress for her role in *The English Patient*

In 1995, cinema celebrated its hundredth birthday. It was on 28 December 1895 that the Lumière brothers, who had recorded the first moving images in their film "Leaving the Lumière factories", gave the film its first commercial showing at the Grand Café in the heart of Paris. This date is taken as marking the birth of cinema and the centenary year was packed with commemorative events all over France. As the birthplace of the Seventh Art, France remains one of the major centres of the film world and has given it some of its legendary figures — from Méliès, a brilliant early exponent, to the 1930s generation of poetic realists (Renoir, Carné and Prévert) and the *nouvelle vague* of the 1960s (Truffaut, Godard, Chabrol, Malle and Rohmer). Along with this tradition of *cinéma d'auteur* France has been home to some outstandingly successful film companies (Pathé, Gaumont) and boasts internationally famous stars such as Brigitte Bardot,

Yves Montand and Alain Delon in the recent past and Gérard Depardieu, Isabelle Adjani and Juliette Binoche today.

In 1998, 148 million cinema tickets were sold in France as a whole, for a total box office value of 5.14 billion francs ($0.85 billion); 57% of the French went to the cinema at least once during the year and 39% at least once a month. Attendances are thus somewhat improved and have returned to their 1980s levels, but there is an underlying downward trend as a result of competition from television and video-cassettes.

The French cinema industry continues to play an acknowledged international role, partly thanks to a comprehensive system of support for creative work, production and distribution administered by the *Centre national de la cinématographie*. This body redistributes the funds derived from a tax on cinema tickets, video-cassette sales and television broadcasts of films. The system of advances on box-office sales is emblematic of France's determination to encourage new talent and to supplement financing from traditional sources for ambitious projects. The success of the policy can be measured quantitatively. France has the second highest number of cinemas in Europe after Russia (4,400), and many have been recently renovated. The drop

in income resulting from declining attendance figures was cause for concern until the end of the 1970s, but this trend was reversed in the following decade. About 100 feature films are produced in France every year, of which approximately one third are first films. This makes France the country with the third biggest film industry in the world, surpassed only by India and the United States. France is unique in Europe in that its home-grown productions accounted for nearly 35% of cinema attendance in 1997 – a healthy performance in the face of competition from the American film industry, which has a virtual monopoly in many foreign markets.

Team responsible for Erick Zonca's film *La vie rêvée des anges*, presented at the Cannes Film Festival, on 17 may 1998, for which E. Bouchez and N. Régnier jointly received the *Prix d'interprétation féminine* (best actress award)

The vitality of French cinema is symbolised by a number of directors whose work is highly personal, such as Bertrand Tavernier (*Que la fête commence* (Let Joy Reign Supreme), *Un dimanche à la campagne* (A Sunday in the Country), *Coup de torchon* (Clean Slate), *L 627, La vie et rien d'autre* (Life and Nothing But), *Capitaine Conan*), Maurice Pialat (*À nos amours* (To Our Loves), *Loulou, Sous le soleil de Satan* (Under Satan's Sun), *Van Gogh*), Bertrand Blier (*Buffet froid* (Cold Cuts) *Tenue de soirée* (Menage), *1, 2, 3, Soleil* (One Two Three Sun), *Mon Homme*), André Téchiné (*Rendez-vous, Ma saison préférée* (My Favourite Season), *Les roseaux sauvages* (Wild Reeds)), and Jean-Jacques Beineix (*Diva, 37°2 le matin* (Betty Blue) and *IP 5*). The more popular quality cinema also has its talents, with Jean-Paul Rappeneau

(*Cyrano de Bergerac, Le Hussard sur le toit*) and Claude Berri (*Jean de Florette, Manon des sources, Germinal*), whose films have been enthusiastically received. Success too for comedy films, a showcase for actors like Josiane Balasko, Michel Blanc, Christian Clavier, Gérard Jugnot and Thierry Lhermitte, where there was something of a revival with the 1993 hit *Les Visiteurs*, the biggest box-office success for a comedy since the 1960s. Some French directors have acquired an international reputation, such as Jean-Jacques Annaud, who made *L'Ours* (The Bear), *Le Nom de la rose* (The Name of the Rose), *L'Amant* (The Lover) and *Sept ans au Tibet* (Seven Years in Tibet), and Luc Besson, whose films include *Le Grand Bleu* (The Big Blue), *Nikita, Léon* and *Le cinquième élément* (The Fifth Element). Finally, a new generation of film-makers are making a name for themselves — Olivier Assayas, Léos Carax, Cédric Klapisch, Manuel Poirier, Eric Rochant, Christian Vincent and others — and some of their successors are probably now studying at the FEMIS (*Fondation européenne des métiers de l'image et du son*) film-school, housed in the Palais de Tokyo in Paris.

Theatre

The dynamic French theatre scene has traditionally owed much to the inspiration of great directors — from Antoine's *Théâtre libre* through the *Cartel* of Gémier, Copeau, Baty and Jouvet between the wars to Jean Vilar's *Théâtre national populaire* (TNP) after the Liberation. Until his early death in 1990, Antoine Vitez trained generations of actors and encouraged them to approach the classic repertoire of French drama from Molière to Victor Hugo, Aragon and Claudel in new ways. Other figures whose experiments have helped to revitalise French theatre include Roger Planchon in Lyon, Marcel Maréchal in Marseille, Ariane Mnouchkine at the *Cartoucherie* in Vincennes, Peter Brook at the *Bouffes du*

A performance of
Jean Racine's *Phèdre*
at the Théâtre de l'Odéon
in Paris, September 1998,
directed by L. Bondy,
with N. Dréville and
D. Sandre

Nord in Paris, Jean-Pierre Vincent at the *Théâtre des Amandiers* in Nanterre, Jorge Lavelli at the *Théâtre de la Colline* in Paris, Georges Lavaudant in Villeurbanne near Lyon, Jacques Nichet in Montpellier, Jérôme Savary at the *Théâtre de Chaillot* and Bernard Sobel in Gennevilliers. Along with Daniel Mesguich, Patrice Chéreau, Gildas Bourdet and Jacques Lassalle, each of them continues to bring a passionate vision of theatre to the French stage.

But listing the most famous directors hardly conveys how many theatre productions of all sorts are mounted each year in France, where there are 42 national drama centres, 170 companies with state contracts and 398 subsidised troupes. The total number of independent companies tripled in the 1980s and today there are well over a thousand. In addition, many theatres have been opened, modernised or restored in recent years both in Paris (e.g. the *Théâtre national de la Colline*) or in the provinces (the *Théâtre de Port de la Lune* in Bordeaux, *Théâtre de la Salamandre* in Lille, the *Nouveau Théâtre de Nice*, etc.).

Another form of live entertainment, the circus, has developed in new directions. Companies like Plume, Archaos and Zingaro – an equestrian troupe – have revolutionised the medium. There are several thriving circus schools, and the Cirque Gruss has made a success of carrying on the big-top tradition.

Literature in France: Tradition and Modernity

Modern French authors have a formidable task, in that they are heirs to a brilliant generation of earlier 20th-century writers whose works have become classics of contemporary literature: Gide, Sartre, Camus, Céline, Malraux, Mauriac, Anouilh, Beckett, Genet and Montherlant. This is made even more difficult by the current lack of clearly identified literary movements or schools, compared with, say, the time of the Surrealists. An exception is the group known as the *Hussards*, which has lost Roger Nimier, Antoine Blondin and Jacques Laurent, but can still rely on Michel Déon to maintain the nonconformist stance they adopted in the immediate post-war years. The *nouveau roman* authors of the 1950s – Michel Butor, Alain Robbe-Grillet, Nathalie Sarraute and others – have continued their literary experiments, while Claude Simon received the ultimate accolade of the Nobel prize for literature in 1985. But the overall impression in French literature today is of a patchwork of individual experiences as each author follows his or her personal bent from one work to the next. Julien Gracq is typical: since the publication of *Le Château d'Argol* he has maintained a solitary pursuit of the great classical tradition. Mention should also be made of Marguerite Yourcenar, the first woman admitted to the French Academy,

Le Salon du Livre (book fair) held annually in Paris provides an opportunity for readers and authors to meet each other: here, philosopher Michel Serres signs a copy of one of his books, 22 March 1998

who died in 1987, leaving a body of work deeply rooted in history (*Mémoires d'Hadrien*, *L'Oeuvre au noir*), Marguerite Duras, who died in 1996, who finally won public acclaim with the publication of *L'Amant*, Michel Tournier too with *Vendredi ou les limbes du Pacifique* and *Le Roi des aulnes*. Amongst the best-known names in the following generation are Philippe Sollers, Jean-Marie Le Clézio, Patrick

Modiano, Patrick Grainville and Pascal Quignard, but since the 1980s a number of new talents have emerged, such as Erik Orsenna, Jean Rouault, Patrick Chamoiseau, Didier Van Cauwelaert, Andrei Makine and Patrick Rambaud.

Novels are still the most popular form of literature in France, but French readers have not forgotten poetry. There have been worthy successors to Aragon, Saint-John Perse, René Char and Francis Ponge. Jean Tardieu, who died in 1995 and Jacques Roubaud, Michel Deguy, Yves Bonnefoy and Jacques Reda have been transforming the vast heritage of French poetry and standing up well to the pressures of an age which unfortunately seems little suited to this form of literature.

The Public and the Arts

As well as new art forms there is now a wider public. True, spending on cultural items and activities still varies according to age, education, social class and geographical origin, but the constant rise in household audiovisual equipment and the boom in museum visits and theatre attendance reflect the growing popularity of cultural activities in all social categories.

Access to Culture

The government is waging an active policy of cultural dissemination starting with the education and training of its youngest citizens. Opportunities for education in the arts, especially music and the visual arts, which used to be limited, were greatly expanded in the 1980s. A close-knit network of regional and municipal conservatories provide low-cost music, theatre and dance tuition. Finally, there are a number of prestigious training establishments for future professionals including the two national music conservatories, the national fine arts school, the national academy for dramatic art, the national school for photography and the European foundation for audiovisual professions (FEMIS).

Artist Ben's *Mur des mots* (wall of words) at the Blois Fine Arts School (Loir-et-Cher)

For many years now, the state television channels have reserved a share (albeit very small) of their air time for cultural programmes. The literary programme *Apostrophes*, presented by Bernard Pivot every

Friday evening for ten years, has been renamed *Bouillon de culture* and expanded to incorporate a broader range of cultural events. Since 1992 one channel has been specifically reserved for cultural broadcasting: *Arte*. This is a joint Franco-German channel with a bilingual schedule, and is the first European experiment of this kind. Since *Arte* broadcasts only during the evening hours, an educational channel, *La Cinquième*, now transmits on the same wavelength throughout the day.

Cultural Venues

At the beginning of the 1960s, André Malraux set up the *Maisons des jeunes et de la culture* (youth and arts centres) to attract a broader urban population to cultural events. Thirty years on, cultural venues have proliferated. There has been a successful effort to build new theatres all over France or refurbish existing houses, whilst rock concert halls and music-hall theatres attract an average audience of 15 million people a year. The Paris-Bercy Omnisports Park can seat up to 15,000 spectators — but giant concerts can also be organised in stadiums, like the Rolling Stones concert at the Grand Stade de France in 1998. The popularity of venues such as the Zénith in Paris and similar projects in Montpellier and Toulon has inspired imitations up and down the country (Lyon, Marseille, Nancy, Caen, Tours, etc.).

Museums too play a major role in extending access to culture, and a new discipline, museology, has been created so that these shrines to beauty, originally designed for conservation, may serve to circulate works of art and promote their appreciation by a broader public. The opening of the Georges Pompidou Centre for Contemporary Art, followed by that of the Musée d'Orsay, focusing on late 19th-century art, the Picasso Museum in the Hôtel Salé and the City of Science and Industry at La Villette in Paris, have given fresh impetus to museums throughout France. In the last twenty-five years nearly 80 museums have been set up or renovated in Paris and elsewhere. A notable example is the Fine Art Museum in Lyon, which occupies the entire Palais Saint-Pierre, a 17th-century abbey renovated by architects Philippe Dubois and Jean-Michel Wilmotte. It was opened in April 1998, following nine years of restoration at a cost of 400 million francs ($66.6 million) and is now the largest and wealthiest in France after the Louvre, with 6,300 works on show in a space of 15,000 m², including the Jacqueline Delubac bequest of Impressionist paintings. Prominent architects have been commissioned to design several museums outside Paris – for example, the Contemporary Art Museum in Lyons, which has been housed, as of 1995, in a building designed by Renzo Piano, or the *Carré d'art* in Nîmes designed by Norman Foster.

In France, libraries continue to be amongst the most frequently visited "halls of culture"

However, the most important project is the refurbishment of the Grand Louvre. The Richelieu wing, which alone is as large as the entire Musée d'Orsay, was inaugurated in 1993. The renovated Denon wing was opened to the public in the autumn of 1994 and presents the Italian, Spanish and northern European sculpture collections, including Michelangelo's two well-known statues of a slave. The whole project was completed in 1997 with the opening of 35 new galleries devoted to French painting from the 17th to the 19th centuries and the reorganisation of the Antiquities section. In all there are 34 national museums in France, of which 19 are located outside Paris, and nearly 900 museums under public supervision, generally belonging to local authorities. They are every bit as successful as was expected, attracting over 70 million visitors a year. Art lovers crowd in to admire masterpieces which form part of the world heritage, as well as major temporary exhibitions (the most recent of which were devoted to Matisse, Poussin, Cézanne and de La Tour).

Libraries are still amongst the most popular cultural venues in France. Apart from school and university libraries, there are about 3,000 municipal libraries. Every departmental authority also runs a lending library, and there are almost 21,000 of these in all, 17,000 in permanent locations and 4,000 mobile (the so-called "bibliobus"). Paris has a number of prestigious libraries, such as those of the Centre Georges Pompidou and the Arsenal and the Sainte-Geneviève and Mazarine Libraries. It is also home to the new National Library opened in 1996, which can hold 30 million works and now houses the stock of the books, printed documents, periodicals and sound library of the old Richelieu National Library.

Cultural Celebrations

A rehearsal of Mozart's *Don Giovanni*, directed by Peter Brook, with the conductor Claudio Abbado, at the Aix-en-Provence opera festival (Bouches-du-Rhône), July 1998

Special occasions are also set aside for culture. Since it was first held in 1982, the *Fête de la musique* has come to symbolise a new approach which tends to cut across the usual divide between official organised events and spontaneous cultural expression. Every year, on 21 June, the *Fête de la musique* brings together tens of thousands of professional and amateur musicians in towns all over France. This French initiative has now spread to nearly 80 other countries. But we should not forget the great summer festivals focusing on opera (Aix-en-Provence),

choral music (Vaison-la-Romaine), theatre (Avignon) and contemporary music (Strasbourg). Variety and rock also have their day in the sun: the *Printemps de Bourges* has become a tradition, and the *Trans-Musicales* in Rennes has introduced Etienne Daho, Niagara and Stéphan Eicher to the public.

Then there is the *Fête du cinéma*, first organised in 1985. This unusual promotional exercise lasting about a week allows people to watch an entire day of films for the price of a single ticket. This festival too is trying to go international, via embassies and the *Alliances françaises*. Just as important are the international film festivals, of which the Cannes Festival is the best known; its *Palme d'Or* is probably the most prestigious of all film awards. There has been a proliferation of film events in recent years, with the Avoriaz fantasy and science-fiction film festival, the Deauville Festival, which presents American films and has its counterpart in the United States with the French film festival in Sarasota, the Cognac festival of detective films and the Biarritz short-film festival. These festivals also play an important role in developing regional tourism.

Literature too has its festivals. Every year in October *Lire en fête*, which succeeded *Le Temps des livres* in 1998, mounts a number of initiatives designed to communicate a passion for the written word to the largest possible number of people. Every year since 1981 the *Salon du livre* (book fair) has presented the public with France's biggest bookshop: on 450 stands, 1,200 publishers display their complete range, from literature to encyclopaedias and art books to works for children. The success of this Paris event has inspired at least ten towns in the provinces to follow suit, and today book fairs are held in Brive, Bordeaux, Nantes, Le Mans, Saint Etienne, Saint Malo, Lyon and Strasbourg. A related area, comic books, has its own festival at Angoulême.

Lastly, one day a year is set aside for the public to delve into the hidden treasures of France's heritage. Monuments open their doors to visitors, who stroll free of charge through the galleries of the Elysée Palace or the Institut de France, the Hôtel de Matignon or the Palais Bourbon, the Bibliothèque Nationale or the Opéra-Bastille. Some two million people take advantage of this opportunity to get a look inside 8,300 or so public buildings. A similar idea inspired the "Visit a French garden" campaign, which invites the public to discover this little-known aspect of French heritage each spring.

Openness to the World

The Mona Lisa is the best known of the art works in the Louvre. Leonardo da Vinci's masterpiece epitomises the debt French culture has always owed to foreign artists and influences. As the third millennium approaches, the tradition of reciprocal influence is as strong as ever.

Access to All Cultures

The French public regularly demonstrates its appreciation of works from all parts of the world. Nearly half the recordings and tapes sold in France are of popular music from other countries, and foreign films bring in two thirds of cinema receipts. The majority of foreign films are American, but Paris is probably the only city in the world where film buffs can indulge their tastes and satisfy their curiosity by viewing recent works or classics from India, Africa, China and Latin America, as well as all the European countries.

This eclecticism is reflected in many other areas – witness the enthusiastic welcome given to foreign choreographers in France, whether they be Swiss, like Gallotta, or American, like Merce Cunningham, William Forsythe and Carolyn Carlson, who directed the Paris Opera research group. The same is true of theatre: Peter Brook, Lucian Pintillé and Jorge Lavelli direct some of France's outstanding theatres. The former Odéon theatre, renamed the Théâtre de l'Europe and now managed by the Catalan Luis Pasqual, gives priority to productions representing the great foreign stage traditions. The same open-mindedness prevails in the visual arts, as is demonstrated by the success of exhibitions of the work of foreign schools or artists regularly organised in French museums. Since it was first opened, the Pompidou Centre has specialised in big retrospectives devoted to the mutual influence of different cultures, from "Paris-New York" and "Paris-Moscow" 15 years ago to more recent tributes to cosmopolitan figures such as Borges, Amado and Brancusi.

Singer Patricia Kaas at a *Fête de la musique* concert at the Paris Parc des Princes, 21 June 1997

The authorities encourage this interest in works from abroad and are doing their part to increase French awareness of foreign cultures. In the literary domain, efforts are made to relieve publishers of some of the extra costs associated with translation: an international translators' college was established in Arles in 1989, and has assisted in the publication of hundreds of foreign-language titles. In addition, two or three times a year the *Belles étrangères* project ("foreign beauties") introduces a variety of foreign literary traditions to French readers by inviting some of their best-known representatives to France; in the recent past, authors from the Netherlands, Israel, Sweden and Korea have been celebrated in this way, and in 1998 it was the turn of Brazilian literature.

Elective Affinities

Thus, no culture and no continent is neglected. Nevertheless, there are certain elective affinities which to this day continue to express the vitality of long-standing traditions of exchange and solidarity. Here, particular mention must be made of Francophony. Since the Ministers of Culture of all the French-speaking countries first met in 1981 in Cotonou, there has been an explosion of initiatives designed to strengthen the ties between creative artists and the public in the French-speaking world. The *Festival international des francophonies* in Limoges has become the annual meeting place for French-language theatres from around the world, while the *Francofolies* festival in La Rochelle brings together every kind of music sung in French. French-language writing is not standing still, so great is the contribution of Francophone writers from all over the world. On all five continents, it is showing renewed vitality: an epic dimension in writing from the French West Indies and the Indian Ocean, a new gravitas in prose from the Maghreb and the Middle East, a heightened sense of mystery in the work of the African poets. The work of Léopold Sedar Senghor, Aimé Césaire, Tahar Ben Jelloun and Ampathé Bâ is ample evidence of this renewed vitality.

Dancers perform in front of the Palais des Papes in Avignon (Vaucluse)

Whether or not they share the French language, many countries in the southern hemisphere maintain a special cultural relationship with France. Some of the places and events where these exchanges take place are worth mentioning: for instance, the *Institut du monde arabe* and the *Maison de l'Amérique latine* in Paris are reminders of the many close ties between French culture and the Mediterranean and Latin countries. The *Musiques métisses* festival at Angoulême first introduced French listeners to African groups such as Touré Kounda or Mory Kante, which have since gained an international reputation. Every autumn the *Festival des trois continents* in Nantes presents a selection of films from Africa, Asia and South America. Finally, the *Maison des cultures du monde*, which was set up in 1982, invites musicians, artists, dancers and artists from all parts of the world to perform or exhibit in France.

As the peoples of Europe develop ever-closer political and economic ties, France is acting to ensure that the cultural dimension is not neglected. To this end, it supports various institutional schemes such as the annual designation of a European capital of culture, the establishment of a European literary prize and programmes of support for European film and audiovisual production. But a "cultural Europe" can also be seen in the profusion of spontaneous initiatives, collaborative efforts and encounters – more and more translations, the growing number of cinema co-productions, the joint training programmes for young creators. Or again, to give just a few typical examples, the regular performances by Milan's *Piccolo teatro* in French theatres, the organisation of a Swedish music week in Paris, the reconstitution of the pilgrim routes to Santiago de Compostela, the exhibition of masterpieces of English painting from French collections, etc.

The Cultural Exception

During the final phase of the GATT trade negotiations, France, acting in agreement with its European Union and Francophone partners, insisted that special conditions must apply to cultural goods and services in international trade.

The above summary of French cultural priorities makes it clear that this stand was in no way dictated by any desire to limit cultural exchanges. On the contrary, by asserting that culture cannot be considered as an ordinary merchandise, and by supporting the right of every state to encourage its own creative artists, France's intention was to help maintain the diverse traditions which make up the cultural heritage of humanity. This ambition also fuels French policy within international bodies dedicated

Château de Chambord (1519-1537) built for King François I, a Renaissance masterpiece

to promoting culture, such as the Council of Europe and UNESCO. France's goal is to facilitate freedom of movement for works of the mind, while at the same time ensuring that all cultures enjoy equal dignity and are enabled to safeguard the conditions necessary for their survival and constant renewal.

Further reading:

Ministère de la Culture et de la Communication, *Chiffres clés 1997 - Statistiques de la culture* (Ed. J. Cardona and C. Lacroix), La Documentation française, 1998.

O. Donnat, *Les Français face à la culture. De l'exclusion à l'éclectisme*, La Découverte, 1994.

P. Goetschel, E. Loyer, *Histoire culturelle et intellectuelle de la France au XXᵉ siècle*, Armand Colin, 1994.

P. Urfalino, *L'invention de la politique culturelle*, Ministère de la Culture, La Documentation française, 1996.

Institutions et vie culturelles, La Documentation française - CNFPT, Les Notices series, 1996.

"Culture et société", in *Cahiers français*, La Documentation française, 1993.

O. Donnat, *Les pratiques culturelles des Français. 1997*, Ministère de la Culture et de la Communication, La Documentation française, 1998.

Ministère de la Culture, Direction des Archives de France, *Célébrations nationales*, 1996.

Ministère de la Culture, Département des études et de la prospective, *Les jeunes et les sorties culturelles*, 1995.

P. Fouché, *L'édition française depuis 1945*, Édition du Cercle de la Librairie, 1998.

300 Yves Saint-Laurent models present a forty-year retrospective of the couturier's work before the kick-off of the World Cup Final between France and Brazil in the Stade de France (Seine-Saint-Denis), 12 July 1998

19

The Media

Freedom of expression is a right in France. Article 11 of the 1789 Declaration of the Rights of Man and the Citizen rules that "every citizen may speak, write and print with freedom, but shall be responsible for such abuses of this freedom as shall be defined by law". Without press freedom there can be no democracy, but winning this freedom in France was not easy. After the French Revolution of 1789, liberal and authoritarian regimes alternated and it was not until the Law of 29 July 1881 that the principle of a free press was permanently established. This law abolished all kinds of obstacles to free expression (prior authorisation, deposit of security bonds, stamps, etc.) and allowed the press to publish with fewer risks of prosecution. A flood of new titles ensued.

During the Occupation, a section of the French press supported the policy of collaboration with Nazi Germany. After the Liberation these publications were rigorously purged. Between June and August 1944 the provisional government announced three decrees to protect the press both from government interference and from financial pressures and subordination to commercial interests.

Since market pressures do not always encourage pluralism, the laws of 23 October 1984 and then of 1 August and 27 November 1986 were designed to guarantee the plurality of the press, vital for democratic debate, and prevent excessive concentrations of ownership. Since then, a single press group has been allowed to control – either by merger or acquisition – no more than 30% of the total circulation of France's daily newspapers.

One of Paris' many newsstands

Concurrently, over the decades, legislation has been passed to protect the individual, guarantee public order and ensure the independence and status of journalists. This is the legal basis on which the press operates in France today.

At the end of 1997, there were approximately

30,000 journalists in possession of an official press card in France, 37.5% of whom were women and over half under 40 years old.

Written Press: a Picture Full of Contrasts

With about 3,100 titles and an annual total print-run of 8 billion copies, the written press is experiencing some difficulties. However, the situation differs considerably from one type of publication to another: national dailies are fighting tooth and nail and the foremost of these, *Le Monde*, *Libération* and *Le Parisien-Aujourd'hui*, have fundamentally reviewed their strategies since 1994 and tried to meet the new expectations of today's readers - successfully, it seems, judging by the greatly improved sales figures.

The regional press reacted earlier to the public's new demands and continues to be the most popular news medium in France, even ahead of television. Finally, the specialist press is enjoying a boom.

There are just under a hundred national and regional dailies, excluding specialist papers, and about 12 million copies are printed daily.

National Dailies

Most French dailies come out in the morning; only *Le Monde* is an afternoon paper. On the whole, they no longer ostensibly espouse a political view; the general tone has become more neutral, except in editorials and opinion pages.

The ideologically aligned daily press, very much in evidence before World War II, has now virtually disappeared. The only remaining examples are *La Lettre de la Nation*, the voice of the *Rassemblement pour la République* (RPR), the Communist Party's *L'Humanité*, founded by Jean Jaurès in 1904, and *Présent*, a platform for the far right. The Catholic daily *La Croix* belongs to the largest religious press group in France, Bayard Presse, but it is more of a general daily newspaper than a religious paper as such.

At the office of *Le Monde*, director Jean-Marie Colombani watches the setting-up of the daily newspaper's new lay-out, December 1994

The leading quality daily newspapers are *Le Monde*, *Le Figaro* and *Libération*. They have an important influence not only on public opinion, but also on the other media. However, their combined circulation (number of copies sold) of almost one million, with nearly five million readers, is lower than that of the other major newspapers in Europe. The star of the popular press is *Le Parisien-Aujourd'hui*. Originally conservative, it has taken radical steps both to improve the financial side of its operation and to gain new readers. It has shifted its political stance, opening up its columns to centre left leader writers and developed a regional strategy; it also produces a national edition entitled *Aujourd'hui*. These efforts have been crowned with success and *Le Parisien-Aujourd'hui*, with a circulation of approximately 500,000 and a readership of two million, has become the second most popular national daily.

By contrast, the popular news daily *France-Soir* has not managed to sort out its problems and its circulation has fallen from 1.5 million in 1955 to 400,000 in 1985 and 173,000 in 1997. Its adoption of a tabloid format in 1998 gives it a new chance to regain a more loyal readership.

Specialist dailies have done better, especially the daily economic and financial papers with *Les Echos* (circulation of 129,000 in 1997) and *La Tribune* (90,000) and the daily sporting press with *L'Equipe*, which has the largest circulation of any daily, with two million readers (average sales of 381,000 copies on weekdays and nearly 500,000 on Mondays).

A new type of newspaper appeared on the streets in 1993 (cf. *Big Issue* in the UK), with an initial total print-run said to be between 45,000 to 50,000. These papers are sold for 10-15 francs in public places (underground and railway stations, etc.) by badged unemployed and homeless vendors who keep a portion of the cover price and, through the scheme, gain entitlement to welfare cover. This "street press" is now experiencing difficulties and sales are falling. Among its best-known weekly and monthly titles are *Macadam-Journal*, *La Rue*, *Sans-Abri* and *L'Itinérant*, which continue to appear, but now have smaller print-runs and lower sales figures.

Regional Dailies

The regional press, with 409 titles and a combined annual circulation of 2.2 billion has weathered the economic crisis better than the national press. Regional newspapers often have the advantage of a monopoly within a given area, giving them a protected advertising market and the local news and services they contain protect them from competition from radio and television.

Regional newspapers began to modernise at the start of the 1970s, with the advent of offset printing, telematics and facsimile; these required sizeable financial resources which could be found only by merging titles and companies. Today the regional press is dominated by a few large groups: the Hersant group controls about 30% of the market (*Le Dauphiné Libéré, Paris-Normandie, Le Progrès de Lyon,*

Les Dernières Nouvelles d'Alsace, Nord-Matin, Nord-Eclair, Le Havre-Libre, Midi-Libre, etc.); Hachette-Filipacchi Presse is also a major force (*Le Provençal, Le Méridional* and *La République*), alongside smaller groups each built up around a flagship newspaper (*Ouest-France, Sud-Ouest, La Dépêche du Midi* and *La Voix du Nord*). *Ouest-France*, the leading French daily (17 editions and a total print-run of over 800,000) is distributed in 12 departments in Brittany, Normandy and the Pays de la Loire. With daily sales of approximately seven million copies and a readership of over 20 million, the daily regional press vies with television as the number-one national medium.

A study carried out by Ipsos Médias revealed that 45.4% of the French over the age of 15 read a regional newspaper every day, with 43.8% of them doing so regularly. Readers aged 35-59, most of whom are in work, are equally divided between men and women. Whilst daily regional papers are read by only 17% of the population in the Paris area, their readership exceeds 50% throughout the rest of France.

Economics of the Press

The written press in France is the 22nd largest in the world and seventh largest in Europe, with 157 copies sold per 1,000 inhabitants. 49% of the French read a newspaper every day, compared with 55% twenty years ago. In 1998, the average amount spent on newspapers and magazines by households was in the region of 793 francs ($132).

On top of the economic crisis and competition from television, which has led to a drop in newspaper advertising, the sector has been hit by the bans or severe restrictions on tobacco and alcohol advertising. In 1980, 60% of advertising revenues still went to the written press, with 20% going to television. In 1996 the share of the press had fallen to 47.3% (including small ads) compared to 33.5% for television.

In addition, the French press suffers from a severe shortage of equity capital and, consequently, is burdened by heavy costs. It has nonetheless had, and is still having, to invest massively to modernise and survive. Rises in the price of paper and distribution costs (which absorb two thirds of earnings from sales) increase the cost price of a product which has to be sold twice over, to readers and to advertisers. French dailies sell at considerably higher prices than their British or German counterparts, despite state assistance: 7.50 francs for *Le Monde*, as against 30 pence (about 3.00 francs) for *The Times*. The price of newspapers, which used to be kept in line with that of an ordinary postage stamp, increased eightfold between 1970 and 1980, although the cost of living increased only by a factor of four.

In 1997, the 60 billion franc ($10 billion) turnover of the press in France was lower than that of its British or German counterparts, which were hit by and overcame the crisis earlier. In 1996, about 2,000 French titles were exported to 107 foreign countries, with a turnover of 2.74 billion francs ($45 million).

Weeklies

The periodical press is flourishing. With 1,354 copies sold for every 1,000 inhabitants, France has the highest level of magazine readership in the world. In 1998, 95.5% of the French regularly or occasionally read this kind of publication.

News Weeklies

France has no fewer than seven major quality news and general interest weeklies, *Le Nouvel Observateur*, *L'Express*, *Le Point*, *L'Evénement du Jeudi*, *Paris Match*, *VSD* and the most recent addition, *Marianne*, founded in 1997. They are, on the whole, in good health. Thanks to economic restructuring, successful changes of formula and membership of large press groups, nearly 2,320,000 copies of these publications are now distributed, including 828,600 for *Paris Match* alone. This magazine, founded in 1949, blends current affairs, culture and features on world celebrities (artists, politicians, royal families) and devotes a great deal of space to illustrated reports. The weekly *Courrier International*, which translates and publishes in French news articles from the international press, celebrated its eighth birthday in 1998 and now has a circulation of 100,000. The price of these periodicals ranges from 12 to 30 francs ($2 to $5).

Alongside these titles, there is also room for more original weekly news magazines. *Le Canard Enchaîné* is probably the liveliest example: this satirical weekly, which maintains its independence by refusing to accept any advertising, serves as a barometre of press freedom in France. Dating back to 1916, it sells for 8 francs ($1.30) and epitomises an irreverent spirit and the freedom to inform, regardless of the political majority in power. Thanks to a formidable network of informants and investigative reporters, it criticises abuses of power and denounces scandals, misappropriation of funds and irregulari-

Some of France's newspapers and magazines

ties of all kinds, with great use of puns and caricature, but always in the most elegant French. It has over 2.5 million readers and sells 550,000 copies each week. *Charlie Hebdo* is another satirical weekly, which now has a readership of 200,000.

■ Consumer, Business and Professional Titles

The last few years have seen an extraordinary boom in specialised magazines in France, with several dozen new titles coming out every year. Magazines for children and consumer titles providing readers with leisure-time information and entertainment are doing particularly well.

Between 1979 and 1991 the economic press jumped from seven to eighteen titles, most of which are thriving. The economic crisis, success of the French stock exchange, growing interest in savings and investment and, more recently, fascination with the workings of business have stimulated this sector. The most notable success story of recent years is *Capital*, which belongs to the German group Prisma and sells 440,000 copies each month; it contains short, practical articles addressing business concerns. *Challenges* (circulation of 212,000), *Enjeux-les Echos* (130,000), *Le Revenu français* (170,000), *Mieux vivre votre argent* (230,000), *Investir Magazine* (115,000), *L'Expansion* (145,000) and *Valeurs actuelles* (85,000) are just some of the publications demonstrating the dynamism of the economic and financial press.

The scientific press is enjoying growing success with firmly established titles, such as *Science et Vie* (320,000 copies), *Ça m'intéresse* and *Sciences et Avenir*; high-level publications like *La Recherche* and *Pour la science* also have substantial print-runs.

Weekly periodicals carrying full details of the forthcoming week's radio and television programmes are among the French magazines with the largest print-runs. In 1997, they had a combined weekly circulation of 20 million copies. *TV Magazine* led the field with 13.5 million readers, followed by *Télé 7 Jours* with 11.4 million, and *Télé Star*, *Télé Z* and *Télé Loisirs* each with nearly seven million readers.

The French are individualists and the press mirrors this trait: every fashion, trend, sport, interest, art-form and way of life has its own publication. Over fifteen magazines are devoted to cars, six to motorcycles, nine to photography or the cinema, twenty to gastronomy, tourism and travel, seven to science, six to music, twenty or so to computers, nearly forty to sports of every kind, eleven to literature, history and the fine arts, twenty-three to homes and gardens, eleven to hunting and fishing, etc.. The press for young people from toddlers to students is also rapidly expanding, with almost 80 titles in 1997. From the birth of a baby (*Famille magazine*, *Parents*, *Enfants Magazine*, etc.) to retirement (*Notre Temps*, 1,054,000 copies), every age group has its own magazine.

Women's magazines, which have a very long history in France, are flourishing and often also sold abroad, where they propagate France's traditional image (fashion, beauty and art of living). Targeted at a very specific section of the population, they have managed to build up a loyal core of readers and advertisers. During the last few years, they have stopped being so focused on Paris and sought a broader, more family readership. Magazines such as *Femme actuelle* (circulation of 1,735,000), *Prima* (1,110,000), *Modes et Travaux* (800,000), *Madame Figaro* (545,000) and *Marie-Claire* (540,000) are among the 28 French titles with circulations of over 500,000. The most prestigious and most influential of the women's magazines is probably *Elle*. Founded in 1945, *Elle* has managed to keep pace with changing lifestyles and with women's issues both in France and abroad, whilst celebrating fashion and style. Sold for 13 francs ($2.40) and with a print-run of 345,000, 29 foreign editions of *Elle* are also published: American, Canadian, English, German, Italian, Spanish, Mexican, Brazilian, Argentinian, Chilean, Greek, Dutch, Portuguese, Swedish, Czech, Norwegian, Polish, Romanian, Taiwanese, Korean, Singaporean, Thai, Vietnamese, Indian, Australian, South African, Hong Kong, Japanese and Russian.

News Agencies

Newspapers and television and radio stations could not operate without news agencies. News wholesalers supply the media and institutions with information of every sort — written copy, photos, graphics, etc., with subscribers paying for their services on a sliding scale based on their print-run or viewing or listening figures. In some newspapers more than 80% of the information published is provided by one or more news agencies, which gather and report in a totally neutral manner news of a purely factual nature, which their subscribers, of varying political tendencies and different nationalities, can then relay.

Newsroom of Agence France-Presse in Paris

Agence France-Presse (AFP) is one of the world's three leading press services (with the American *Associated Press* and British *Reuters*). It has 150 offices around the world and is the only French-language international news service. It employs 1,200 journalists, including 200 photographers, and also uses 2,000 freelancers in 165 countries. It transmits two million words a day in six languages and 70,000 photographs a year. Its customers include 650 newspapers, 400 radio and television stations, 1,500 government departments and businesses and 100 national news agencies. So, directly or indirectly, it reaches three billion people and informs 10,000 media organizations. It also supplies radio features and reports, computer graphics and multimedia services on the Internet and Intranet.

There are also photo news agencies; the three world leaders – Sygma, Gamma and Sipa – are all French.

Boom in French Broadcasting

The written press has lost ground in the face of the growth of the broadcast media and, to a lesser extent, to books, which, when it comes to immediate past history, have taken over the traditional preserve of the press. In 1997 the French spent an average of three hours and twenty minutes a day in front of their television sets, but only 30 minutes reading the press.

Up to 1982, radio and television broadcasting was a state monopoly in France. In that year eighteen commercial radio stations were authorised to broadcast. Then, to protect the independence of the media, especially from political pressure, the Law of 29 July 1982 placed all radio and television networks in France, except the Franco-German channel Arte, under the supervision of an independent administrative body, as is the case in the United States and Canada; in 1989 this body was named the *Conseil supérieur de l'audiovisuel* (CSA – Higher Council for the Audiovisual Sector).

Higher Council for the Audiovisual Sector

One of the tasks of the CSA (French broadcasting authority) is to monitor the time allocated to each candidate or party during election campaigns

The CSA is responsible for seeing that broadcasters honour their legal obligations. It also assigns television and radio frequencies, appoints the chairmen of the governing boards of the public broadcasting channels and advises the government or Parliament when its opinion is requested. It must ensure respect for the principle of political pluralism, encourage free competition, protect the interests of children and defend the French language in the broadcast media. Legally, it has the power to apply sanctions such as fines or the suspension of transmission.

The country's three highest authorities - the President of the Republic, and the Presidents of

the Senate and National Assembly - each appoint a third of the CSA's nine members and its chairman is appointed by the President of the Republic. The councillors serve a six-year term of office, with a third of the Council replaced every two years. To reinforce their independence they may not be removed from office or serve more than one term.

Mushrooming of Television Channels

The French audiovisual sector entered the competition era when commercial television stations were authorised in 1982. In ten years the number of broadcast channels jumped from three to over thirty (including cable).

Overall, regardless of channel, French viewers prefer above all films, drama, light entertainment and informative programmes (news, coverage of current affairs and documentaries). Viewers all over the nation gather around their televisions sets for the daily *TF1* and *France 2* 8 p.m. news. However, as was the case for the written press, alongside the relatively few general-interest television channels, France has seen a burgeoning of increasingly specialised subscription or pay-per-view TV channels targeting people with specific interests such as sport, music and concerts, films, etc..

In addition to the 20 or so cable TV channels, there are now seven terrestrial television channels in France, four of which - *France 2*, *France 3*, the Franco-German channel *Arte* and *La Cinquième* - belong to the public sector and are financed by the television licence fee - 735 francs ($122) in 1998 - government subsidies and the selling of advertising time. The three others are independent: *TF1* and *M6* are both financed by private shareholders and funded solely by advertising, while *Canal Plus* offers a scrambled subscription service, but also sells advertising time.

New headquarters of France Télévision in Paris

Since 1989, *France 2* and *France 3* (originally *Antenne 2* and *FR3*) have been part of the *France Télévision* group, under a single chairman, thereby rationalizing their output and encouraging complementarity. *France 2* is a national general-interest channel with a brief to inform, entertain and educate, attracting around 25% of viewers. Much of its early evening schedule is devoted to French and European drama.

France 3 has both national and regional responsibilities, since at certain times of the day it broadcasts regional and local news bulletins and programmes. Thanks to a strengthening of its national identity and the high quality of its programmes, *France 3* is steadily gaining larger audiences and is currently attracting close to 20% of viewers. *19-20*, its evening news programme, has the highest audience ratings for the early evening largely because part of it is handed over to regional broadcasters who cover local issues and events.

Arte, which transmits on the fifth channel from 7 p.m. to 3 a.m., is a high-quality cultural channel also broadcast in Germany (by cable), which specialises in whole evenings given over to films, discussion programmes and reports with the same theme. Established as a result of the Franco-German treaty of 2 October 1990, *Arte* is destined to be a European channel: the Belgian *Radio-télévision belge* has already linked up with it and other nations may soon follow. *Arte* still has modest viewing figures in France, but these are steadily increasing: in 1997, 19 million regular viewers in France, 5.6 million in Germany and 27 million in Europe as a whole.

14 December 1994 saw the birth of *La Cinquième*, France's first educational channel devoted to "education, training and employment". It broadcasts on the same channel as *Arte* from 6 a.m. to 7 p.m. when *Arte* is off air, offering educational programmes and documentaries appealing to a very wide audience and particularly to schools.

There are two general-interest channels in the commercial sector: *TF1* and *M6*. Privatised in 1987, *TF1* is the most popular French channel, watched by an average 35% of viewers. It has benefited from the long experience, reputation and know-how of what was the first and for a long time only public television channel in France. It is a general-interest channel whose schedule contains a high proportion of game-shows, sports programmes, variety shows and films appealing to a general audience. It attracts 55% of television advertising and is controlled by the civil engineering group Bouygues in partnership with Bolloré.

M6, whose principal shareholders are the Compagnie luxembourgeoise de télédiffusion (CLT) and the Lyonnaise des Eaux-Dumez, focuses particularly on drama (during the first half of the evening) and music. It also broadcasts specific local news programmes to 12 key French cities. Half of its viewers are under 35.

Canal Plus, set up in 1984, is the oldest of the independent channels. It offers a scrambled subscription service (it is necessary to rent a decoder device to watch all its programmes, except those which are not encrypted). Although initially greeted with widespread scepticism, *Canal Plus* has done exceptionally well: with almost 5 million subscribers and a turnover of 13.5 billion francs ($2.25 billion) in 1997, it is the outstanding triumph of the French audiovisual sector and has exported its success to other European countries such as Spain, Belgium and Poland. Its strong points are films and sport. It also broadcasts one of France's most famous television programmes, *Les Guignols de l'Info*, whose rubber puppets extremely irreverently parody leading figures from the worlds of politics, the arts and sport. *Canal Plus* is now controlled by Vivendi (former Générale des Eaux), which centres the media side of its business on this channel for the audiovisual sector, on Havas, for its publishing, multimedia and advertising activities and Cégétel for the telecommunications industry.

In addition to these seven terrestrial channels, some 250 French and foreign channels can be received by cable or satellite. In practice, however, for the moment most French homes receive packages of themed channels transmitted by a single satellite. Over three million homes either have a satellite dish or cable connection and half of these subscribe to a basic service which provides access to fifteen or so channels; the terrestrial channels, the French themed channels (i.e. concentrating on specific areas of interest) and some foreign channels (BBC, MTV, CNN, TVE, RAI and ZDF, etc.) along with the European news channel *Euronews*.

Today the most important themed French channels are *Canal J*, (young people's channel) which is on the air every day from 7 a.m. to 8 p.m., before handing over to *Canal Jimmy* which shows programmes mainly aimed at fans of the 1960s and 1970s, *Planète* (documentaries and current affairs), *Eurosport*, *MCM* (music) and *LCI* (*La Chaîne Info*), France's first 24-hour news channel, set up in June 1994. *LCI*, a *TF1* subsidiary, broadcasts a full news programme every half-hour as well as continuous news when events so warrant. It also offers discussion programmes and interviews. Two cable film channels are available in return for a higher subscription.

Studio of the TF1 subsidiary, LCI (*la Chaîne Info*), the first French 24-hour news channel, founded in June 1994

Digital television got off to a flying start in France in 1996 and has gained over a million subscribers in less than two years. It is essential for France to develop satellite broadcasting of multichannel packages for two reasons: firstly, to maintain its position and influence in tomorrow's world - where so many cultural and economic interests are at stake - so as to fight off competition from foreign channels and, secondly, to diversify by giving subscribers more than is currently available on the terrestrial channels. *Canal Satellite*, a multichannel package managed by *Canal Plus*, already provides 750,000 subscribers (1998) with nine themed channels.

Following right behind, *TPS* (a subsidiary of *TF1*, *France Télévision*, *M6* and the *Compagnie luxembourgeoise de télé-commications*) is now marketing a multichannel package to which 200,000 households have subscribed. Other newcomers in the sector include *AB Sat*, which already has 50,000 subscribers. All these operators are waging a ferocious battle in a rapidly expanding market: the satellite TV market had a turnover of around 5 billion francs in 1998, exceeding that of cable television (4 billion francs). Digital compression will also encourage the development of pay-for-view television enabling viewers to see the programmes they choose when they choose, a service already offered by *Multivision 1*, linked to over 25 cable networks, and *Multivision 2*, which was set up in January 1995.

Finally, the television channels actively support French cinema through a policy of buying up and co-producing films. In 1996, *Canal Plus* bought up about a hundred feature films at a total cost of 605 million francs ($100.8 million) and co-produced 22. *TF1* invested 221.2 million francs ($36.8 million) in the co-production of 17 films; *France 2*, spent 120.9 million francs ($20.1 million) on co-financing 23 films and *France 3* spent 99 million francs ($16.5 million) on 15; *La Sept* co-financed 11 and *M6*, 15.

Shooting on the banks of the Dordogne (Lot) of the very successful television film *La rivière Espérance*, shown on France 2

INA: the Television Archive

For over twenty years now, the *Institut national de l'audiovisuel* (INA - National Institute for the Audiovisual Sector), a public corporation, has been responsible for managing France's television archives. The INA, the architect of "the memory of the future", firmly intends to continue and strengthen this task of conserving and capitalising on this heritage, making use of new IT technology, in particular high-speed digital networks, and of the *Inathèque de France*, which began operating on 1 January 1995. This body conserves and makes available for consultation, for research purposes, French television and radio archives, on which researchers, academics and doctoral students can work, using computer and multimedia tools such as the "Vidéoscribe" system, which allows analysis of television archive material, frame by frame, while varying the lighting, shots and sound. In addition, publication of the research results and studies by academics who use the *Inathèque de France* is opening up to serious critical discussion the audiovisual media, which are going to become increasingly present and influential.

Huge Popularity of Radio

The success of television has not led to a decline in the popularity of radio, quite the contrary. The mushrooming of radio stations, in the wake of the 1982 law ending the state monopoly, and their growing diversity, have given a new boost to this medium, which is still the favourite of the French, except in the evening, when they prefer to watch television. However, the success of radio and television has been at the detriment of the written press. The French as a whole, over the whole age range, spend an average of over two hours a day listening to the radio, doing so especially during meals, household chores and journeys.

Public radio broadcasting is grouped together under the umbrella of the national radio company, *Radio France*, which devises and programmes broadcasts on a network of 53 radio stations of which five are national and 39 local; there are also *Fip*, first set up in 1971 to provide traffic information for Parisians, which now broadcast round-the-clock news and public service messages (weather, traffic, job vacancies, what's on at the cinema and on radio and television, etc.) against a background of non-stop music, to ten or so localities. *Radio France* employs over 3,000 people, including nearly 450 journalists, and has 124 studios, of which over half are in the provinces. It can also call upon two orchestras, the *Orchestre national de France* and the *Orchestre philharmonique*, as well as its own choir, the *Choeur et la Maîtrise de Radio France*. Altogether, *Radio France* broadcasts nearly 500,000 hours of programmes per year. Public radio stations are financed by the radio and television licensing fee and in some cases directly by the state and advertising is severely restricted.

The one o'clock news on *Europe 1*

France has five national radio stations: *France-Inter*, founded in 1947 and France's second most popular station (after *RTL*), broadcasts round the clock; *France-Culture* provides a very wide variety of programmes including music, interviews, discussions and in-depth coverage of major international events; *France-Musique* broadcasts more than 1,000 concerts each year, including those produced by *Radio France*; *Radio Bleue* principally targets the over-50s, with French songs (*la chanson française*) a special feature of its programmes - indeed *la chanson française* is a popular musical genre in France and abroad, characterized by the quality of its lyrics -; and, finally, *France Info*, created in 1987 and the first, and very swiftly successful rolling news station not only in France but in Europe, broadcasts 24 hours a day, offering frequent news headlines and a full news bulletin every half-hour.

Radio-France Internationale (*RFI*), broadcasting in France and in all five continents, is one of the cornerstones of France's external audiovisual policy. *RFO* (*Société nationale de Radio et de Télévision d'Outre-mer*) schedules, produces and broadcasts radio and television programmes in France's overseas departments and territories.

France has three national general-interest commercial radio stations: *RTL*, *Europe 1* and *Radio Monte-Carlo*. There are also national frequency-modulation (FM) stations much of whose output is music, such as *NRJ*, *Radio-Nostalgie*, *Fun Radio*, *Skyrock*, some 30 regional commercial radio stations including *Sud-Radio*, *Radio-Service* and *Radio-1*, and over 350 radio stations run by voluntary organizations, providing a total of 450 radio services on about 2,650 frequencies. At the end of the 1980s, general-interest commercial radio stations lost a large number of listeners. To redress the situation, *RTL*, *Europe 1* and *RMC* formed closer and more personal relationships with their listeners, stepping up direct contacts with local communities and introducing phone-in programmes. They also bought FM networks (*RMC* acquired *Radio-Montmartre* and *Nostalgie*, the *CLT* acquired *Fun Radio*, while *Europe 1* bought *RFM*) or set up their own FM radio stations (*Europe 2* was established by *Europe 1*, and *RTL2* by *RTL*).

To protect French culture, the Law of 1 February 1994 requires that at least 40% of the songs broadcast in any one popular or light music programme be sung in French, with half performed by "new talent" or be "new productions". In addition, this same law stipulates that an individual or corporation can have legal or de facto control of several networks only if the total potential audience does not exceed 150 million inhabitants.

The CSA (see above) has jurisdiction over radio as well as television broadcasting.

French Radio and Television Abroad

France was one of the first countries to conduct a genuine policy of cultural diplomacy through schools, cultural centres, the

Alliance française and scientific and technical cooperation. Today it also has an external audiovisual policy, for which the government has set out new guidelines aimed at developing the operations of France's major worldwide communications channels - *TV5*, *Canal France International* (*CFI*), *Radio-France Internationale* (*RFI*) - and the SOFIRAD radio stations; SOFIRAD manages all the French state's interests in independent radio and television stations in France and abroad. These guidelines have three broad aims: to make TV5 the international showcase for French television programmes, to support the export of French radio and television programmes and increase financial aid for satellite TV channels.

To this end, public funding of France's action in this sphere was raised from 900 million francs ($150 million) to 1.4 billion francs in 1998. *TV5*, now responsible for the bulk of the broadcasting of French programmes to foreign countries, is a multilateral French-language television channel transmitted by satellite and cable. Founded in 1984, it is a joint venture run by the French public audiovisual sector (*France 2, France 3, SOFIRAD* and the *Institut national de l'audiovisuel*) and the Swiss French, Belgian, Canadian and Quebec public television networks - hence its name: *TV5*. In 1998, it had a budget of 350 million francs ($58 million) and was transmitted via about 20 satellites to over 80 million homes in around hundred countries in Europe, America, Africa and Asia. Twenty-four hours a day, it puts out top-of-the range programmes, 75% of them in French, including its own news broadcasts and those of the French, Swiss, Belgian, Quebec and Canadian public television networks, magazine programmes, drama, films, variety and game shows, etc..

Canal France International (*CFI*) was set up in 1989 as a film/video library for French satellite channels and was essentially intended to serve the African national television channels. In 1997, *CFI* broadcast 27,500 hours of programmes to over 80 countries in partnership with over 100 foreign channels. It can reach up to 354 million viewers, thanks to six satellite channels covering the five continents. With a budget of 180 million francs ($30 million) in 1998, *CFI* broadcasts 11 news bulletins per day, including two in English, and many live sporting events (Roland-Garros tennis tournament, World Football Cup, Tour de France cycling race, etc.). *CFI* also offers more than 150 full-length feature films a year, as well as documentaries, drama and current affairs, variety shows and programmes for young people. Under the new external audiovisual policy guidelines, *CFI* is concentrating on its role as film/video library and scientific and technical cooperation tool, and maintaining its role as broadcaster to African countries.

Finally, to encourage the two instruments of French televisual policy abroad to work together, *CFI* and *TV5* now have a joint chairman.

RFI, the World Radio Station

Another pillar of France's audiovisual policy abroad, *Radio-France Internationale* (*RFI*) presents to listeners throughout the world French and international news as seen from a French and European angle. It has been on the air since 1931. Today *RFI* has a huge variety of programmes, makes use of every available broadcasting technology and has journalists known for their professionalism. Its 45 million regular listeners tune in to programmes in French and eighteen other languages.

In autumn 1996, *RFI* launched a non-stop, 24-hour news and information service, with ten-minute news bulletins every half-hour and programmes covering every aspect of French culture, economics and society. European and African issues and international economic relations are also given substantial airtime. These programmes are also available (although not round-the-clock) in 18 foreign languages.

RFI also has a service specifically devoted to French song and has two websites, one for news and the other for song. Its budget is in the region of 775 million francs ($129 million).

With high-quality digital satellite coverage, *RFI* has set up a network of relay stations operating 24 hours a day and allowing rebroadcasting of its programmes on FM, medium-wave or cable in over 140 cities world-wide, including almost all the capitals of Francophone

The worldwide broadcasting network of Radio France Internationale

Pacific Ocean

Paris

Pacific Ocean

Atlantic Ocean

Indian Ocean

Source : RFI

Area covered by short-wave transmitters

RFI relay stations rebroadcasting 24h/24

Areas covered by each of the eleven satellites

Africa and Central and Eastern Europe, as well as cities like New York, Amman and Phnom Penh.

In 1991, *RFI* took over *RMC Moyen-Orient*, a station which transmits on medium-wave sixteen-and-a-half hours a day in Arabic and one-and-a-half hours a day in French to 13 million listeners in the Middle East and, on FM, to a growing number of Arab capitals.

In addition, *Medi 1*, with 19 hours a day of programmes in Arabic and French, reaches 11 million listeners in the Maghreb countries.

France in the Internet Age

The French entered the multimedia era later than the Americans and their European neighbours largely because the Minitel was and continues to be so successful. With over two billion calls a year and 115 million hours spent on line to the Minitel, France leads the world for use of on-line services (electronic telephone directory, business and professional services, practical information, stock exchange listings, messaging services and games and leisure activities).

Half-way through 1996, 21% of households had a computer, including 17% with multimedia software, and this percentage is expected to rise substantially by the year 2000, mainly thanks to the drop in price of the equipment, a proactive policy conducted by the various French governments promoting the use of IT in schools and the reduction in telephone charges resulting from the opening-up of the telecommunications market in 1998.

Half-way through 1997, France had 1.12 million Internet users, i.e. 2.4% of the population aged over 15. The projected growth rate for the ensuing twelve months was 90% and in mid-1998 it had 2.1 million net surfers, i.e. 5% of all those over 15, and over 25,000 websites. In June 1997, French sites accounted for about half total connection time, compared with a third in 1996. Almost all the national dailies and weeklies are now present on the Net. The business daily *Les Echos* has the most visitors, 350,000 a month, followed by the general-interest newspaper *Libération*.

Further reading:

Les réseaux de la société d'information, rapport du Commissariat général du Plan, Ed. T. Miléo, Éditions Aspe, 1997.

D'Internet aux autoroutes de l'information, in *Regards sur l'actualité*, N° 217, La Documentation française, 1996.

L'Internet, un vrai défi pour la France, La Documentation française, Rapports officiels series, 1997.

Programme d'action gouvernemental, *Préparer l'entrée de la France dans la société de l'information*, Premier Ministre (Prime Minister), Service d'information du gouvernement, La Documentation française, 1998.

L'abrégé du droit de la presse, Éditions du Centre de formation et de perfection-nement des journalistes (CFPJ), 1994 (full bibliography).

Indicateurs statistiques de la radio, SJTI, CSA, La Documentation française, 1997.

Indicateurs statistiques de l'audiovisuel. Cinéma, télévision, vidéo. Données 1995, SJTI, La Documentation française, 1997.

Chiffres clés de la télévision et du cinéma. France 1995, INA, CNC, CSA, La Documentation française, 1996.

Daniel Junqua, *La presse écrite et audiovisuelle*, Éditions du CFPJ, Connais-sance des médias series, 1997.

Pierre Albert, *La presse française*, La Documentation française, Les Études series, 1998.

H. Pigeat, *Les agences de presse. Institutions du passé ou médias d'avenir ?* La Documentation française, Les Études series, 1996.

Internet et les réseaux numériques, La Documentation française, Rapports du Conseil d'État series, 1998.

The Internet sites of La Documentation française:
http://www.ladocfrancaise.gouv.fr
http://www.admifrance.gouv.fr

APPENDICES

General Index

Index of Proper Names

Acknowledgments for photographs

Figures are page numbers:
h = top, m = centre, b = bottom.

7 D. Repérant / Rapho

8h La Documentation française / ph. D. Taulin-Hommell ; **8m** T. Perrin / Hoa-qui ;

8b La Documentation française / Interphotothèque ph. Sodel-M. Brigaud

9 G. Sioen / Rapho

10 D. Repérant / Rapho

11 La Documentation française / ph. D. Taulin-Hommell

12 Office national des forêts / J.-P. Chasseau

13 F. de la Mure / Ministère des Affaires étrangères. Diffuseur La Documentation française

19h F. de la Mure / Ministère des Affaires étrangères ;

19b La Documentation française / ph. F. Saur-Visum

20 La Photothèque EDF

21 La Documentation française / ph. D. Taulin-Hommell

25 F. de la Mure / Ministère des Affaires étrangères. Diffuseur La Documentation française

31h Yan / Rapho ; **31m** D. Repérant / Rapho ;

31b La Documentation française / ph. J.-F. Marin-Editing

32 La Documentation française / ph. J.-F. Marin-Editing

34 E. Valentin / Hoa-qui

36 Debaisieux / Rapho

37 X. Richer / Hoa-qui

41 Photo Josse

43 Photo Josse

45h Fournier / Rapho ; **45b** CNDP-collection historique

46 Photo Willy Ronis / Rapho

47 Archives La Documentation française

49 Ministère des Affaires étrangères

51 Photo A.F.P.

53 Photo A.F.P.

54 Photo A.F.P.

56 Premier Ministre / Service photographique

58 L.-N. Bonaparte : La Documentation française, d'après nature/Lafosse ; **A. Thiers** : La Documentation française ; **Mac-Mahon** : La Documentation française ; **J. Grévy** : Bibliothèque nationale de France, diffuseur La Documentation française ; **S. Carnot** : Présidence de la République, diffuseur La Documentation française ; **J. Casimir-Périer** : Présidence de la République, diffuseur La Documentation française ; **F. Faure** : Présidence de la République, diffuseur La Documentation française ; **E. Loubet** : Présidence de la République, diffuseur La Documentation française ; **A. Fallières** : Présidence de la République, diffuseur La Documentation française ; **R. Poincaré** : Présidence de la République, diffuseur La Documentation française ; **P. Deschanel** : Bibliothèque nationale de France, diffuseur La Documentation française ; **A. Millerand** : Bibliothèque nationale de France, diffuseur La Documentation française ; **G. Doumergue** : Bibliothèque nationale de France, diffuseur La Documentation française ; **P. Doumer** : Bibliothèque nationale de France, diffuseur La Documentation française ; **A. Lebrun** : Présidence de la République, diffuseur La Documentation française ; **V. Auriol** : photo Harcourt, diffuseur La Documentation française ; **R. Coty** : Présidence de la République, diffuseur La Documentation française ; **C. de Gaulle** : La Documentation française, photo J.-M. Marcel ; **G. Pompidou** : La Documentation française, photo F. Pagès / Paris Match : **V. Giscard d'Estaing** : La Documentation française, photo J.-H. Lartigue ; **F. Mitterrand** : La Documentation française, photo G. Freund ; **J. Chirac** : La Documentation française, photo B. Rheims.

61 Présidence de la République

63 Premier Ministre / Service photographique

65 Premier Ministre / Service photographique

66 La Documentation française / ph. F. Le Diascorn

ACKNOWLEDGMENTS
FOR PHOTOGRAHS

67 D. Repérant / Rapho
68 La Documentation française / ph. R. Allard-Vu
72h Epamarne / Ph. Morency. Diffuseur La Documentation française ; **72b** SAN de Sénart / J. Dupeyrat.
Diffuseur La Documentation française
73 La Documentation française / ph. S. Challon
75 A. Le Bot / DIAF
78 Photo Branger / Viollet
79 Photo A.F.P.
80 Moschetti / Réa
84 B. Bisson / Sygma
85 J.-B. Vernier / Sygma
94 F. De la Mure / Ministère des Affaires étrangères
97 F. De la Mure / Ministère des Affaires étrangères
98h F. De la Mure / Ministère des Affaires étrangères ; **98b** Commission européenne
99 F. De la Mure / Ministère des Affaires étrangères
100 V. Maaski
102 Premier Ministre / Service photographique
103 Trois Têtes. A l'Amitié. Henri Matisse 1951-52. Héritiers Matisse 1998
107 Droits réservés
109 Ministère des Affaires étrangères / DGRCST
112 Ministère des Affaires étrangères
113 J. Marces / SIRPA / ECPA
115 F. De la Mure / Ministère des Affaires étrangères
116 ECPA
117 ECPA
118 ECPA
119 ECPA
124 S. Cuisset / Réa
125 D. Faget / A.F.P.
129 Th. Rousseau / Sygma
131 J.-P. Amet / Sygma
133 P. Wang / Hoa-qui
134 D. Maillac / Réa
135 La Documentation française / ph. J.-F. Marin-Editing
136 Ministère de l'Emploi et de la Solidarité
138 J.E. Pasquier / Rapho
140 Sygma / Tempsport / T. Orban
141 J. Van Hasselt / Sygma
144 J.-P. Amet / Sygma
145 J.-P. Amet / Sygma
146 La Documentation française / ph. P. Dewarez
147 La Documentation française / ph. J.-P. Bajard-Editing
149 D. Giry / Sygma
154 La Documentation française / ph. F. Ivaldi-Viva
155 La Documentation française / ph. J. Guillaume-Editing
156 La Documentation française / ph. F. Boucher
157 Epamarne / Ph. Morency. Diffuseur La Documentation française
158 Epamarne / Ph. Morency. Diffuseur La Documentation française
159 La Documentation française / ph. F. Boucher
160 M. Denance / Archipress
171 Bartoli / Réa
178 Conseil régional du Centre / B. Voisin. Diffuseur La Documentation française
180 La Documentation française / J.-F. Marin-Editing
183 La Documentation française / Interphotothèque ph. Sodel-M. Brigaud
185 B. Decoux / Réa

ACKNOWLEDGMENTS
FOR PHOTOGRAHS

187h Peterson / Saba / Réa ; **187b** La Documentation française / ph. Ph. Guignard

188 D. Maillac / Réa

189 S. Cuisset / Réa

190 M. Fourmy / Réa

192 A. Devouard / Réa

194 P. Sittler / Réa

196 C. Ena / Réa

197 A. Wolf / Hoa-qui

200 M. Fourmy / Réa

203 J.-M. Charles / Sygma

209 D. Repérant / Rapho

210 M. Denance / Archipress

214 P. Sittler / Réa

215 A. Devouard / Réa

216 Allard / Réa

218h Ministère des Affaires étrangères ; **218b** V. Macon / Réa

220 B. Marguerite / RATP-Audiovisuel

221 A. Devouard / Réa

223 La Documentation française / ph. P. Dewarez

225h F. Eustache / Archipress ; **225b** Archipress

227 Delluc / Réa

228 B. Annebicque / Sygma

230 Archipress

231 La Documentation française / ph. T. Carre

232 C. Masson / Enguérand

233h Q. Bertoux / Enguérand ; **233b** A.F.P. / ph. T.A. Clary

234 S. Cardinale / Sygma

235 F. Fogel / Sygma

236 D. Sauveur / Sygma

237 F. Eustache / Archipress

238 C. Stephan / Ministère des Affaires étrangères

239 F. Fogel / Sygma

241 M. Attar / Sygma

242 Photo M. Enguérand

243 D. Thierry / Maison de la France

244 Sygma / Tempsport / S. Compoint

245 Ministère des Affaires étrangères

246 G. Leimdorfer / Réa

249 Ministère des Affaires étrangères

251 G. Leimdorfer / Réa

252 G. Leimdorfer / Réa

253 Photo France 2 / G. Schrempp

255 G. Leimdorfer / Réa

256 D. Repérant / Hoa-qui

257 G. Leimdorfer / Réa

Infographie : Graffito, Paris

Compogravure - Impression : S.N. imb IMPRIMEUR - 70000 Vesoul - Dépôt légal n° 4627 - October 1999 - Imprimé en France